KAZOONIE

JOHN DIENER

◆ FriesenPress

Suite 300 - 990 Fort St
Victoria, BC, V8V 3K2
Canada

www.friesenpress.com

Copyright © 2017 by John Diener
First Edition — 2017

All rights reserved.

No part of this publication may be reproduced in any form, or by any means, electronic or mechanical, including photocopying, recording, or any information browsing, storage, or retrieval system, without permission in writing from FriesenPress.

ISBN
978-1-4602-9661-5 (Hardcover)
978-1-4602-9662-2 (Paperback)
978-1-4602-9663-9 (eBook)

1. BIOGRAPHY & AUTOBIOGRAPHY, CRIMINALS & OUTLAWS

Distributed to the trade by The Ingram Book Company

Table of Contents

PREFACE VII

CHAPTER ONE 1
    The Gun
    Where I Lived

CHAPTER TWO 7
    One Near Death
    One Death

CHAPTER 3 15
    The First Robbery
    Introduction to Okalla

CHAPTER FOUR 25
    Penitentiary

CHAPTER 5 63
    My First Parole
    My Escape

CHAPTER 6 75
    King County Jail Immigration Lock Up
    Back to the Pen to Finish My Time

CHAPTER 7 83
    Vancouvers East End
    Arrested Again
    Okalla Prison Farm

CHAPTER 8 107
    Ducan and the Henslowes
    Employment in Port Alberni
    America and the Gun

CHAPTER 9 137
    Stealing a Car
    Robbing the Bank
    Capture, Trial, and Back to Jail

CHAPTER 10 161
    20 Years a Long Jolt
    Appendicitis, Admission to Hospital
    Music and a Few Incidents

CHAPTER 11 185
    Williams Head Medium Security Penitentiary
    Back to the Maximum Security Pententiary
    A Few Escapes that Didn't Last Long
    A Few More Incidences and My Final Parole

CHAPTER 12 219
    Royal Jubilee Hospital
    Work in the Kitchen
    And as an Orderly on the Wards

CHAPTER 13 243
    Unionization of the Hospital
    Morgue Attendant
    1St Autopsy
    Checking for Possible Infection

CHAPTER 14 257
    Viewing of Bodies by Relatives
    Signing over the Disposal of Newborn
    Infants to the Hospital
    A Few Situations Regarding Bonuses
    The Difficulties of Picking up and
    Transporting the Bodies to the Morgue

CHAPTER 15 275
    Problems with the Pathologists
    Nursing School
    Fainting at Autopsies

CHAPTER 16 287
    Wage Dispute
    Blood in my Urine
    A Kidney Stone
    A Suspicious Autopsy
    Rude Relatives and a Few Difficult Times
    Final Closure

PREFACE

This is not a story of my whole life nor is it an attempt to make excuses for a part of my life that was a complete disaster. It's just a story about a young man who started his adult years by making one mistake after another and having to endure the punishment dealt out to those who break Societies Laws. I'm sure there will be others who follow in my footsteps and who eventually look around and ask themselves why and get the right answers and endeavour to change their lives for the better. I hope that their efforts don't take as long as mine did and that their decisions bring better results than mine did. Some do not have complete control and you have to make the best of it no matter what happens. If any readers of this narration find themselves in the above mentioned position just think, and act in a positive way and there's always an open door to walk through that leads to a better way with a little effort made on their part.

MY story started in 1949 and I walked a long path to my door. I was one of the lucky ones because I met the right woman who stuck by me through some very trying times and a little help went a very long way. This story in my mind is all true just as I lived it and if I have made mistakes in some of my descriptions of events then I apologise for my slip in memory. Fifty years have passed since then and I still remember it like it was yesterday.

This is my first and will be my only effort at writing a memoir. Whoever reads this story will not find in the pages the writing of an educated man just a series of chapters that talked about events that came to mind at the time of writing. I have tried to protect those people who may be alive by using a pseudonym or not naming them at all. I wrote this memoir to

John Diener

remember and never to forget a part of my life that could have been avoided if I had of taken a little time to seek out a little advise when I reached the door of no return. In my case I just got tired of being a Kazoonie.

JOHN DIENER

KAZOONEY

DOING TIME IN THE CANADIAN PROVINCE OF
BRITISH COLUMBIA PENITENTIARY
IN THE YEAR 1949

CHAPTER ONE

The Gun

Where I Lived

The rack of guns in the Second hand Store on Government Street in Victoria British Columbia was covered with dust and grime like everything else in the store. The proprietor, a fat man with traces of his last meal on the fringes of his unkempt mustache asked in a gruff voice,

"What can I do for you kid?"

I pointed to the Remington pump action gun.

"What calibre is that one?" I asked.

"44-40 a real canon," he replied.

"How much do you want for it?"

He stared at me trying to estimate my age, and whether I was wasting his time or not. I stood six feet two and a half and weighed one hundred eighty pounds, but my juvenile acne and dress gave my eighteen years away. After a few minutes of doubt he replied in a conspiratorial tone

I'll let you have it for fifteen bucks"

He took the gun down from the rack and handed it to me. It was heavy but the cold steel felt good as I put it to my shoulder, and looked down along the barrel. I pulled the pump action toward me and listened to the sound of the breach opening. It felt smooth and gave me a sense of power I had never felt before.

"Do you want it wrapped in some paper?"

"Yes I better keep it covered until I get home." I said as I counted the fifteen dollars. He wrapped the gun efficiently using paper from a big brown roll on a stand beside an old ornate cash registrar. He handed me my bill of sale, and I walked home.

I lived on the corner of Spring Road and Denman Street in the Fern wood district one of Victoria's oldest neighbourhoods. The house was a very large frame house built on a corner lot, with a yard that was big enough to hold a large barn, a Chicken Coupe and seven fruit trees. The house also contained six large rooms on the main floor. A bathroom with a tub that was no longer useable, because the plumping had rusted away. The hinges on the door had long ago rusted, and the door offered no more privacy, and so the room was never used anymore. The toilet was situated in a small separate room on the back porch, so if nature called you stepped outside onto the closed back porch, and opened the bathroom door, which was situated on your left. The toilet was a regular flush design so you, couldn't really call it an outhouse although it was outside the main building. The small room did not contain a sink for washing your hands.

It never occurred to me at the time how anyone took a bath, because in my early years the only baths myself, and my brother got were administered in a large galvanized wash tub, which was filled with hot water and placed on the kitchen floor. This only happened when we got so filthy it became too hard to live with us. I assume my older brother bathed at the Y.M.C.A. which he was a member of. My parents and two sisters must have taken discrete sponge baths late at night when no one was around. When my youngest sister obtained work as a live in housekeeper she had the luxury of a complete bathroom.

Upstairs there were four bedrooms, and each one had a window overlooking each side of the house. The whole upstairs area was in an unliveable condition. The kitchen was large with the usual wood burning stove, and the living room was heated by a round sheet metal stove, which glowed cherry red in the winter from overheating. I often wondered why the house never caught fire and burned to the ground. The rest of the rooms were heated by fireplaces which were used very rarely, because of lack of firewood. Eventually we chopped down all the fruit trees for firewood.

One particularly tough winter, I resorted to stealing wood from our next door neighbor, so we could have fuel to cook with. In the winter all available coats and sweaters were spread out on the beds for warmth, and nothing was thrown out when worn out. The children never chased the family dog from their beds, for its warmth was a big help on a cold winter night. The house was affectionately called by my older brother and sister "Wuthering Heights"

My father came from a wealthy family in England, and my mother was a live in servant in my Father's Parent's household. His father spent most of his time at his club, and when he came home his wife would become pregnant and he would go back to the club. As fate would have it my father fell in love with my mother and ask her to marry him. The caste system was very rigid in those days, and his mother and father disapproved of the marriage completely. It was just not acceptable for a maid to marry a man of my Fathers breeding, but love won the day, and they were married.

The family decided to put as much distance between them and there errant son as they could, and sent him to Ontario, Canada to be a gentleman farmer. During the Great Depression and one particularly cold winter they decided to pack up and move to Victoria, British Columbia where at least the weather was more civilized. My father held numerous jobs during the depression and was lucky enough to get a position as a caretaker and handyman for the owners of "Wuthering Heights. Eventually the owner died, and the son sold the property to the City of Victoria. During this time my father obtained employment as an Elevator Operator in an office building down town, and was allowed to stay in the house to maintain the premises. But then disaster struck. My father had a serious heart attack, and never worked at gainful employment again.

There we were a family of six with no money and a crippled bread winner. There was no alternative but to go to the Government Welfare Offices and ask for assistance. We then began eighteen years of abject poverty, and if it wasn't for my mother's Herculean efforts in feeding and clothing us in our youth, our existence would have been deplorable. My father just sat by the radio in the living room, and stared out at the coming and goings of our neighbors, or worked half-heartedly on the make shift chicken coupes in the backyard, but other than this he left the day to day running of the household to my mother.

MY mother was a large woman with an olive complexion and beautiful jet black hair. She was twenty years younger than my father. She was given the rudiments of an education in her youth and then trained in the skills of home making, which were prestigious. She never ceased to amaze with her ability to feed and clothe us in very difficult times.

When my mother married my father, I can imagine her great joy and elation, and her belief that she was going to rise to the top of her social position, gaining wealth, and prestige, and then her total frustration and anger to have her dreams dashed, by being banished by the family patriarch to a strange faraway land, and a life even more harsh and mundane than the one she thought she was escaping from. Her heavy handedness and sometimes cruel words during the times of discipline I blame on this great disappointment in her life. My father in all the years I knew him left the child raising to my mother and only engaged in the occasional bit of advice during our very short conversations.

My mother opened a credit account at the local corner store, and was so far in debt that she couldn't possibly meet the required payments to keep things under control. When the grocer suggested she send one of her kids to work to help pay the bills she chose me. I had been a very poor student at school. I was more a truant than student and when the grocer offered to speak to the man in charge of The Department of Transport, a local Government Agency, explaining with some pride that he was a friend of his. I jumped at the chance even though an agreement to pay 25% of my wages towards the grocery bill was struck between the grocer and my mother. A few days later my mother received a phone call and was told to send me down to the Coast Guard Wharf located in the inner harbour and that I was to report to the First Mate on the C.G.S. Estevan which was a Government Light House Tender which plied the West Coast Waters of Vancouver Island off the coast of British Columbia I liked the job. The Hardy life and hard work combined with the beautiful scenery and comradeship of the young deck-hands appealed to my sense of adventure.

A few months went by and my brother-in-law who was a Sergeant Major in the army had me convinced that there was a better future in the army and that I should enlist. I left my job on the Estevan and went down to the local Army Barracks and sat for an I.Q. test. The Recruitment Officer, ask me what branch of the army I wanted to be in, and as he was wearing the Red Beret of the Airborne, and looked marvellously fit. I told him I wanted to be in the Airborne, and that I was a good fighter, but it was obvious by the expression on his face that he wasn't impressed at all. He told me to wait in the other room, while he checked my papers. After what seemed like forever, he called me back to the examination room, and told me that I had failed the I.Q. tests, and the aptitude tests, and everything else that he had given me. A profound feeling of embarrassment swept over me. I felt totally inadequate, and angry that I wasn't being accepted into the army. As I walked across the parade ground, I stopped for a minute to watch some troops smartly drilling in the sun, and a feeling of rejection and disappointment swept over me. My brother-in-law commiserated with me but it only fanned the flame of anger.

To my surprise the Second Mate on the ship phoned me up the next day and when he found out I had not been excepted into the army he told me my old job was still available , and I went back to work. The first day back was a quiet day, the cargo had been stowed away and the ship was ready to sail up the West Coast the following morning. Most of the crew had disappeared below decks and found places to hide. I had been given the job of washing down the Well Deck with a hose by the Second Mate. In the past if it wasn't a busy day, it was not uncommon for the crew to break off early for lunch. I noticed that it was 11:45 so I left the deck and proceeded to the Mess which I found empty. Just as I was making myself comfortable the Second Mate appeared in the doorway saw me lounging in my seat and asked me.

"What the hell are you doing here?"

I explained that it was slow and that I was breaking of for an early lunch.

"Have you finished washing the deck down?"

"No."

"Well if you don't get out there and finish the job you're fired."

A feeling of anger and then rage boiled to the surface of what I thought was total unfairness.

"You can't fire me I quit."

I yelled back at him. A look of surprise swept over his face at an unsuspected act of total defiance. But I had created an intractable situation.

"Sparks will give you your walking papers." He yelled at me.

I stormed out of the Mess and proceeded to the Radio Shack behind the bridge. I found Sparks, and told him what I wanted. He tried to talk me out of it but I wasn't having any of it. I left the ship and the last job I was to hold for any reasonable length of time for ten years.

CHAPTER TWO

One Near Death

One Death

After I had left the ship I found a few short construction jobs and made enough money to buy a few rounds of ammunition for target practice, which consisted of going into the back room of the kitchen when no one was home and blowing very large holes into blocks of- Firewood. The entrance hole was small but the exit hole was at least six inches in diameter, and the bullets trajectory left small pieces of lead embedded in the wood. The bullets were large flat nosed copper jacketed slugs and when the bullet struck, the impact of the flat nose tore the wood to pieces with tremendous power.

My oldest brother and my mother were annoyed that I had purchased the gun. My mother because she thought it was a waste of money and my brother because of its age and its uselessness after all I couldn't go hunting in my backyard.

The following Christmas, the family got together for Christmas Dinner. Marjorie, my oldest sister, Mom, and me were in the kitchen. The women were setting the table, and I was admiring the turkey on the stove. Suddenly a loud sharp report came from the living room. The shock reverberated through the house. My head snapped up.

Jesus what's that?" I said.

Then it dawned on me, "The Rifle." I leaped to my feet and dashed into the living room. My heart was full of dread for what I might find.

My brother in law, Sargent Major Bert Harrington was sitting in a chair with the rifle butt on his knee and the barrel directly in front of his face pointing at the ceiling. His mouth was wide open, and his complexion was pasty white, and this was very pronounced because he was part Indian on his mother's side, and leaned more towards the Indian complexion than Caucasian. My father was sitting in his usual position by the window, looking very surprised and annoyed. My youngest brother "Billy," was standing with a look of great delight on his face. Wow!" he exclaimed when he got his breath. "Look at the hole in the ceiling." All heads snapped up to stare at the gaping hole in the ceiling. Everybody in the family had dashed to the living room at the sound of the gun going off.

"Jesus Christ John," you left the damn rifle loaded in the corner of the living room."

My oldest brother Alan's face was twisted in anger. He gave me a shove out of the way as he strolled over to Bert.

"Are you all right," he said.

"I didn't know the bloody thing was loaded, I was just showing Billy a little arm's drill and for a finale I pulled the pump and trigger and "BANG!"

"I sure hope it doesn't rain." Billy said.

The near tragedy had not registered with him at all, for at his age the firing of the gun was merely an unexpected thrill.

"What are you talking about?" said my mother," recovering her composure.

"The hole in the ceiling," he said, jabbing his finger in the air. This earned him a cuff to the side of his head.

"Go on into the other room for now," she said.

All eyes now turned on me. Alan walked over to Bert who was struggling to regain his composure.

"Give me that thing." He said. Bert handed it to him slowly.

"How do you unload it?"

"You just pump it up and down and the shells will eject." I said.

"I'm going to put this thing inside the door to the stairs I'll decide what to do with it, and you put those bullet's away where no one can lay their hands on them."

Alan had taken charge of the situation, and was verbally pushing me around. The rest of the family were merely showing their disapproval by the odd nasty comment and stare

"Don't blame him too much, with my experience with guns, I should have known better," Bert said.

I thought (don't blame me to much!) I shouldn't have been blamed at all you had no business fooling around with my gun in the first place. I totally ignored the fact that they were well within their right to admonish me all they wanted, because it was a stupid thing to do, leaving a fully loaded heavy caliber rifle in a corner of the living room.

Finally in my mind I was finished with the criticism being heaped on me, and I stormed out of the house. Christmas was a bust. The first time in my seventeen Christmases this had happened. In a totally selfish way, the thought that Bert could have blown his brains out never entered my mind. All I could think of was that I was being unduly picked on over his carelessness.

During the uproar my father sat quietly in his chair by the radio and stared out the window that overlooked the street, only perturbed with Bert for disturbing his quiet reverie of what things might have been, and said nothing.

I came back late in the evening after walking the down town streets thinking about how hard things were, losing my job, and what a mess Christmas had turned out to be, but not a thought of the fact that a little common sense on my part would have adverted these disturbing incidents before they had happened. As far as I was concerned, it was everybody's fault but my own. I ate my Christmas Dinner, opened my presents in a quiet house and went to bed.

My father began to deteriorate slowly due to his heart condition, and the effects of old age, to the point where my mother decided to have him put into a nursing home. The first home was too far away from his family. He would try to walk the two miles or so to get home every day, and became exhausted, and passersby would usually come to his aid by calling the police or an ambulance, to take him back to the nursing home, where he lived a very lonely life cooped up in his room just vegetating. Finally my mother realized what the problem was, and had him moved to a private nursing home run by a young single woman in her residence. She lived on the ground floor and the quests occupied the upstairs quarters. The establishment was just a few blocks away from Weathering Heights, which he could navigate although with some difficulty due to his bad heart, but he made it home on a regular basis.

One of the few pleasures my father enjoyed was a cigarette after his meals, and before retiring for the evening. The cigarettes were McDonalds roll your own tobacco which he rolled by hand. But as time went by, and arthritis slowly crippled his hands, he invariably got most of the tobacco in his lap, and not in the cigarette paper. Every so often one of us would buy him a package of tailor made cigarettes, which he enjoyed immensely. While I was working on the Light House Tender, I made a point of getting him a carton of cigarettes and going down to the nursing home to visit when the ship was in port. After I left the ship I tried to carry on this little tradition which I knew he looked forward to.

At the nursing home part of the usual routine for my father was to take before going to bed, was to drink a small jigger of brandy to help the heart, and improve his sleeping. He had made it up to the house that day, and when he got back home, he had taken his brandy. He opened the drawer in his side table, and lit up his evening cigarette. He turned on his radio, and settled into his armchair before calling it a day. Being relaxed and comfortable in his chair, he invariably fell asleep. He was comfortably dressed in a pair of heavy cotton Pyjamas, and a warm dressing gown. Unfortunately the dressing gown was made of a very inflammable material, and as his tired old hands relaxed in sleep, the lighted cigarette fell into the folds of his dressing gown, and lay smoldering for a few minutes before bursting into flames. The excruciating pain of his burning flesh yanked him awake and sent him stumbling into the hall at the top of the stairs screaming.

"I'm burning, I'm burning," where he collapsed in a ball of fire.

The young proprietress of the property was quietly settling down for the evening, with her fiancé, when my father's screams brought her and the young man rushing out from the kitchen, to find my father engulfed in flames. The young man immediately rushed to his aid, and ignoring the pain began to beat out the flames with his bare hands. His hands were severely burned during the procedure. The young lady called an ambulance, and my father was rushed to the closest hospital with sixty percent third degree burns to his body.

I came home from a bout of job hunting to find the family gathered around the kitchen table very quiet and subdued. I knew there was something wrong right away.

"What's going on?" I said.

"There's been an accident," my mother said, "Your Fathers been burned in a fire.

"Where is he?"

"He's at the Royal Jubilee Hospital."

I had a premonition, that I would never see him again. For although he never took part in the child rearing and never contributed any visible acts of affection, he was always there by his radio, and window, in my mind's eye. He lived for sixteen hours, but eventually his general state of poor health, and terrible burns killed him. I cried in my grief over his loss in such a horrible way and often wondered if I hadn't given him the cigarettes, would he have just died quietly in his sleep as we all thought he would. Then I would have cried not because he had died but for what he might have been.

My first brush with the law came over the rifle. I had moved it from the stairwell, and hidden it under the old bath tub in the unused wash room, for fear of my brother or mother getting rid of it when I wasn't around. My mother decided that because of my increasing belligerent attitude towards her, and the rest of the family, and my petty thievery, it would be better to turn the gun into the local Police Department for disposal. But the problem was she couldn't find it, and she didn't want to ask me where I had put it. She knew I wouldn't allow her to do anything with my possessions. She phoned the Victoria Police Department, and told them the situation. They told her not to worry they would come around and talk to me about it, and pick up the gun.

I arrived home from a bout of job hunting one afternoon to find two large burly Police plain clothes Detectives in the kitchen waiting for me. My mother introduced them as Police Detectives, and told me what they were doing there. One of the Detectives said in a quiet reasoning voice.

"Your mother wants us to take the gun off your hands son, so if you'll just tell us where it is we'll take it down town and get rid of it."

"Wait a minute," It's my gun and I never ask you guys to come for it."

"We know that, we just think it would be much safer with us, and out of your mother's house."

"Well I don't care," I said. "I'm not giving it to you."

A feeling of rage, and frustration swept over me, and tears began to well in my eyes. The Detectives noticing this closed around me preparing for any sudden moves on my part. Their attitudes were much less condescending and becoming more demanding. My over wrought and emotional condition had put them into an alert stance

Although I had done nothing to provoke it, I was suddenly attacked by both Detectives. One of them suddenly grabbed me around the throat with his right forearm, and dragged me to the floor, holding me in a sitting position from behind. With his left hand he held my left arm. The other detective immediately pinned my legs, I was completely helpless, unable to kick or use one of my arms and unable to reach either of my attacker's with my right arm. The Detective with his arm around my throat proceeded to strangle me with his right forearm until I was unable to breathe at all. This was all performed with the skill of years of practice. In the mean-time, my Mother and my sister Marjorie did nothing at all while I was being choked within an inch of unconsciousness. Finally, they decided it was enough and let me go. I staggered to my feet gasping for breath, and managed to sputter through the tears of rage.

"What was that for? I didn't do anything."

"Where's the gun?"

One of the detectives shouted at me, oblivious to my distress. The more he shouted at me the more stubborn I got, and I refused to tell them anything at all. Finally the detectives gave up, and proceeded to talk to me about getting psychiatric help. I just couldn't understand what he was talking about, because all I could think off was total strangers had come to take away my possessions, invited by my Mother without my permission. What really annoyed me was when they humiliated me in front of my Mother and Sister, and to top it all off they had the nerve to try to conciliate with me to obtain what they wanted.

"Not a chance."

After a half hour of futile persuasion, they talked to my mother for a while, and left. Although I had never been taught any respect for the Police, the chance of gaining any in the future was gone. The seeds of total rebellion were sewn.

During the next few weeks I went through the act of going down to the Unemployment Office to apply for work. I picked up a few part time jobs, but nothing permanent, which only made me feel sorry for myself while I loafed around home, and listened to my mother nag me about getting out, and finding a permanent job.

When no one was around I would get my gun out from its hiding place, and stand in front of the dresser mirror in my mom's front bedroom, and point it at my reflection, and utter tough commands like "Freeze," or "This is a stickup," while trying to look as tough as possible. I even tied a kerchief over my face as a mask, like in the westerns at the movies. The whole thing was totally ridiculous, but it made me feel like I was a potential force to be reckoned with, and not the frustrated and lost kid who needed some guidance, which just wasn't there. Unfortunately there was not anyone to show me how to get a job, or to take me aside, and give me some advice on the ways of life, and I was left alone to my own thoughts, which dwelled on how hard done by I was, and how I would get even for my lot in life. I was now totally antisocial in everything I did.

Time went by while a cauldron of resentment for my lot in life boiled until finally it bubbled over, and I decided to take the easy way, and use my rifle to hold up a store to get some quick money. I had this feeling if you had money in your pocket your troubles would evaporate, and, everything would be just fine. No thought of how this magic potion should be obtained ever occurred to me or that I would be causing anybody any harm seem to matter, or the consequences of my actions would bring me any grief. It just didn't matter at all.

CHAPTER 3

The First Robbery

Introduction to Okalla

I took the rifle out to the back shed and using an old saw, I sawed of the stock at the level of the hand grip. I took an old over coat I had and ripped out the right hand pocket. I could now put my hand in the pocket and hold the rifle under the coal out of sight. That evening I walked the few blocks to where a couple of small grocery stores were located. I could stand on the corner and watch the customers coming in and out. I waited until a small confectionary was empty, and then with a feeling of fear and excitement all rolled into one I walked over, and stepped through the door.

A young attractive woman was standing alone behind the counter looking at me a bored expression on her face.

"Yes can I help you?" she asked.

I reached down with my left hand lifted the coat up and brought the rifle to bear holding it waste high. A look of total surprise and fear swept over her face. For a moment we just stood there staring at each other. She turned and started toward the back of the store, I made a menacing gesture with the gun, which stopped her in her tracks. She screamed hysterically towards the back.

"Mrs. Smith there's a man with a gun here."

But no one appeared. She was rushing back and forth in a complete panic. Then a look of understanding swept over her face.

"You want the money don't you?"

Without waiting for an answer, she punched open the cash register grabbed a hand full of bills, and placed them quickly on the counter between us. I picked them up and backed slowly out of the store. During the two or three minutes while the previous events were going on, I hadn't spoken a single word. I just stood there pointing the gun at her. I hadn't levered a shell into the breach or taken the safety off. I couldn't have shot her even if I had wanted to.

I backed out of the store and when I found myself out on the side walk with the cold evening air slapping me in the face, bringing me back to reality. I ran as fast as I could toward town. When I had gone a couple of blocks I realized I was still holding the rifle out in the open for every passerby to see. An alley appeared to my right. I dashed in, and dropped the gun in a grassy corner. I took of my coat and threw it down on top of it. I then continued to run as fast as I could to put distance between myself and the robbery.

As I rounded a corner I could hear the sirens getting closer, so I stopped running and just strolled along like I was out for an evening walk. In a few minutes a Motorcycle Cop roared out of a side street, and passed right by in a move meant to cut anybody off who was fleeing in that direction. A Police Car was right behind the motorcycle. They made a sharp turn, and proceeded in the direction I had just come. None of the police noticed me at all, and soon I was out of there encirclement and downtown.

I realized I had to get off the street so I went to a local movie, and sat through the show to the end. When the movie was over I caught a bus home. It was getting late, and was very overcast, and dark out. I walked slowly up Denman Street Hill, feeling very tired and emotionally drained. I noticed a car parked a little farther up the street from my house with its lights on. As I approached the lights went out. I didn't think much of it. Just someone coming home, but no one got out of the car   I entered the house through the back door, and turned on the kitchen lights.

There didn't appear to be anyone home. Just as I was about to turn on the radio, a knock came on the back door. I shouted, "Come," but nothing happened. A feeling of finality came over me. Another knock came to the door. "Just a minute," I shouted. I walked over, and opened the door. A big man dressed in a Suit, and Overcoat and wearing a Fedora was standing directly in front of the door with his hands in his coat pockets.

"Yes, what can I do for you?" I asked.

"You know what were here for?" He asked.

I leaned out, and looked through the covered porch to the back yard, and saw another big man dressed identically to the man in front of me. He was obviously covering his partner although there were no drawn guns visible.

"Yeah I know what you're here for," I said. I stepped out onto the porch. "Let's go."

A slight look of surprise came over the Detective's face, as I walked out into the back yard. The Detectives flanked me, and we walked to their car.

When I saw the Policeman standing there, a feeling of complete dejection came over me, and so I thought, "What the hell!" Just give up and go with them. Nobody gives a damn anyway, and so rather than running for it I just stepped out and walked away with them. From the moment I saw the car with the lights on, I subconsciously knew who it was when the knock came on the door.

It never occurred to me before I set out to rob the store, at how easy it would be for the Police to remember the emotional kid who lived on Denman Street who wouldn't turn in his rifle, or was it a twisted way of shouting for help, and getting revenge on a thoughtless society. In the years gone by since that night, efforts of trying to analysis the reasons for my straying into the adversity of crime have come up with countless answers and none of them pass for a reasonable excuse.

One of the Detectives handcuffed my hands behind my back and shoved my head down so I could get into the backseat of the car. We drove a few blocks in silence, and then he asked.

"Where's the gun?"

"I'll show you."

We passed the store on Cook Street.

"Turn up North Park St. and stop at the first alley," I said.

I showed them where the gun was, and we proceeded to the City Jail where I was put in the open cells with the rest of the prisoners.

A uniform cop came in, and issued me with an arm load of blankets and said, "Pick an empty bunk," and then he left. The bunks were two tiered with no mattress just steel straps woven to make a platform to sleep on. The walls were covered with graffiti, and were in need of a paint job. A few local drunks and petty thieves sat around staring at me curiously. I just ignored them, and proceeded to make up- a bed the best I could with what I had. I lay down and the exhaustion of stress soon had me falling asleep.

The sound of what seemed to be running water splashing on the concrete floor woke me up with a start. It was just a drunk in the bunk across from me in a stupor laying in his bunk, and pissing through the blankets onto the floor. I thought, "Well he's not worried about a damn thing," and then I realized that I had a great deal to worry about. A small timid looking man with a nervous manner came over and leaned on the edge of my bunk.

"What did you do?"

"I held up a store," I said.

"Whoa, you're in real trouble." He said.

"Yea, I said with a sigh, "I guess I am."

"I'm in for assault with a deadly weapon," he said.

I thought Oh! Oh! What have I got here?

"My wife was cheating on me, so when I went to work in the morning, I just went back to the house, and found two guys sitting in my living room. I asked them to leave and they just laughed at me."

"What happened then?" I said, forgetting my problems.

"I went into the bed room. I've got a shot gun in the closet. I loaded it, and went back into the living room, and told them to leave or else. They just laughed again."

"What did you do then?"

I blew a hole in the Coffee Table, and some of the pellet's hit him in the groin, boy did he scream. The other guy ran into the bathroom and locked the door. I yelled through the door, and told him to come out, or I was going to shoot through the door. He came out on his hands and knees begging me not to kill him. Their attitude sure changed in a hurry."

While he was narrating his story his outward personality changed before my eyes. A man who had enough of his wife's infidelity, and was determined to act to put a stop to it emerged.

"Well, my wife phoned the cops and here I am, but I showed her a thing or two,"

He wandered away lost in his own thoughts, and sat on the edge of his bunk, a man who came out of his shell and surprised everybody.

The peep hole on the solid steel door to the cell block clanged open. A key rattled in the lock, and a cop came in with a list of prisoners for the day's court session. Five men got on the elevator and went up to the second floor and were put in a holding cell behind the prisoners dock, out of sight of the courtroom spectators.

When the Bailiff called out your name, a guard opened a solid door leading into the prisoner's dock where you stood until told to sit down. The Court Bailiff reads out the charges against you, and you are ask,

"How do you plead guilty or not guilty?"

I pleaded guilty, and then the young lady who I had scared the day lights out off was asked to identify me. She stood up before the court, and pointed a finger at me and quickly sat down.

The Judge rummaged through some papers on the desk in front of him and sentenced me to three years in the Penitentiary. The next day two Royal Canadian Mounted Policemen arrived, and picked me up and took me to the Victoria Airport, where I was flown to the Vancouver Airport, and placed in a Patty Wagon with steel mesh over the small windows. I sat on a bench and watched the pedestrian's go about their everyday business and thought, well I won't be doing that for a while.

We drove to the Vancouver City Police Cell Block, where they picked up four or five other men. One of them was a young man not much older than me. He was engaged in earnest conversation with an older man probably in his forties. He was dressed all in black, suit, overcoat, and shoes. I watched him slip the wavy haired kid a condom full of small white capsules. The condom was twisted at the top and secured with a rubber band. The kid loosened his belt and stuffed the package with his right hand under his rectum and with some discomfort by the look on his face forced the condom into his Anal Canal. The guy in black asked,

"Is everything alright Kid?"

"Yeah it'll be okay."

Then I realized that somehow the sinister looking guy in black had smuggled drugs into the local jail when he was arrested for trafficking in narcotic's and was using the kid for a courier, probably for a share of the drugs later in the prison. One of the prisoners was obviously mentally ill, for he just kept rambling incoherently about nothing in general. I noticed the rest of the prisoners just ignored him like it was and everyday occurrence to be riding around in a Police Van with an insane man as a companion. I didn't know it at the time but I had already entered the insane world of the prison system in British Columbia.

After a short ride, we stopped in front of a barrier blocking the entrance to a portal. I could see a uniformed guard dressed in a Khaki Uniform and a Tan Shirt approaching. After a few minutes the van proceeded down a winding road and stopped. The back door of the Van opened and we filed out. I found myself standing in front of a large red brick building, with bars on all the windows. There were two large compounds on each side of the concrete steps leading up to the bared doors of the front entrance. We were hustled single file inside. I asked the prisoner next to me in a low voice.

"What's this place?"

He looked at me a little surprised and then he grinned and said.

"First time eh kid?"

I said "yeah!" and shrugged my shoulders.

"Well this is Okalla B.C. Provincial Jail."

We were taken into a reception room with a small cell in one wall with a bench along one side. The cell couldn't have been more than five ft. by ten. The guard herded us into the cell. Three or four managed to sit down, but the rest had standing room only. It was a very tight squeeze. The guard behind the reception counter called out our names and we were let out of the cell one at a time to approach the counter. Each person's valuables were catalogued and placed in an envelope. The prisoner was then signed into the prison. When we were finished we were herded down into a large room with a long counter on one side with uniformed convicts behind it. There were benches lining the walls to sit on. A prison guard shouted,

"Everybody strip of their clothes."

So I sat down and stripped naked. I felt a little embarrassed because I had never been stark naked in front of anybody at least when all dignity, and modesty were also stripped along with your clothes. You were then instructed to put your clothes on the counter. The convicts then took them for cleaning for when you were released.

"All right everybody into the showers," the guard barked.

We were herded into a large room with rows of shower nozzles hanging from the ceiling. The concrete floor was studded with drains, and showed the wear of years of running water. There were stands bolted to the floor with dishes holding bars of soap for use under two rows of shower nozzles, and the other row was for rinsing and was not equipped with soap dishes. The man in front of me was huge he weighed at least 250 pounds and stood at least six ft. six inches.

Before he stripped he was wearing the clothes of a street bum. He obviously hadn't changed his clothes in weeks, and smelled of the gutter. He was obviously familiar with every aspect of what was happening to him, and the guard called him by his first name in a disgusted but friendly tone.

"Rinse yourself off good Harry I don't want any of those lice getting up in the cell blocks."

He saw me step back away from him, and I guess the look on my face was something to see because he broke out in laughter at my discomfort. Harry just grinned vacantly, oblivious to the insulting tone of the guard. Then I realized he wasn't working with a full deck, and I needed to keep my distance.

When we were finished showering we lined up in front of the counter, and one of the inmates barked at us.

"Waist, and Shirt size?"

We were issued a blue striped shirt and brown pants and a coat and work type boots. Those prisoners who were waiting to be transferred to the penitentiary or waiting appeals to be settled were moved to one side of the prison and the others to various other wings to start serving their sentences.

The next day a guard came down the tier to my cell and ask me if I was appealing my sentence. I said "No," and the door to my cell was opened, and I was told to follow him up to the front rotunda with a group of prisoners. I stood in line in front of a small holding cell, and waited my turn to be admitted. In front of everybody because the cell was just a cage I was told by a small dapper man dressed in civilian clothes that he was a doctor, and this was a short arm inspection.

"Let's have a look,"

So I had to stand there while one after another we all pulled out our Penises and squeezed them while this joker scrutinized them.

When it was over we filed back down to our cells in time to stand in line for a noon meal of stew and large steamed potatoes, served by inmates out of large cast metal kettles onto sectioned trays, then we paraded back to our cells where we ate the best we could with spoons that were issued at the time of the meal. The spoons were counted carefully when we brought our trays back in an hour.

In the afternoon those who wanted to go were allowed out into the yard next to the cell block for fresh air and exercise. The yard was reached from the floor of the Prison Wing. It was a large compound dug out of a bank, which sloped down the cell block wall and was lined with concrete. The exercise consisted mostly of walking back and forth in the fifty foot concrete passageway, and gazing up at the guards who lined the top to see that no one tried jumping up the side of the ten ft. wall to escape. We were all carefully counted when we went into the yard, and carefully counted when we came out.

During one of these exercise periods, one of the convicts had been studying the layout of the yard carefully, and had discovered a blind spot where the inmates couldn't be seen from the main building. It was the section at the bottom of the stairs leading to a small courtyard which had an opening leading into the main exercise area which was bigger than the courtyard opening. When the prisoner's time came to go back into the main building, the guards patrolling the top of the wall around the exercise area advanced forward to the courtyard to watch the inmates going up the stairs into the main building. The inmate loitered back as the cons. All filed through the opening in the exercise area's wall and when the last person passed through he ducked into the corner beside the courtyard opening and flattened himself up against the wall. The guards watching the inmates come up the stairs to the cell block couldn't see him and the guards who were up on the Courtyard Wall were watching with their backs to the Main Exercise Area. Even if they had turned around and took a few steps to see if the area was clear they wouldn't see him unless they looked straight down, which they didn't.

As soon as the last prisoner entered the main building, and the guards moved away the Con. Leaped up grabbed the edge of the wall and climbed out of the exercise area. He walked a few yards along the fence found a blank laying nearby, propped it up against the fence's barbed wire top. Climbed up, and was gone. This was accomplished with a great deal of luck and ingenuity. Eventually he was recaptured. I found out later on that he had escaped prison before, and was a notorious criminal.

There was another daring escape from Okalla where a couple of Bank Robbers managed to have two guns smuggled into them and when they went out for an exercise period they got the drop on the guards on the other side of the Chain Link Fence. After they scaled the fence, and picked up the guards rifle they made their way to the prisons front entrance area, and overcame the guard there. Just outside the entrance there was a line of cars parked with visitors coming and going. They commandeered a car, but before they could drive away an alert man, who was there applying for a job at the prison rammed his car into the escaping vehicle. One of the Cons fired a shot from the rifle through his vehicles windshield narrowly missing him. The convicts abandoned the car and escaped into the nearby woods only to be captured a short time later. The story goes that the alert man who foiled the escape was immediately hired by the Warden. The two convicts were given long prison sentences.

A few days went by of the routinely monotonous existence of sitting in my cell staring out through the bars at the small piece of prison grounds I could see through the buildings barred windows, directly across from me. This was what I did for about fifteen hours a day. The rest of the time I slept, or went to the yard or collected my meals. Finally after what seemed like an eternity my name was called out to be transferred to the British Columbia Penitentiary. I was led down to the reception room and told to strip. I was then handed my clothes by a convict at the counter, and I dressed.

CHAPTER FOUR

Penitentiary

After a long drive through Greater Vancouver we finally arrived at the small community of New Westminster on the banks of the Fraser River, home of the British Columbia Federal Penitentiary.

A couple of other guys who were making the trip with me were gazing out the small windows in the sides of the van. Both exclaimed at the same time.

"Well there she is."

Room was made for me at the window. I looked out on the grim sight of massive wooden gates in front of us. I could hear the clanging of steel on the other side, as the large double barred gates were being opened. Then the wooden doors were opened, and we drove into a small covered courtyard.

When the wooden gates and the steel barred gates were closed we were let out of the van, and told to line up by a guard dressed in the drab khaki Jacket, and Pants and Tan Shirt similar to the military garb of that time. His shoulder patches bore the legend B.C. Penitentiary. And peaked military style hat, was embellished with a badge in the shape of a Crown. On his lower sleeves he sported another patch in the shape of a Crown.

"All right, single file into the hallway. No talking."

He barked, as he pointed to a heavy Oak Door in the opposite wall, with a small glass peephole in the center for observation purposes. He opened the door and we filed in.

"Come on you! Line up properly."

He said, as he took one of the prisoners, and pulled him away from the wall he was leaning on. His demeanor was menacing and obviously he was used to getting his own way. When we were all lined up, he stepped outside locking the door behind him. In a few minutes, the door at the other end of the hall opened, and another guard came out holding a clipboard with a pen dangling from it on a string. The only thing that differed from the first Guards Uniform was he was lacking the Cloth Crown Patches on his sleeves. I realized then that the Crowns were an insignia of rank.

The guard stood there for a minute gazing at us with a look of disgust on his face. Then he said.

"When I call out your name answer," he growled. "Jones," The prisoner next to me muttered, "Here." "Two years," the guard bellowed, as he checked off the name. "Diener," I hesitated a moment. I thought "What the hell is he doing." We know how much our sentences are. "Diener", the guard bellowed getting more impatient.

"Yes," I said.

"Next time I talk to you answer promptly," he said. I just looked at him. I was thinking this guy is really wrapped up in his own importance. "Three years," he yelled, I knew then he was enjoying himself. As the guard went down the line with his clip board, I heard a prisoner mutter under his breath.

"Abandon hope, all ye who enter here." I thought, "How true, how true."

When the guard was finished with his admission, he went to the door leading to the courtyard, pressed a button which sounded a buzzer and soon the first guard came and opened the door.

"All right single file."

The second guard said as he waved us out. The first guard opened a single barred gate into the prison yard itself, and we filed through.

I glanced around, at the prisons front grounds. The prison had towers built on each corner which were manned during the day by a single guard with a rifle. The front of the prison was facing the river, consisted of a concrete administration building, the large barred front gates, and a small courtyard previously described. On top of the building were two towers, identical to those of an Ancient Medieval Castle. None of the building's walls were painted. They were just grey plaster to match the concrete walls.

Running up the center of the steeply sloping front yard was a long set of concrete steps leading to the massive grey prison cell blocks, and Work Shops set at the back of the square. The front of the yard was neat and tidy, with a sloping lawn, and flower beds. In the distance I could see a small green house with a couple of Convicts (cons,) staring our way.

"All right single file. Follow the wall around and up the hill." The guard barked in a military type command. I thought why not just go up the concrete steps, which were in front of us, and led in a straight line to the distant buildings. Then I realized there was a method in all that was happening here. By marching us up the path beneath the massive grey walls, we would get a feeling of hopelessness as we looked up at the sky for the outside world was permanently shut out, except for the sky above.

We reached the top of the hill, and walked up a few steps where a guard opened a barred door, and let us through into a hall way, I could see a few inmates standing in the door ways along the hall watching curiously as we were paraded to a flight of stairs leading down to the first floor.

I glanced to my right as I walked down the hall and I noticed a large room with shelves full of books. Convicts were sorting and stacking magazines and books at a table. I thought at least they have a library here. We were hustled down the stairs and into a reception area with a counter, and the usual desks. A big rugged looking guard sporting Crowns on his sleeves was waiting for us.

"Some new comers amongst them Harry,"

He said to an accompanying guard. "Yeah," he said, looking at us with unveiled indifference. A Barber's Chair and an old style Porcelain Bathtub stood in one half of the room. A Shower Stall was against the wall. Over to the left of me was a room with bundles of civilian clothing piled on shelves.

"Line up, and strip naked," was the next command.

As we stripped off our clothes the big guard with the Yorkshire accent checked over our belts to see if there was any contraband sewn between the leather before he gave them back.

"Okay, step over here one at a time," he commanded sitting in a Desk Chair.

"Turn around and bend over and spread your cheek's he growled.

I thought "What the hell is this," and then I remembered the young guy in the Bun Wagon stuffing the dope up his rectum, and I knew what it was all about. One by one we bent over and he fingered us with a rubber glove. He found nothing. I felt absolutely soiled, and I could feel the heat of rage warming my face but I realized I was helpless, and so I said nothing. When the guard finished with humiliating us he said.

"Alright one at a time, get into the tub."

I looked and noticed a dark grey fluid filling the tub about half full and thought "What the hell is this," and then I realized it was a kind of disinfectant. The guy in front of me hesitated a second.

"Come on get in. The guard said. It's only Sheep Dip and laughed at his own crude joke, and then I realized he wasn't far wrong. What else do you use for Sheep?" One after another we climbed into the tub and were ordered to lay and dip our heads. When we were through in the tub, we stepped into the shower, and rinsed ourselves off thoroughly.

After we had dried ourselves off, we were given underwear, socks, black boots, a blue and white striped shirt, and tan pants. A white patch was sewn at the back of the pants at the belt line and a number was stamped in ink on it. The shirt had a patch over the left chest stamped with the same number. A brown jacket made of a heavy cloth was issued also with the patch and number sewn onto the chest. Finally a peaked cap with a patch and number sewn across the front topped it off.

After dressing we were ordered into the Barber's Chair and our hair was cut a half inch on the top, and a quarter inch on the sides, by a convict with a pair of electric sheers who never spoke to anybody at all.

Finally we were issued three blankets, sheets and a pillow with a cover, a mirror, and small dust broom, and a tooth brush with a box full of a white chalk, which turned out to be the prison issue toothpaste, a metal plate with a lip bent in the upper half for hanging. Painted on the plate was your name and number in black if you were Protestant or Anglican or similar faith. Red was for Catholic or Jewish. Finally a small wooden box was issued with a wheel and flint. The box was full of small scraps of burnt rags for punk. This was your punk box for lighting your cigarettes if you were a smoker, and along with this came one package of McDonalds fine cut tobacco, and a package of cigarette papers.

Before the tobacco and cigarette papers were issued you were ask if you smoked. This was where I made my first mistake in my prison indoctrination. Not being a smoker when I was asked, I said, "No," I didn't need it." I noticed several intense stares coming from some of the prisoners who were repeaters, but I didn't pick up on it until later.

"All right get your gear together, a guard ordered. All you men who don't know listen up. The number that's been assigned you will be used instead of your names from now on, so remember it, because that's who you are." I looked at the name plate and read 6208 in big black letters. I didn't know it at the time but it was never to be forgotten.

"Put your caps on," the guard ordered, not on the back of your heads, forward over your eyes," he bellowed, for most of us had just stuck them on the back of our heads.

"Line up single file."

When we were lined up he checked the angle of the caps one by one. When they met his approval we were marched out into the dome.

The dome was a large square in the center of the building. Branching out from each side were the cell blocks like spokes coming from the hub of a wheel.

"Follow me." The guard ordered, and we walked in single file across the floor towards a large door with the inscription B.7, above it. Our footsteps echoed with every step, for everything was steel and concrete. There were steel stairs running up the front of the two large cell blocks, with cat walks running around the square dome on each level. A few convicts were busy sweeping and mopping the floor. As we walked by nobody spoke. A guard stood by a small wooden table near the door we had just emerged from. This was the only piece of furniture in the place.

I noticed as we entered the B.7. Corridor that the floor turned from concrete to granite terrazzo, and I realized it was new. The right side of the passage had large windows which looked out onto an outside court with basketball hoops set up at each end. The court was surrounded by the buildings walls except for one corner which had a large chain link pen with barbed wire topping.

When we reached the end of the corridor we were ushered onto a landing, which over looked another dome, which was lined by cell blocks on each side, but was obviously much newer than the area I had just left, and smaller. We were taken into the cell block on our right as we came in. It consisted of a long room with large windows facing out onto the inside exercise yard we had just past on our way in. A long row of cells faced the windows, but didn't give a view because the windows were set to high. Directly above this row of cells was a cat walk with a steel pipe railing, and another row of cells with a glimpse of the exercise yard. All of the cell blocks in B.7 were identical and were marked with an identification number and letter such as 1A, 2B, and so on. I found out later on that the tier had a nickname "Fish Tier."

When we were allocated a cell on the Fish Tier we were told to hang our name plate on what looked like two large steel railroad ties which ran along the top of the cells front bars. At one end just outside the cell blocks gates there were two large wheels, like the wheel of a sailing ship only made of brass. Next to the wheel was a brass gauge with the numbers of the cells stamped on it. Pointing at the numbers was a brass arrow which moved when the wheels were turned. This arrangement allowed the guards to open the cells all at the same time, or individually. When the wheels were turned a hole drilled through the steel ties could be separated, preventing a steel bar which ran down to a handle attached to a latch which opened and closed the cell gate. When the handle was lifted the bar entered the aligned hole, lifting the simple latch allowing the gate to spring open. When the handle dropped, and the steel ties were moved, the hole divided, effectively blocking the bar from entering the hole, and stopping the handle from being lifted, creating a permanent lock without a key. I was to learn that ironically a convict had invented this ingenious method of incarceration.

The guard said "6208, 2B Number 3."

I stepped out of line and climbed the steel stairs to the upper tier, and walked along to the third cell, hung my name plate up while the guard spun the wheels until the needle on the gauge reached number 3. He shouted, "Lift the handle," I lifted and the gate sprang forward a couple of inches with a loud clanging noise as the steel latch was released. I could hear other cells on the block being opened and shut in the same way.

I stood there taking in my surroundings for a minute. On the left wall, bolted in place was a wooden cupboard painted light grey. The front door opened down and was suspended by a chain which created a small table. Bolted to the right wall was your steel bed, which folded up on heavy steel hinges against the wall. The legs folded flat against the bed for compactness sake. The back wall contained a small porcelain sink which fitted snugly against the wall with no facets just a nozzle protruding from the back. Fitted just above the sink in the wall was a stainless steel button, which when pressed caused the water to pour into the sink, this procedure caused a loud banging noise when the water was released, and when it was shut off, for it was under very high pressure. In the right hand corner of the cell directly behind your bed was the toilet, which operated in the same principal as the sinks. There was no tank visible for the toilet and no visible pipes at all. They were all behind the back wall of the cell. Above the sanitation facilities was a single wooden shelf, which ran the width of the cell.

The cell was about five feet wide by ten feet long. If you paced your cell, three good steps were all you got. On the wall beside the cupboard some wooden pegs were attached for hanging your clothes. A folding wooden chair leaned against the wall. In the back wall about waist high was a slot or peephole penetrating the concrete, on the other side was a walkway and the various plumbing that only a very few inmates ever saw. A set of head phones, the only bit of luxury we had were hanging from the bars at the head of the bed. Music and prison messages were piped through to the Inmates during their eighteen hours spent in the cells during the day. This proved to be the major contact the men had with the outside world. I set the bed down, and proceeded to make it up, and to stow my meager possessions in the cupboard. I found that by sitting on my bed I had just enough room for my legs to fit in front of the cupboard table.

This was my first moment of total privacy with nothing to do but think. As I sat there looking around. I felt a feeling of total hopelessness, and despair. Suddenly a guard walked by and glanced into my cell through the bars causing me to snap out of my feelings of self- pity, and I thought well you're here now and if you can't do the time you shouldn't do the crime.

Approximately an hour went by, which I spent lying on the bed listening to the music on the earphones, which was coming from a radio situated somewhere in the prison. A guard came up to the cell, opened the door, and said.

"Get up I'm going to show you how you make up your bed every morning from now on."

I hung up the earphones and stood aside. He said.

"Strip off those blankets and sheets."

I stripped the bed down to the thin tick mattress, and the guard showed me how to fold the blankets length wise, and then the two ends to the middle, and once over again to make a compact bundle of the sheets and two blankets. The third blanket was left folded lengthwise and wrapped around the others. The bed was then folded up to the wall and the bundle was placed on top of the turned up edge of the bed with the pillow on top.

"You will leave the bed made up in this manner while you are absent from your cell five days a week, weekends excluded. "Do you understand?" he snapped. I just looked at him, and he left slamming the cell door behind him as he went. Suddenly a loud bell went off and in a few minutes I heard the low rumbling of the wheels being turned, and the steel rails moving. The convict in cell number 1 ran by my cell lifting the door handle as he went. I could hear the loud clang, clang as he went from door to door down the tier. I pushed open the door, and stepped out looking around. The other convicts were gathered outside the cells. Most of them stared at the newcomers. I noticed that a few were shaved totally bald, and that the rest were showing some new hair growth in various stages. I was to learn that I had escaped having my hair cut off by just a few days. The Penal Services had decided that it was an unnecessary punishment, which could be dispensed with. I thought they probably realized that foul sheep dip would kill any parasites in the hair, so total shaving was really unnecessary. Another bell rang and a guard stationed at the end of the tier shouted. "Let's Go."

We walked down the stairs in single file. On the landing I noticed a guard standing beside a large bell controlled by a button. There were three or four other guards in attendance watching as we filed single file up the long corridor towards the main dome.

After passing through the dome we turned to the right through a gate which led into a corridor with several openings in a tiled wall where your meal was dispensed. The main meal came on a metal sectioned tray with the days offerings in their appropriate compartments. Another slot served up a large steel mug which contained tea for most of the meals, and occasionally on other days half a cup of milk was issued. Another opening served sliced bread, which because of the meagreness of some of the meals was usually picked up in a large quantity, although most of the inmates thrived on the three meals a day.

After picking up our trays, we all proceeded back to our cells in single file. The corridor was wide enough that a line of inmates could pass each other without being able to come in contact with one another. I noticed that the Fish Tier was sent to pick up their meals before any of the other cells proceeded.

After re-entering my cell I sat there on the edge of my bed and ate my meal of mashed potatoes, stew and corn. One of the sections on the tray held a desert of creamed rice. The portions weren't very large but along with the tea and bread were adequate. I was to find as the days went by that the food was alright but very monotonous and I did not look forward to it at all.

After eating, there was nothing to do but lie down and listen to the radio on the earphones, and occasionally when I got tired of that the noise of the other inmates rustling about in their cells, and occasionally talking back and forth about the day's events. At 10.00 o'clock, the bell rang, and fifteen minutes later the lights went out. The routine had begun.

Kazoonie

In the morning, we dropped off our empty supper trays, and picked up our breakfast. After breakfast was dispensed with we were let out of our cells and told to congregate on the cell block floor below. A few of the prisoners seemed to know each other, and were engaged in quiet conversations while the others just stood around staring at each other. A guard came into the room and said.

"Everybody outside, and line up on the landing for your tobacco issue."

I thought I don't want any tobacco, so I just held back, while the rest of the cons made a rush for the door.

A guard was standing with a large canvas bag full of packets of Macdonald's Fine Cut Tobacco, and Cigarette Paper's. Another guard stood and called names from a list on a clip board, and as each name was called he picked up his weekly issue of one packet of tobacco and papers, and walked back into the cellblock. Eventually my name was called, and I said.

"I don't smoke, so I don't need any."

The guard just stood there for a minute staring at me in surprise, and finally said "O.K." and wrote something on his clipboard. When I said, "I don't need any," all the cons head's snapped around, and stared with disbelief written all over their faces.

I walked back into the cell block, and immediately I was left standing alone in the corner as the cons backed away from me. I knew that I had made a mistake in not accepting the tobacco, and even worse, telling the guard I didn't need it. I couldn't make a connection to why I was being ostracized so quickly, but I knew the tobacco was the key to the problem. I just stood there and waited for something to happen. I didn't have to wait long.

A small group of cons slowly walked over towards where I was standing. The obvious leader of the group was powerfully built, with a head which just seemed to sit on his massive shoulders. He was thickly built from head to foot. His small beady black eyes looked right through me.

"Why didn't you take your tobacco?" he asked.

His voice was high and sounded nasal, and he smiled a humorless smile, as he tried to ingratiate himself. I felt a little fear touch at my heart as the other cons circled me quietly.

"I don't smoke," I said half-heartedly.

"Yeah, well we do, and we can use an extra packet of weed," he said as he scratched his partially bald head, grinning at me. I don't think I had ever seen a more evil grin.

"Well, I said as I shrugged my shoulders, it's a little late now you should have told me."

"I didn't think you'd be so dumb," he said.

"Look if it's so important I'll get it next time," I smiled back as ingratiating as I could trying to ease the tension that was hanging as thick as fog. "I'll give it to you, I don't need it."

"I don't need it."

A falsetto voice bantered from a group standing a few yards away. I just grinned uneasily, and said nothing. The rest of the cons thought that it was funny, and some laughed outright, while others just grinned. I didn't realize I was being tested. Just then a guard came onto the tier.

"The new cons over against the wall, the rest of you pick up your sand paper, and go to your assigned tier," he shouted.

The cons were issued long pieces of emery paper, as they filed out the door to their work areas.

"All right you guy's over here," the guard ordered.

He was standing by a cell door holding a long strip of emery paper about an inch wide and two feet long. He wrapped it around one of the bars in the cell door took a hold of the ends and began to pull it back and forth on the bar, sanding it until it shone.

"I want to see these bars shine like silver with no exceptions."

He handed out a strip to each one of us, and assigned us to a tier, and told us to pick a cell door, and to get with it.

At one end of the tier was a small room, equipped with a sink, and the necessary janitorial equipment, such as a broom, and mop, and bucket with squeegee. One of the cons who's Hair had begun to grow back, was sweeping the tier floor. As he passed by me he glanced over to the tier door, to check whether the guard had gone or not. When he stopped sweeping, he leaned on his broom staring me up and down for a minute. I was looking at a man with close set eyes and a low hair line with heavy black eyebrows. He had a thick powerful torso with unusually long arms, and a narrow waist with short bowed legs. Finally he said.

"How much time you doing?"

"Three years, I said, how about you?"

"A deuce," he snapped, following with a quick "What for?"

"Armed robbery," I said.

"B&E," he volunteered and continued to sweep the floor.

Around noon the bell rang and we filed up to the Fish Tier. After the count, we proceeded to the kitchen to pick up our lunch trays and spent another hour in our cells.

After lunch was straightened away, we were escorted to the Exercise Yard, located outside the B7 corridor. The guard produced a basketball, and an impromptu game started up, and I joined in for a little exercise. The con was playing to. He was athletic but clumsy. I played basketball a lot in school, and was obviously the best player on the court. After about twenty minutes of play, the high falsetto voice began to make smart cracks about my game, implying crude remarks about my manhood etc. This goaded some of the others to pick up with the idea of fun. I realized that I was becoming the center of attention, and this was not in my best interest, so I walked over towards where a couple of cons were playing Horse Shoes. I sat down on the dirt bank facing the B7 outside wall and watched hoping I would be soon forgotten. A deep gravelly voice broke into my reverie.

"Giving you a rough time kid?"

I looked up, and saw a big man standing there. His face was broad and flat. His jacket was far too small for him, the sleeves were at least three inches too short, and his massive hands stuck out like a couple of hams. His cap sat on top of his large flat head. He sat down beside me and said.

"What your name?"

"John," I said.

"Getting a bad time in the game?" he asked.

"No I just ignored them."

"Monk has got his group, and he doesn't like not being the center of attention," he said.

"Who's Monk?" I ask.

"The guy with the long arms," he said.

I looked over to the group on the court and realized he was talking about the sweeper

"Well Monk sure fits anyway."

"My names Lynch I'm in for bad Cheque's," he said laughing.

"You?" he asked.

"Armed robbery," I said, just a grocery store."

"Oh," he said, lots in for that look over there, now see the group gathering," he said.

I looked over to the edge of the court, and saw five or six cons. all young, about my age gathering around Monk. They were glancing over my way, and occasionally making disparaging remarks about the play that was going on the basketball court. They were laughing, and snickering, trying to gain Monks attention and support.

"There all graduates of various reform schools and Vancouver's streets, and they all know each other, he said, keep away from that bunch. The little shrimp with the big coat," he said.

I looked over, and picked out who he was talking about right away. He looked years younger than he was, small, and slight of build almost like a small boy not yet out of grade school. He was engaged in animated conversation with one of the other Cons. I could just make out some of the conversation. "Bang, Bang," he said in a high squeaky voice swinging his arms like he was playing baseball.

"I smashed him with a steel pipe and knocked him down, and grabbed his wallet," he was bragging.

He was getting more animated and excited as he told the not too interested con about some mugging he'd pulled off somewhere.

"That's Mousey, don' let his looks fool you he' a full- fledged member of that group."

Suddenly a murmur of excitement rolled from the yard and then silence as everybody strained to see what was happening. Two guards were opening a door at the far corner of the yard in front of an enclosure surrounded by a chain link fence, about ten feet high topped off with barbed wire. A convict shuffled out and stood there for a minute blinking his eyes in the unaccustomed sunlight. One of the guards opened the gate to the enclosure and ordered him inside. He ambled in slowly, not paying any attention to who was gawking at him. He then proceeded to walk up and down on the well-worn track in the thirty foot square.

"What's going on there?" I asked.

"Oh, that's just some guy who's in the Hole getting his exercise," he said. "Only suckers get thrown in the Hole."

"What do you mean?"

"Well if you go to the Hole you lose some of your good time, so it pays to keep your nose clean. You don't gain anything by going to the Hole not even respect from your fellow cons remember that kid," he shot back as he wandered away

In about an hour we were lined up, and marched back to the Fish Tier. We were issued our sand paper, and sent back to work. Just before lock up a convict delivered a wagon load of books from the library, and we placed them on the cell bars of the tier according to the con's number which was on a slip of paper slipped between the pages.

The bell went on schedule, and we all proceeded up to the Fish Tier to assemble, and wait a few minutes for supper. I was standing minding my own business, When Monk wandered over to me and took a fighters stance and began to throw fake punches into my body. The punches were thrown hard but were checked just before they made contact. I said.

"Cut it out Monk,"

But he just ignored me. I brushed past him but he just kept doing it. He knew it was annoying me, and knew that I was not going to do anything about it. I knew he thought I was afraid of him, and that his intimidation would bother me. Well he was right on both counts. He was like a cat playing with a mouse he had just caught before he killed it. The rest of the convicts were watching me to see how long I was going to put up with this bully, with anticipation. Then I knew if I didn't do something I was going to be the brunt of every cruel bastard in the place, when they needed to torment someone to let off their frustrations.

I stopped avoiding the taunting menacing game he was playing, and stared him in the eye. My feelings of anger and disguised frustration came boiling to the surface. He realized that he had finally got to me, and with a smirk on his face increased his taunting punches. I thought two can play at this game, and lashed out with a punch aimed at his shoulder. I figured a good sharp jolt would let him know his little game was over, and he'd tire of it. The punch missed its mark. He had seen it coming and shifted his weight to reduce the force, but what happened then surprised both of us, mostly him. The punch ricocheted of his shoulder, and cracked into his jaw with a considerable amount of force like a baseball glancing of a bat when not hit solidly, increasing the balls forward velocity. A total look of surprise came over his face. As he staggered back clutching his chin.

"Jesus Monk, I'm sorry I didn't mean that,"

He stood there in a daze, not saying anything just staring at me in disbelief. Finally he brushed my hand away and walked carefully over to the wall and crouched down on his haunches looking all in the world like his nickname intimated. A quiet had spread over the Con's when the worm turned, and they walked in groups whispering about the sudden turn in events. Mousey walked over to Monk and said.

"What happened to you?"

"He throws a pretty mean punch."

Monk said, staring at me with a pale worried expression on his face. Mousey looked at me with a look of curiosity, shrugged his shoulders, and left Monk to his own thoughts. The Convicts who had talked me into giving my tobacco to him came over and said.

"You had better watch your back from now on," and grinned at me

"Hell, I didn't mean to hit him so hard, I was just trying to get him to lay off me. That little game he was playing was bloody annoying.

"Look my name is Chuck, and I know this guy, you've embarrassed Monk in front of friend's and he's going to try some-time or another to get back at you."

He laughed. He seemed to be taking pleasure in my predicament. The bell went, and we filed out for supper.

That night I lay on my bunk, digesting the day's events, and I came to the conclusion that I would be much more careful about what I was doing, and who I was associating with. I stared at the Confining - Walls, and bars surrounding me and felt for the first time a feeling of security and realized it wasn't the prison confinement itself that was going to be tough, it was the fellow inmates that were going to make my life miserable if I allowed it.

Saturday morning a change of clothing with a towel was delivered to each fish, (New Convict) and we were let out for a shower. Before the first cell was a single shower room, which we used according to your cell numbers. Once a week, hot water and razors were given to the Convict's to shave. The blades were carefully accounted for after each session.

One evening during the second week of my stay on the Fish Tier, the usual noise of the inmates in their cells was suddenly broken by an incessant steady pounding, like someone was hammering a nail repeatedly with a steady unbroken stroke. This was interrupted by the smashing sound of porcelain and wood.

"What the hells that?" One of the con's hollered, tell that bastard to cool it."

"Hey quiet down there," another one called.

Soon the quiet was broken by the shouts from several inmates all clamouring for quiet at once. Finally someone shouted.

"Wolseski's, flipped out he's smashing his cell up."

"Christ, that's all we need," an insensitive voice said.

The only sound from then on was the incessant banging on the wall, a steady drumming. It seemed like an eternity, but in reality it was probably just a few minutes. Finally I heard the cell wheels being turned, and the sound of running feet. Someone said.

"It's about time the screws got here."

A cell door opened with a clang, a few muttered words were spoken, and then a shrill high scream came up from one of the cells below me. I could hear the sounds of a scuffle going on, and the screaming got loader and louder. Finally it slowly faded away as they took the convict away to isolation. The wheel turned, a few toilets flushed, and then silence. I lay there on my bunk, my nerves as tight as violin strings. I felt like leaping to my feet and screaming, and smashing my way out, and then the utter futility of my situation settled in, and I went to sleep.

Near the end of my stay on the Fish Tier, I was called to the front foyer, and introduced to a tall elderly guard with a clipped mustache and sporting two brass Crowns on his shoulders. I realized that this was a higher ranking guard than those that I had seen so far.

"This is the Chief Engineer," a guard said.

He stood there staring at me for few minutes, sizing me up.

"Would you like to work in the Engineering Department?" He said.

I thought Engineering, What the hell sounds alright.

Kazoonie

"Sure." I said.

"All right you will start Monday."

"OK, back on the tier," the guard said.

The few Con's that came in with me, and some of the others on the tier were given their job assignments that afternoon, and we knew we were getting off the Fish Tier, and out into the general prison population at last. The anticipation of not having to shine cell bars any more was a welcome break from the monotony of the day. I thought just a couple more days of this and things will get better. I ate my supper with a little more enthusiasm that night.

The next day I was assigned my tier to clean and service, but when I arrived I found the cell's still occupied, nobody had gone to work.

"Hey!" a voice called down from the upper deck. I looked up and saw this lanky Con staring down at me. His cell name plate said "Mears"

"Yes!" I said.

"Are the other guys sloughed up in their drums on the other side?"

"Sloughed up in their drum's?" I asked hesitantly.

I didn't know what he was talking about.

"Jesus Pat! We've got a real green one here," he called out to the man in the cell next to him.

"Yeah!" he said, he means in their cells," he said dryly.

I felt my face getting hot and flushed with embarrassment, and I just shrugged my shoulders.

"I don't know, I haven' been over there this morning," I said.

"Shit! Mears said, I guess they haven' found it yet."

"Yeah, I wonder how long were going to be sloughed up?" Pat said.

I found out later, that the Con's on this tier were all from the Engineering Department, and that someone had stolen the week's issue of tobacco, and that they were all being held in their cells for the day, while they searched the building where they worked. The Convicts were hoping that by stealing the tobacco issue, the prison administration world decide to issue another package to those who were the victims, and thereby obtain a double ration that week. But the guards didn't see it that way at all and a further issue was not given out. Subsequently the stolen tobacco mysteriously reappeared, but it was all to no avail. Nobody in the Engineering Department received any tobacco that week, so they were without their precious weed for almost two weeks driving some of them closer to the brink of insanity. I never heard of anyone trying that caper again.

The following Sunday, instead of being assigned a tier to clean, I was told to pack up my gear, and get ready to move. I folded my blankets and got my meagre belongings into a pile and waited for my new assignment. I noticed Joey Cramer, Monk, Irving Walker, and Bobby Shaefer standing in a group waiting to move to their new quarters.

Finally a guard stepped forward with a list, and started calling out our names. I was to go to Tier H cell 6 B7. I was pleased to find I was located on a top tier, where I could look over the front wall through the tall windows in the front of building. The Petallo Bridge spanned the Fraser River on my right, and I had a panoramic view of the river and its far shore. I could hear the cell doors on my right and left opening and closing, and I wondered who my neighbours were. Then Monk's voice came over.

"Hey, number 6 is that you Joey?"

"No! It's 6208 Diener

"Jesus Christ, not you?" He growled.

Joey's voice came over.

"I'm in number 7 Monk," he said, "Where's Walker?"

A voice came up from below.

"I'm down here in number 5 below."

"Hey we got a view up here," Joey said obviously pleased with his location.

"Yeah, you'll soon get tired of that," an unknown voice said. A spattering of laughter echoed through the tier at this sardonic comment.

"Jealousy will get you nothing," Monk muttered weekly.

The rest of the morning was fairly quiet, just the usual banging of sinks, and toilets being used and the constant rustle of twenty-four men going about the usual activities available in approximately a 12 ft. x 6 ft. cell.

When we were let out onto the tier for lunch, I looked around to see who was there, and I immediately noticed there was no one there who was older than twenty-one. Both tiers on the range were full. There were a few surprised comments about this, but it was soon shrugged off as a coincidence and forgotten.

After lunch we were let out to drop off our trays, and were then directed out through the Dome to an enclosed courtyard on the opposite side of the building, nestled in between the East Wing and the South Wing, this was called the Exercise Yard. The yard consisted of a weight lifting area on the top of a bank just opposite the South Wing of the main building. All along the bank wall were wooden benches placed so you could sit and watch the Asphalt Basketball Court below. Over at the end of the cell block were a couple of Horse Shoe Pitches. This area was surrounded by a high chain link fence, held up on a wooden frame work. Beyond this was the approximately thirty feet or more of high main concrete wall of the prison.

Men were engaged in weight lifting, and there was a Base Ball Game going on in the Basketball Court. Because the yard was far too small for a proper baseball field, the fielders were outside the fence standing on the road, which ran alongside the enclosure. Two prison guards were stationed nearby to watch they didn't run too far, when chasing a fly ball. I thought that's kind of silly, where can they go?

I walked along the bench lines and sat down to watch the game which was being played with a great deal of enthusiasm below me. The convict next to me gave me a poke in the ribs with his elbow to get my attention. I looked up, and saw a nervous face staring at me from under his new hat brim. A voice on the opposite side said.

"Move to the bench in front, and sit up straight."

I turned and glanced at this new problem, and saw another earnest character sitting next to me. It suddenly dawned on me that they meant business, and they definitely wanted me to move. The nervous guy said.

"Look your sitting over our brew, and we want to check it. It should be ready now."

I said. "Brew?" in a questioning tone.

"Yeah, it's buried under your feet. Potatoes and prune juice, it's been brewing for a couple of weeks, and we want to check it."

I thought these guys have got to be kidding, but then I realized by their nervous furtive glances around at the guards mingling with the convicts, they weren't at all. I got up and stepped over the low bench in front of me. I noticed most of the cons. around us had drawn into a tight group to shield what was happening. I just sat up straight, and stared straight ahead. Someone said, "Now." I turned to see what was happening. An inmate was hurriedly digging with his hands in the soft dirt between his legs. Quickly he uncovered a quart preserve can, unscrewed the lid and drank some of its contents. He then quickly put the can back, and covered it up. The other Con looked on expectantly.

"Well!" He said.

"Not quite ready yet," his partner said, wrinkling up his face.

I turned back to the ball game, and when I looked around again they were both gone. I sat there thinking, all that for a crummy drink. There nuts. If they get caught they'll go to solitary confinement for punishment. As far as I was concerned the risk wasn't worth the effort. Then I thought. It's a game between guard and convict. The guard to catch them in the act of breaking prison rules and the convict in an act of defiance a planned action to kill the endless monotony of time. I was to change my mind about this theory several times in the months ahead.

After we were returned to our cells, and the count finished. I lay quietly listening to my head phones. It was Matt Dillon, United States Marshal a radio western. The count was carried out by the guards each time the prisoners returned to their cells from outside activity, such as exercise periods, or work. They just walked down the tiers and counted heads in each cell, and matched the count with the total prison population count.

The next day I reported to the dome, where the men who worked in the different shops were joining up in groups before marching off to work. I found the Dome Commander who wore a crown on his sleeve and he directed me to the appropriate group. I noticed some of the men who had been sloughed up in their drums because of the tobacco theft, and they nodded and grinned, but didn't say anything. A guard checked off our numbers on a clipboard, and when he was satisfied he had his full crew we went out a barred gate in the side of the dome, and walked down to a single story building in front of the complex overlooking the front inside grounds, which gave us a bit of a view of the daily activities going on down at the front gate, and we could see the manicured lawns, and flowers grown by a few convict grounds keepers.

The Engineers Department was the name used by the convicts and guards, to identify the Electric, Plumbing and Heating Plant. The Steam Engineers and the various tradesmen also acted as prison guards, while teaching the convicts how to do the various duties required to run an institution of close to Five-hundred men and growing.

"6208," a guard called. I stepped out of line "6200," and Chuck stepped out. He had been assigned to the Electrical Department. The next number that was called was a very low number, and a few heads turned to see who it was. A small built boyish looking man stepped forward his uniform was clean and pressed, and his shoes shone. There was a wild look in his eye. Later on, I found out he had been transferred from the Taylor Shop which explained the neatness of his prison uniform. Apparently he was an American Sailor who was in Vancouver visiting his girlfriend, and he found out she had another suitor, so in a jealous rage he shot her and broke her back, leaving her a cripple for the rest of her life. The courts found him guilty and sentenced him to life in prison, which explained the low prison numbers. I had not seen any numbers which were as low as his, but as time went by I came across several more wearing low numbers and most of them wore pressed clothes and wore better boots then the majority. I could only suspect this was because of the cons respect for the length of time they were doing which led to better treatment in the laundry, Tailor Shop and the Shoe Shop. Another explanation could be when they ask for something and they mentioned the length of their time to be served, the word life brought forth some sympathy. Sympathy was not apparent in most transactions amongst the cons, but barter was.

"You, and you," the guard pointed to me and the long timer.

"You stay here, the rest of you are dismissed."

The rest of the group ambled off to their various duties. The guard came over looking at his clipboard, and said to me.

"You're Diener?"

"Yes."

"You're going to work on the boilers with Sailor Mack here."

I was surprised when the guard spoke to us and used our last names instead of the numbers. I almost didn't reply. I believe that using the numbers was just another method of making us understand that we were just another number in the institution and it was much easier for record keeping etc.

I looked over at the three large steam boilers, to the right of a large open room. In the back I could see piles of coal. There was an iron wagon for bringing coal out to the front of the boilers. A door on the side of the wagon was opened and the coal fell out onto the floor for easier shovelling into the furnace. I thought "one shower a week, and I'm going to be shovelling coal into a bloody furnace all day. This is not good at all." The guard said.

"Come on out the back with me, were going to fill the Coal Cart."

Mack and I, walked out to the cart, and pushed it into position beside the pile of coal, and began shovelling. When we were finished we pushed the cart out to the boilers, and released the catches on the side door, and the coal slid out onto the floor in front of the furnace doors.

The rest of the day was spent learning how to bank and clean the fires, and to keep them going to maximum capacity. Near the end of the day we were told we could use two showers situated in the corner of the Boiler House, but there would be no clean change of clothes. A buzzer went off around noon, and the Engineer Gang all lined up and marched up to the dome, where we were searched. When that was finished with, we picked up our dinner trays from the kitchen, and marched down to our cells for an hours break. In the middle of the afternoon we were given our exercise period which consisted of an hour in the exercise yard. Then we went back to the boiler house to tend the coal fires until supper, and then we were locked up for the night.

The next day I was escorted up to the South Wing of the dome. This wing held the Prison Library, Hospital, Dental, Admitting, and Discharge. In general it was the Administration Wing of the prison. I was taken to the top floor of the wing and ushered into a large open room with a few school desks, and a black board. I was told to sit down at one of the school desks. A young guard at the end of the room introduced himself, as the officer in charge of the school, and Correspondence Courses. He asked me about my education, and then said.

"You have been assigned to our Engineering Department, on the boilers."

"Yes."

"Its customary for inmates assigned to this position to take the B.C. Government Correspondence Course on Fourth Class Engineering. So that when they finished they will be able to write for a Fourth Class Engineers Steam Ticket. The other inmates who are assigned to the boilers are all taking the course. Are you interested?"

I thought, why not, it'll give me something to do other than just reading and lying around in my cell, so I said.

"Sure, I'll take the course."

"Fine, I'll get you to fill out the application papers to-night. Put them on your cell bars in the morning, and they'll be picked up. "That's all," he said, and he handed me a brown vanilla envelope. When I got back to the Boiler House Sailor Mac came over, and said.

"I see your taking the Fourth Class Course to eh."

"Yea, it'll give me something to do at night. Are you taking it?" I ask.

"No I'm doing life it won't do me any good."

His eyes took on the wild look, and he said.

"My girlfriend was cheating on me, and I caught her. I was in the American Navy, and my ship was visiting Vancouver when I met her, I thought we had an understanding, but when I came up to visit her, she said she had met somebody else, so I shot her with a .45 and crippled her for life."

He looked at me for a minute, and said with a hopeful look on his face,

"Maybe they will deport me."

"Yea, maybe they will who knows," I said and walked away.

Time went by and to try and keep clean on one of our trips to the Prison Barber. I had my hair all shaved off, in the hope I could wash the coal dust off of my head easier.

I observed that tobacco was used as the instrument of barter in the prison amongst the inmates. Your clothes could be pressed for a few packages of tobacco every few months. You could get new shoes made for you in the Shoe Shop, even tailor made clothes from the Taylor Shop, and if you were a gambling man, you could place bets on the horses which were run every week on our radio earphones.

I was handing my weekly tobacco issue around to the other convicts on the tier, not trying to gain any favor's it was just that I didn't need it, so why not. But when I found out about its value, I stopped that immediately, and started to save it instead. Of course when I was asked for the odd hand out, and I turned them down there was a few very disappointed people around me, but when they found out I had smartened up, they seemed to respect this more than when I gave it away. So my fears of possible heavy handed retaliation didn't materialize. In a few months after I made a few connections. I was feeling a lot better about my appearance, with my new pressed clothes every week, and a new pair of shoes. My appearance was a bit of a status symbol.

In the meantime the reputation of my tier on B7 was beginning to spread around the prison. The word about all the young punks confined to one cell block was going around, and so we were given a name the Kazoonies. We were the Kazoonies in B7. I never was able to find out who started this, but it stuck for the rest of my stay. Twenty-four young men serving time for crimes ranging from murder to car theft, most of them minded their own business, and did their own time, but there were one or two who were natural bullies and couldn't do their own time. I tried to avoid them as much as I could, but sometimes it wasn't always possible.

On Sunday morning after breakfast, there was Church Parade. The North Wing was the original cell block, and it contained the smallest cells in the prison as well as the kitchen and Prison Chapel. The Chapel was used strictly for Protestant Church services. The Roman Catholics had their own chapel, which was located in the West Wing of the prison. Most of the Kazoonies went to the church services the first time, not because of any religious verve but just to get out of our cells, and see what the chapel was like.

The Protestant Chapel had a stage, to allow extra entertainment, which was put on occasionally by inmates, or an occasional movie was shown. There were two elevated chairs on each side of the typical arrangement of two rows of large Church Pews, which filled the high ceiling hall. During services guards occupied the elevated chairs for a better view over the inmates. Later on after attending a few services I noticed the attendance was never very large, and always the same group seemed to attend, for the services were designed to be about as boring as they could get, and after a few months I stopped attending, and spent my Sunday mornings cleaning up my cell, or reading.

The library was probably the most important source of entertainment in the prison. Everyone made out a list of books and magazines which were available to them from the Prison Library. On your admission a library Catalogue was given to you so you could pick out what you preferred to have delivered to you during the week. You received a magazine every day during the working week, and your library book was replaced when you returned the used one.

There was quite a variety of sports played in the small exercise yard, Hand Ball, Basketball, Soft Ball, and Horse Shoe's to name a few. I had learned how to play Basketball when I was going to school, and I became fairly skilled at it, and so when the guard in charge of prison athletics made an arrangement for us to play in the local town Basketball League under special conditions, which of course meant we didn't visit. The opposing teams came inside the walls to play us on our outside court. I was asked by the Inmate Manager and Coach to try out for the team. The players picked for the team were the cream of the prison program, and so when I was finally chosen as a player, I felt quite pleased about it, until I saw the click that was apparent among the players. The Coach tried to mould us into a team, but it was apparent from the start that the team work wasn't there, and would never be there, and without team work in Basketball you cannot win. None of the players except for a few who had played the game at school had any real experience in the intricate play making of Basketball, and most of them didn't want to be told anything by anybody especially another con, and so most of the practices were more a series of arguments about who was right, and who was wrong, during the game. After a few sessions of this I took the coach aside and told him I wasn't interested anymore, and advised him to get someone else.

The big day came for the first visiting team to come. Nearly the whole prison population was sitting on the Wooden Benches overlooking the court. After the first period of play, it was apparent that our players were over matched, and that the visitors were playing with us, although occasionally we would make an individual basket that brought a cheer from the crowd. In the second half the score was so lopsided that the visitors put out their second string, but even with that it was a disaster. After finding out that the league they were in was too high. And that they needed considerable more training, the Basketball League fizzed out, and there never was another league game.

After about six months in B7, the Kazoonies were told to pack up our gear, and that we were being sent to the North Wing. The worst wing in the prison, because it was the oldest, and the cells were considerably smaller. There was just enough room on one side of the cell for your bunk and toilet, and when the bed was laid down and your cupboard door was open you could not get from one end of the cell to the other, without lifting the cupboard door. There were five floors of cells. The main floor ended at the entrance to the kitchen. Starting at the second tier, thin bars and wire enclosed the tiers to the top of the block so no one could commit suicide by leaping off the top tiers. Compared to B7 it was grim.

The third tier ended at the entrance to the Protestant Chapel landing, this is where I was located with half of the Kazoonies on one side of the wing and the other half around the corner facing the other way on the other half of the wing.

The first night was like being admitted all over again. It was considerably noisier, for we were exposed to the noises made by the North Wing, and the East Wing. More than half the prison population in cells which were not confined in closed blocks like B7, so the running sinks and flushing toilets, and the calling back and forth of the inmates were deafening compared to B7. This went on every night until ten o'clock when the lights were turned out, and the cell activity settled down for the night. It was a kind of mutual agreement that after the lights went out extra noise would stop. I never saw the guards having to discipline anyone over excessive noise after ten except the occasional inmate who cracked under the crushing monotony of everyday existence, and had to be taken to solitary screaming. An added disturbance to those on my tier was the Church Parade on Sunday morning, which marched down our tier to get to the Church, and occasionally when the Chapel was used for entertainment activities.

My occasional harassment by Monk and Chuck had slowed down, when we were released from the Fish Tier, and consisted of the occasional taunts in the exercise yard which seemed to satisfy their twisted sense of humor. I made a point of trying to avoid them, if I could, and associated with what I thought was a more amicable crowd. Until one evening after I had picked up my supper tray, and was settling down to eat. My cell door was suddenly opened and Monk was standing there staring at me. I thought what is he doing here, his cell was over on the opposite side, and to get to my cell would put him in an area he had no business being in. I then realized that this was payback time, probably for the crack to the jaw I had given him on the Fish Tier. He had been sitting in his cell thinking of revenge for months, and finally built up enough courage to form his plan of attack.

"What do you want Monk?" I said.

He didn't answer he just made a couple of furtive glances up the tier to see if anyone was coming. I slowly reached out and took hold of my heavy stainless steel cups handle. It was full of hot tea, and I'd heard it had been used with devastating effect in other brawls in the prison before. I could see he was building up his courage to rush me. I just kept slowly eating my supper using my free hand, never letting go of the cup, all the while keeping an eye on him. He suddenly stepped back, made a glance down the tier, and then to my surprise wheeled and hurried away down the tier to his cell on the other side. Then I heard the clanging of the doors being closed on the tier, and realized it was lockup time and he didn't want to be caught on the wrong tier. I breathed a sigh of relief and let go of the cup handle and noticed my hand was shaking. I don't know whether it was from fear or anticipation of violence. It took me a while that evening to unwind. From that evening on I was never approached by Monk again in a threatening manner. During the evening after supper, I spent my time studying my course and doing my tests, and I found it helped do the time much easier.

After a year of banking and tending the furnaces and steam pumps, an inspector came in from the outside, and six of us were ushered into the plant office and issued provincial examination papers for the Fourth Class Steam Engineers Diploma. A couple of the cons hadn't studied very hard, and were whispering questions about some of the answers during the course of the written examination, and I helped them out as best I could. I had some trouble with the area of starting up the boiler after shut down, because I wasn't present when they did this the one time during my stay, and so I left it blank. There was a short break after the written examine before we started the oral examination, and the Third Class Engineer asked me how I did, and I told him about my problem. He laughed and gave me a bit of a bad time about it, but he also explained the question in detail, so when I was asked about this in the oral, I got by with flying colors and that was all I was asked about. I felt good about being able to help the other con with some of the questions when I found out that one of them was writing for a second time. It was the con who made fun of my lack of knowledge of the prison slang when we first met on B7 over the stolen tobacco incident. He was easier to get along with after he had past and received his diploma.

A few days after writing the exam' we were called into the plant office and told we were going to be moved to new jobs to make room for new Fourth Class Students. I didn't mind, I was tired of being dirty all the time. It wasn't helping my acne at all, besides I felt a change would help break the routine for a little while anyway. Two days later I was assigned to the Carpenter Gang.

The Carpenter Gang was a group of about five convicts who roamed about the prison doing maintenance and construction. Our boss was a fully trained Carpenter who also had the job of training us how to work as Carpenters. After about nine months working on various projects around the prison, we were told that our gang was going to be enlarged, and that our net job was to build two H. Huts, one on each side of the B7 corridor. This was going to be our biggest job yet.

The usual laying out of the foundations was accomplished without much trouble, and we were in the process of putting in the floors, when I was asked to get up onto the roof of a small shack that had been constructed for an operations office, to keep the blue prints out of the weather etc. I was told to cover the roof with Tar Paper, so I climbed up on the roof with a couple of 2x4's to hold the paper flat while I tacked it down, but the width of the paper was wider than the roof, and as I moved the 2x4's around one of them was accidentally pushed onto a section of paper with no roof under it and unfortunately the Carpenter Boss was standing under it talking to the head of the Carpenter Shop. It bounced of his shoulder, but as it only fell about four feet before hitting him, the only damage he sustained was to be extremely startled and surprised. He looked up, and saw me staring down at him.

"What are you doing?" he said.

I shrugged my shoulders and said.

I'm sorry, I didn't notice the paper was extended over the roof edge, and pushed the board too far."

I could see by the look on his face that he didn't believe me. I knew he thought I had deliberately tried to injure him.

"Come down off of there," he yelled.

I climbed down and said, "Look, It was an accident." But he wasn't having any of it.

"You go over there," he said pointing to a pile of flooring, "and help those men supply the Floor Layers with planks."

The rest of the day I carried planks for the huts flooring. I felt like I had been unfairly treated, and as the day went by I became obsessed with what I felt was a bum rap. For the rest of the week I wasn't given any meaningful jobs. I was ignored, and reduced to Joe Boy.

The following week the framing for the walls was completed and the rafters were being installed. The Carpenter Boss asked me to climb up on the Roofing joist's that had been erected and give a hand nailing up the rafters. I just stood there looking at him not making a move.

"Come on we haven't got all day you know." He said.

"Hell! I'm not getting up there," I said. If I can't be trusted to nail some tar paper on a shack roof without dropping a plank on you what makes you think I wouldn't drop a bigger one on you when I'm up there on purpose this time." I laughed and walked away.

That afternoon after lunch I was called up to the Warden's Court, and this only happens when you've been charged with some prison offence. The slang expression used by the convicts was crimed. The Warden's Court was situated in the South Wing. It was built like all Judges Court Rooms which consisted of a railing and then a higher platform with the Judges Bench and chair on top of that, so the prisoner and spectators had to look up to the Judge. A guard escorted me down the hall to the Wardens Chambers.

I was kept standing for ten minutes. All I had been told was I was going to see the Warden and the questions I ask about the reasons were ignored. Finally I was ushered into the chamber, and told to stand in front of the bench. The warden sat looking down on me. He was dressed immaculately in a tailored prison guard uniform with gold braid on his cap's visor and pips on his shoulders. He looked more like a Military Officer than just a Government Public Official.

"Take off your hat when you stand before me."

He screamed at me. His face was scarlet with rage. He was yelling so loud I jumped with the shock of it, and snatched the hat off my head.

"Stand at attention," he screamed, his voice getting shriller by the minute. I glanced over at my escort with a questioning look on my face, and he just grinned at me saying nothing. The Warden then proceeded to go into a long tirade about how I had been treated well, and that I had better pull my act together, or I would find myself in solitary confinement if there were any more incidents during my work assignments. Now I knew what this was all about and it only made me very bitter and resentful, about being treated this way. I felt the frustration and rage running through me, and I hardly heard what he was saying towards the end of his tirade. It wasn't a disciplinary lecture. It was a man screaming threats at me. He had only brought his mentality to the level of some of the prisons worst prisoners, and I had lost all respect I might have had for him because of it. I heard the words, "You are dismissed," being shouted at me through my red haze of anger, and I turned on my heel and walked out, oblivious to any beneficial council he might have had to offer. For all his actions had done was to increase my growing hatred towards the system.

The following morning, I approached the Dome Commander, who was looking after the prisoner's requests as they mustered for work. Such things as sick parade, job changes, and any other requests were given to him for his consideration. I wanted a move to the farm.

The prison had a large piggery, and several acres of land were used to grow farm produce for the prisoner's consumption. It was located directly behind the prison outside the walls. Only prisoners with less than a year remaining on their sentence were assigned to work there, and as I only had nine months to go that made me eligible. The only advantages to working on the farm, was to get out of the prison environment, away from the bars during the day and the fresh air of open fields around you or so I thought at the time. I had neglected to consider the weather, and as it was November it was raining most of the time.

Two days after making my request, the transfer was granted. And I stepped out of the Carpenter line up, and into the Farm Gang. Some of the Farm Gang was assigned to the Piggery, and were responsible for feeding and butchering the pigs, and performing any other duties that were required to run an efficient operation. The senior guard in charge of the Piggery was an older man who treated his crew fairly, and ran a very efficient operation. Most of his crew were hustlers who had been in and out of jail all of their life's and knew all of the angles to beat the system.

One of the inmates on the Piggery staff was a thick set blond, who was doing three years for armed robbery, with several other major related offences. He had led the American, and Canadian Police Forces on a merry chase through lower British Columbia, and down into the State of Washington with some women and two other men. They broke into an American Arsenal, and made off with a whole car load of guns and ammunition, and proceeded to break into gas stations and pull several armed robberies which netted them very little in the way of loot. Finally they made their way back to Canada and were subsequently arrested by the Canadian Police. Two of them were sentenced to short sentences in the Penitentiary and he hadn't changed at all. All he talked about was getting back out on the streets and back into action. In one of his past crimes he had been shot in the ankle by a small caliber hand gun while making his getaway and even that hadn't deterred him at all. While trying to evade a road block in the United States during his latest escapade several shots were fired which discouraged the local sheriff from continuing, and he managed to get clean away. He was absolutely incorrigible.

The first day on the Farm Gang was discouraging. It was raining on and off all day. We were given picks and shovels and put to work digging some new ditches around the Piggery for drainage. Our guard was a big young strap who pushed us hard all day, some of the convicts talked him into approaching the kitchen staff for extra rations because of the hard manual labour we had just done. There was always somebody hustling to get something. I often thought if some of this twisted imagination, and ingenuity, was put to sensible use on the street they could be successful in any enterprise they should care to undertake.

To get to the farm and then back to your cell you marched to the back of the prison. The left corner guard tower had a pair of massive gates, which opened into a small court. These gates were opened by the tower guard who turned a large wheel, allowing a gear arrangement to lift the gate for access into the court. At this point the guard would close the gate behind us. The tower guard would then lift the gate on the other side of the compound allowing us to walk outside to the prison farm. The gate was then closed behind us. Both gates were never lifted at the same time. At the end of a day's work you marched back to the compound where we lined up between the gates and were searched for contraband before being allowed back into the prison

All the pig slop given to the pigs was cooked in large steamers before being given to them, and during butchering days the convicts would steal pig livers, and cook them in the steamers. I was offered some of this fair, but thought of eating steamed pigs livers didn't agree with me, so I declined by saying "I wasn't hungry," no offence was taken. I guess they thought all the more for them.

During the return frisk, very little contraband was ever detected by the guards, because it was usually passed to someone in the row directly behind and when the guard was finished his frisk it was passed back again. Why the guards never caught on to this I'll never know. Whenever the opportunity presented itself to beat the system the convicts usually worked with precision. And the extent of the deception knew no bounds.

A few years before I came on the scene, a gun was smuggled into the prison piece by piece. This was accomplished by a prisoner who was serving time for attempting to tunnel into a bank and was wounded in the leg in a gun fight. The wound hadn't healed properly and he wore a bandage over it constantly. A gun was hidden on the farm property by

59

an outside accomplice, and picked up by the Farm Gang, and smuggled into the prison by hiding it under the bandage piece by piece each day, until it was smuggled into the main prison, but before it could be brought into use it was found by the guards, and confiscated with no harm done. The prisoner was sentenced to an additional very long sentence and was just finishing it when I arrived. His leg was badly deformed from his past injury and he walked with a pronounced limp. He was more known for the fact that he refused an anesthetic when having his teeth extracted by the Prison Dentist. I don't know whether he was allergic to the anesthetic or did it to obtain pain killers. The large population of Dope Addicts would go to great lengths to obtain drugs. Any kind of drugs it didn't matter at all.

It was just a few weeks after being transferred to the farm, that the Quonset Huts were finished, and as many prisoners with less than a year left of their time to go as possible, were being transferred to these accommodations. The huts were built in the shape of an H. The center section contained the washrooms, and a large area enclosed in chain link mesh for the guards. From this enclosure he could walk back and forth and see what was going on in both sides of the hut. Each arm of the hut was lined with single cots except for one corner which held three or four double decker bunks. The center of the two rooms contained a group of tables which could seat about six inmate's each and were used for eating and playing cards etc. Each sleeping area was equipped with a wooden locker and a small table. The entrance to the huts was off the B7 corridor, with the usual barred gate and door. The huts were well supplied with high windows which were covered with a heavy screen mesh. These windows afforded no view at all because they were situated high up on the walls.

I knew there was homosexuality going on in the prison. Every once in a while you would hear some whispered innuendo, but during my stay I never saw anything actually happening, just a few rude gestures, and comments exchanged between individuals once in a while. I think the fact that I spent most of my stay on B7 on the Kazoonie tier accounted for that.

The H. huts were full of short term prisoners, prisoners near the end of their sentences. Due to the increasing population the exercise yard was now full to the point of bursting at the seams, and it was impossible to engage in any organized sports. The most exercise anybody got now was fifty men all fighting for the basketball on the packed court. This usually resulted in some pretty brutal fights before the period was over. I had long before given up any contact sports to avoid this problem, and spent my exercise time just walking around the benches or watching the uproar on the basketball court.

Because of the overcrowding the prison administration had decided to build a new exercise yard at the back of the prison. The land had to be dug out considerable to make it flat for a soccer field, two Baseball Diamonds, Tennis Court, Horse Shoe Pitch, Hand Ball Court, and Volley Ball were available. They even built a Barbeque Pit for Summer Track & Field events. The whole enclosure was surrounded by a high Chain Link Fence, topped with Barbed Wire. Two sides were covered by Gun Towers, which were there to cover the farm and the back fence. The two towers, one on each corner of the back prison wall covered the rest of the yard. There was a wire set about two feet off the ground, which ran around the entire inside of the yard, about three feet inside the fence. This was the Dead Zone, supposedly any inmates caught inside this wire, and the fence were liable to be shot, but I never saw any incidents when an inmate was foolish enough to rescue a ball from the area, just a lot of shouting and threats. I was careful not to put it to the test myself.

The section of the H hut I was in, held a lot of the yard gang, which consisted of some of Vancouver's worst toughs and hustlers. There was never a dull moment. A mild mannered con, was bunking across from me who kept very much to himself, he seemed very nervous, and agitated most of the time. He was obviously out of his element. One morning during breakfast I noticed he wasn't there anymore. The convict, who sat across from me at the table whispered to a big hulking hustler next to him. The conversation went something like this.

"Did you guys get him last night?"

"Yeah," he said.

"How was it?"

"Beautiful," he said with a sly evil grin on his face,"

He nodded his head with a knowing smirk, and went back to eating his breakfast. For a minute I didn't get what was being said here then I realized that these bastards had taken advantage of a latent homosexual they had discovered in our midst and abused him somehow. How I didn't want to know. I just felt a deep feeling of disgust came over me. The only thing you could do was mind your own business, to survive. I later found out that the victim had ask the guards for protection that night after his ordeal, and been removed to a cell in the East Wing.

CHAPTER 5

My First Parole

My Escape

Just before my transfer to the Farm Gang. I had applied for permission to write for a parole, and I had filled out the application form and handed it in for mailing. When a decision is made by the Federal Parole Board, you are informed when it is refused by a small note placed on your cell bars merely stating "not at this time," with no explanation why you have been refused. If you are fortunate enough to be successful it is a little more formal, and you are called up to the Administration Office's and informed by a Prison Administration Officer, that your Parole Application has been successful, and what day you are to be released. In most instances it is usually within a week of being informed that you are released. If you just finished your sentence without parole, you are taken to the Tailor Shop and measured for a suit and to the Shoe Shop for a measurement. When the big day arrives you pack up your gear and carry it out to the Admission Office exactly like the day you arrived. You change into your New Suit and Shoes, and you are tried out for a new Fedora, and when you find one that fits, you are told to wear it. When you are dressed in your new finery you are given your old belongings wrapped in brown paper and tied with a string, and then you are marched down beside the wall, the same way you came in to the Accounting Offices at the front gates of the prison, to receive any personal valuables that you may have had when you were brought in to the prison. At the same time you are given ten dollars in cash from the prison. The ten dollars is given to everybody whether they were incarcerated for ten years or two years every one received the same amount, and it was supposed to keep you until you could get employment and start earning a living. You might as well have been given nothing at all. Those inmates who had no family or friends willing to help them on release would go into Vancouver and start hustling in any criminal activity they could to just survive, and this would lead to arrest and imprisonment. As time went by the above financial conditions were changed for the better.

When I was granted my parole I had about nine months left on my sentence, and I was told I had a week before I was to be released. During that week I went through the usual preparations for release. The Suit measurements, and Shoe measurements, done in a day, and I waited for them to be made in the shops. Everything went off with the usual prison precision.

Nobody bothered to tell me what was going to happen on my release, and I didn't care. All I was concerned with was I was getting out of this hole. I would have walked out naked if they had of asked me. Finally the magic day came, and instead of walking out for the line up in the dome, I was told to stay behind in the huts until I was called.

Two days previously some Heroin had been smuggled into the prison, and some of it was being hidden on one of the huts high window sills. Johnny, a convicted Dope Addict and trafficker was worried it was going to be found by another convict or a prison guard, and when he approached me the concern was written all over his face. I had discovered that these men would go to great lengths to protect their dope even murder. I had grown to totally despise drug addicts. I had not a trace of sympathy for them at all, and to this day I do not understand this need to be sent into a world devoid of reality, and to risk anything even death. For a Narcotic Addict it is not the tremendous profit, for that goes back into his arm. It can't be because he comes tremendously sick when he quits, because he never stays free for long even when he does quit, and it is definitely not because he has a low I.Q. because a lot of them are very intelligent in regards at least to learning and knowledge. A more cunning lot you'll never find. There has been Dope Fiends for a thousand years, and I'm sure there will be Dope Fiends for another thousand.

"Keep an eye on the cache on the sill for me." Johnny said nodding towards the window sill.

"Look John I'm not going to be here all day, I'm getting out this morning." His brow rose a little in surprise. And he said.

"Well keep an eye out for as long as you're here," he said.

He wasn't a bit interested in the fact that I was getting out all he was concerned about was his precious dope. I thought to hell with you John, but I said.

"I'll watch out for it."

The whole thing was ridiculous. How could he think for one minute that I could protect his dope, or that I was going to even make an attempt, I wasn't even going to be there that afternoon, if I hadn't been released that day it could very well have been a dangerous situation. Knowing the mentality of these Dope Addicts, if anything had of happened to their cache while I was supposed to be watching it. There was good chance I would be subject to some sort of retribution, a beating during the night or worse.

Finally I was called to go to the Front Admission Office in the South Wing where I was decked out in my new Suit, and Shoes, and given my Hat, and my Brown Paper Bundle of my old clothes. I was then marched down along the wall to the Front Administration Offices, and issued my ten dollars, and told to sign my release papers.

During the waiting period for my release I wasn't told by anyone what was waiting for me on my release, and I was only interested in the fact that I was getting out. They could have sent me to hell, I wouldn't have cared. Since the day I was arrested I didn't have to worry or think for myself, everything was done for me. I was literally the trained monkey responding to my master's commands, although if I got a chance to bite him, I did if I could get away with it. I got up by a bell, I went to work by a bell, and I went to bed by a bell. I spent eighteen hours a day in my cell, and the rest of the time working, exercising and eating. After a while you stopped thinking ahead, and just waited for the Prison Guards to tell you of any changes in your routine, and you didn't question anything, because you knew you just did as you were told anyway.

After signing my release papers, I was told to wait in the hall, and I would be given a ride into Vancouver in a Prison Van. Eventually I was driven to the Bus Depot in Vancouver, given a bus ticket to Victoria, and told that I would be met at the Victoria Bus Deport by a Parole Officer from the John Howard Society. The John Howard Society was an organization that helped ex- convicts and prisoners on parole get employment and saw that they abided by the terms of their parole.

The trip over to Vancouver Island was uneventful, and when I stepped off the bus, I was met by a distinguished gentleman who introduced himself as my Parole Officer. He offered a limp handshake which sent an uneasy feeling through me, and I felt that this was a man that I could not trust, and the following events were to prove me right.

We drove to his office, and he handed me my Parole Papers and told me to read them, and to remember what they said in detail, which was basically that I was not to leave Victoria without his permission, and I was not to possess Firearms or Explosives. And I was to obtain a job. I could not quit the job without permission. All in all I was not to do anything in regards to my social obligations without permission, and if I did the penalty would be immediate arrest, and sent back to the Penitentiary to serve out the remainder of my sentence. With the loss of any good time I had earned for early release. I would have to start earning my good time all over again upon my return, which meant, that I would have to serve a longer sentence than if I had not been paroled, and that any time I spent on the street before my return did not count.

I was then told that I would be staying at my sister's home, and we would be going over to her place. I was a little surprised at this because I hadn't seen or heard from my family since I was arrested, and I had not given them any thought at all.

My sister, Betty had married a veteran, and was raising two small children. George was a milkman, and had built with financial help of the Canadian Veterans Affairs a small two bedroom house. His father also boarded with them he had a small room in the basement. The arrangement that had been made on my behalf was I would sleep on the sofa in the living room, and stay there until I got established in the community. I was expected to pay room and board when I found work.

The next day, I was taken to a local sawmill and introduced to the manager, and told I would start work the next day as a laborer assisting the Millwright in various maintenance jobs around the mill. That afternoon I went back to the old neighborhood, and visited some girl friends who went to school, and lived there as long as I had, and were probably the only friends of my age I had who were still around, and didn't care about my past.

While all this was going on, the arrangements for my accommodation with my sister, the efforts made to get me a job, and to get me established in the community, nobody consulted with me or asked me how I was managing or if I liked what was happening.

After about a week of work, a Father Munn a local Anglican Minister appeared at the house. I knew him from when I was in the Church Choir. He had replaced Father Smith who had retired due to old age. Father Smith was admired and respected by all the Church Parishioners. I cannot say the same for Father Munn at least not for myself. I did not like him very much at all. He spent most of his time trying to raise money for the Church where as Father Smith looked after his parishioner's religion needs, and the Churches social activities flourished while he was in charge. When he left and Father Munn took over all the social activities disappeared, and so did the neighborhood family involvement with the church, and my interest along with it.

I was very surprised to see him at the door. It was obvious that my sister Betty had arranged this, probably through coaching from my parole officer. In any event I tried to be agreeable by saying I would turn up for Choir Practice again after all these years. Father Munn's money raising efforts had been a success for they had built a new Church, and I was to show up at the Vestry for choir practice the following Friday.

After about a month of working at the mill I was able to buy some work cloths, and pay some rent to Betty, and go out to the odd movie. Things were beginning to fall into place very slowly, but there was still one big problem. I was still not being allowed to make any decisions, and my living conditions had a lot to be desired. Sleeping on a couch in some ones living room for a month did not allow for any privacy, and I was getting bored and restless. Eventually my sister began to see this, and started dropping hints it was time for me to move.

As I was supposed to report to the Parole Officer periodically, I dropped by his office to talk to him about my activities during the previous two weeks. I found him in a particularly nasty mood. He accused me of spending all my money on my old girl friends, and not saving anything, and that these girls were a particularly bad lot, and were using me for my money. I was totally astounded by this absolute nonsense, and denied it vigorously. But he wasn't going to listen to my side of it, and the more I told him he was wrong the madder he got. Finally he told me if I didn't smarten up, he would have me sent back to the Penitentiary to finish my time. I ask him where he had got this gossip from, and he told me he had been in close contact with my sister, and she had told him that she didn't like the girls I was associating with, and felt that I was spending all, my money on them. I was shocked. She hadn't mentioned anything at all to me about my leisure hours, and she was as far away from the truth as she could get. I had not spent any money on the girls at all. I had not even taken them to a movie. They were my age, and I had known them for years, and I could talk to them at my level and they didn't care about my past. I had to start socializing somewhere, and nobody else had any ideas. Maybe they thought I was supposed to associate with a group of middle age people in a Church Choir, and live a titillating life. The whole thing was totally ridiculous. I had been working at the mill for a very short time, and paying room and board. I needed bus fair and money to buy gear and boots. The little entertainment I paid for was the occasional movie and after these few extravagances I was nearly broke until my next pay check came in. After looking back and trying to understand what was happening. I think Betty had my welfare at heart and didn't realize she was playing with a powder keg. She had decided that with her and the Parole Officers help I was going to be put on the straight and narrow path, and to discuss anything with me was just not necessary, because I was just a young man who didn't know the error of his ways and, needed to be put in my place whether I liked it or not. This approach was definitely not the proper procedure in my case it only enraged me. I felt betrayed by my own sister going behind my back to the enemy. The Parole Officer was supposed to be helping me, and he was. He had obtained employment for me, and found me accommodation, but he had failed in the most vital thing. He had not gained my trust or friendship during are short association. I was watching him. His comments and attitude towards other Parolee's under his supervision when they were not around was expressed openly in derogatory remarks showing his contempt for them, and I realized it was just a job just like the prison guards, who I had no respect for at all. I was surrounded by freedom but not free at all.

That night at supper I could barely keep my anger hidden from Betty. I had decided not to confront her at all with her betrayal. I had decided not to talk with her for fear I would say something she didn't like and she would run and tell my Parole Officer, with the possibility of being sent back to prison as a consequence.

During supper, Betty and George said that they felt it was time I went out on my own, and suggested I go and check into the Y.M.C.A. Up until this time there had been no discussion about my future, or anything at all in the way of advice from Betty and George, and I didn't know what was going on at all. I had been invited into their home, and now I was being invited to leave, just like that, with no preparation at all. At that moment I decided I had had enough of being pushed about and it was time I left all together.

The next morning, I got up, ate my breakfast, changed into come clean work clothes like I was going to work and left on the first ferry to Vancouver. I had the major part of my last pay check left so I still had enough money to get by for about a week. When I arrived in Vancouver I didn't have any idea where I was going, or what I was going to do, all I wanted was to get away from Victoria as far as I could. l was walking along Main Street and I began to think about the Patella Bridge, which spanned the Fraser River just to the right of the Penitentiary. From my cell

I could look out the front windows and see the bridge and I often thought about the American Border on the other side and if I would get there someday. Well now was a good time. I stopped at the first bank I came to and exchanged my money into American Dollars, and then headed for the bridge and the United States.

When I passed over the bridge I walked on the left hand shoulder of the road so if any police cars passed they would be to the right and probably wouldn't stop. I was right about that theory because an R.C.M.P. car passed, and gave me the once over but didn't stop. I figured I had a good head start and the alarm wouldn't be out for me yet anyway.

I hitch hiked for a while, and finally caught a ride to the town of White Rock on the American & Canadian Border. I booked into a small hotel on the main street, and slept until it was dark. I then left quietly by the back door, and made my way down to the beach. White Rock is situated on the Strait of Georgia and is famous for its beautiful beaches. I noticed a railway track running along the edge of the beach heading into the United States and I proceeded to follow it to the border. I was well along the track when a Freight Train appeared, so I ducked down in the underbrush beside, the track so the Engineer couldn't see me. A short distance down the track in front of me the train stopped, and when I approached I had to hide again because a Switchman and a Border Patrol Officer were searching the outside and under the cars for anyone trying to cross over the border illegally. In a few minutes they were finished and the train continued on its way down into the United States.

Situated in front of the train when it had stopped, was a small Train Station and when I raised my head to see if the coast was clear, I could see the Border Patrol Officer standing in the window watching the track to see if anyone had jumped of the train when it had stopped. I was well concealed alongside the track, and he didn't see me. When he finally disappeared into the station, I leaped up and ran across the track and out onto a small side road leading into the suburbs of Blaine, a small border town on the American side. I carefully skirted around the main street and the center of town, and when I felt I was well clear of the Border Patrol and their most likely patrolled areas, I cut across on an angle which I felt would take me back towards the sea and the railroad tracks, and after a short walk I located the tracks and started to follow them without any idea of where I was going or what I was going to do when I got there.

It was very dark and the railway tracks ran directly alongside the highway for miles and every time I saw some car light coming in the distance I would hide in the brush alongside the tracks until they had passed. Eventually the highway and the tracks parted and I found myself well out into the American Country side.

The weather was fine and I was wearing a light jacket which was adequate, and it only rained for a few minutes during my walk, and fortunately this happened when I was passing an abandoned shack beside the tracks which gave me adequate shelter until the shower had passed. A Fright Train roared by, but I felt they hadn't noticed me. Some dogs came from a farm house and followed me down the tracks barking for a few hundred yards, but they soon gave up when I didn't run from them.

I had no idea what time it was or how far I had come, but I did know I was getting very thirsty and needed a drink and I started watching out for a source of water. Eventually I came up to a Gas Station, which was on a small side street near the tracks. After watching it for a while I decided there was nobody inside, and I located the wash rooms I found the door wasn't locked. The place was filthy and it hadn't been cleaned or washed in a very long time but the taps on the sink were working and I took a long healthy drink. Rather than risk making any more noise or tripping an alarm of some sort, I didn't try breaking into the front office, because it was well illuminated with overhead front lights. I just continued on my way down the tracks.

The sun came up just as I was coming into my first town. It was very early in the morning, and nobody was stirring, as I walked by the railroad station I noticed the sign on the front which said "Ferndale." I hurried, not wanting to be noticed at that time of the morning on the railway tracks and bring unwanted attention to myself. I was soon clear of town and making good time, and I was soon on the outskirts of Bellingham. I left the tracks and walked down the main street and came to a small Convection Store where I bought a package of doughnuts for breakfast. I was feeling a little tired after my long walk and decided to find a place to get some rest. I found a cheap hotel and paid four dollars for a sleeping room which was very cold, and I couldn't get any sleep so I decided to just keep going.

I walked for a few blocks and asked a young lady where the Bus Depot was. I followed her directions and found the depot and bought a ticket to Seattle. When it was time to get on the bus there was a delay of some kind, and the driver was lining the passengers up on each side of the door, and not letting them onto the bus. I stood there watching this, and noticed he wasn't giving any explanation to the passengers who were asking what the delay was. I felt uneasy about this, and decided to just keep walking and not take the bus, and so I quietly walked away and continued towards Seattle on foot.

On the edge of town I started hitch hiking and soon picked up a ride which took me as far as Mount Vernon another small town along interstate 5. It was beginning to get dark and I was very tired and feeling sorry for myself. As I walked through town, I passed a couple of better class hotels, but I thought I would arouse suspicion if I tried to check in dressed the way I was, with no luggage. I was nearing the far edge of town when I noticed a sign on an office building which said State Police. A couple of Police Cruisers were parked outside.

I stood for a while thinking about what I was doing, and what my future plans were, and I realized I really didn't have any plans which were very viable. I realized I had better get a start with a clean slate, and the first thing I had to do was to go back to the Penitentiary and finish my time, besides I was tired and disillusioned. I walked over to the State Police building and through the front door and up to the counter. A State Trooper came over and said.

"Yes sir what can I do for you?"

When I told him I was a Parole Violator from Canada a look of total surprise came over his face, and he became all attentive and much more alert,

"I see! Step this way please into my office,"

He showed me into a small office in the back behind the counter

"Empty your pockets on the desk please."

After I had placed the contents of my pockets on the desk he gave me a thorough frisk, and took my finger prints. He asked me a few more questions pertaining to my previous record and then he placed me in a small holding cell.

The cell had no furniture in it at all. There was a Stainless Steel Bunk built into the wall with no blankets or any means of making myself comfortable. I figured it would take them a little while to check my story out so I lay down on the steel bunk and to my surprise I fell asleep almost immediately. Now that my haphazard escape had come to an end, and I had a plan of sorts, a weight was lifted from my shoulders

CHAPTER 6

King County Jail Immigration Lock Up
Back to the Pen to Finish My Time

I woke up with a start when someone rattled a key in the door. A different trooper than the one I had met the night before was standing there looking me over.

"Come on, you are going back to Blaine to the Border Patrol," he said.

My hands were handcuffed behind my back, and I was put into the back of a patrol car. Two troopers got into the front. I noticed the one who was not driving held the drivers gun in his belt as well as his own holstered revolver. They weren't taking any chances with a punk as a prisoner.

I was surprised at the distance I had walked from Blaine because it seemed like sometime before we arrived at the border station, where I was taken down to a basement room and locked up. This room was equipped with a proper bed and mattress. After an hour or so I was given a decent meal. The first thing I had eaten in at least twenty four hours. I hadn't realized how hungry I was. After I had eaten I tried to sleep some more but found I was to wound up for that.

Nobody asked me anymore questions and I began to wonder what was going on. I figured I would be picked up by the Canadian Police and taken back to the Penitentiary in an hour or two. After a while I was taken back up stairs and my picture was taken. Two Border Patrol Cops loaded me into a car and we started to drive back the way I had just come.

"Hey! Aren't you guys taking me back to Canada?" I ask.

The cop on the passenger side turned and said,

"You have to be tried for illegal entry first."

"O! I didn't think of that."

The cop sneered and said, "Hell you didn't think of a lot of things." Then I realized I wasn't going to get back to Canada as quick as I thought. The rest of the trip to Seattle was done in silence.

When we arrived in Seattle we drove down into what I thought was an underground parking lot of a large office building.

"Where are we?" I asked.

"You are at the King County Jail," the cop told me.

I was ushered out of the car and the hand cuffs taken off. There was a group of other prisoners who had arrived at the same time mostly Mexicans. Among them, was a tall black man who was well-dressed, I glanced around and saw several Policemen milling around the garage, probably going about their patrol duties for there were a number of police cars parked on the landing.

"Hey!" Wet Backs,"

One of the cops called over, referring to the Mexicans in our group.

"Make a run for it, I'd like to shoot you in the Ass," he laughed. Several snickers came from the Uniform cops standing around. I thought, someone should shoot you in the Ass you bastard.

"Okay." A tall blond man wearing a Light Grey Suit barked at us. "Line up and follow me."

I noticed he was wearing a Plastic Identification Badge and I could see he was a Federal Marshal. He even had Cowboy Boots on.

We all filed onto a large elevator and rode up to the reception area, which consisted of offices and two large holding cells. We were placed in the cells which already contained three young well-dressed blacks. The tall black that was with our group asked to be moved in with the other three, who were in the cell next to ours, and this was granted by the Marshal. One of the Mexicans told me he was a drug dealer who had been caught with Heroin when his Cadillac had been pulled over for a routine check and searched. He had made a deal and been sentenced to three years in McNeal Island Penitentiary.

After a while a small man was ushered into our cell. He was dressed in a Suit and Tie and wearing a tan Rain Coat. I was told by one of our guards that he was a Convict who was confined to a sanitarium because he had Tuberculosis and as he was nearing the end of his sentence he had been given a day pass to come to town for some tests but instead had robbed a Bank for Fifty Thousand Dollars and went back to the sanitarium as if nothing had happened, but one of the sanitarium staff read about the robbery and remembered that the prisoner had been in town that day, and reported it to the Police which led to his arrest.

After a short stay in the holding cells we were taken to a courtroom for a hearing, and I was handcuffed to the Bank Robber. As we were being led down a hallway we were ambushed by reporters and photographers all shouting questions and taking pictures, until we were ushered into the courtroom. The Bank Robber and the Dope Dealers all received remands to higher courts. When my turn came I was asked if I was guilty or not guilty. I said guilty and I was ordered deported back to Canada. I thought I would be sent back quickly but it was a month before they finally got around to me. In the meantime I was confined in the King County Jail Immigration Tank while the wheels of justice turned.

I was led from the reception area through a barred gate up a series of long ramps. At the top of each ramp was another barred gate with a guard who could see anybody approaching. It was unique in that there were no stairs. This allowed wheeled vehicles easy access and a clear view of anybody approaching the different floors. The floor I was on had a large room with a caged in passage running along the entrance, so the guards could walk along the outside with a clear view of anyone in the room. Anyone who was leaving was confined to this passage for several feet before coming out onto a landing, and then the ramp. The big room was divided in half by bars one half had tables and chairs and a smaller section had a solid partition which hid the toilets and shower. The other half contained steel double decker bunks for sleeping. During the day, we were confined to the section with the bathroom and the eating area and at night moved to the sleeping half and locked in.

There were only two Caucasian's in the lockup, myself and a man from Manitoba, a Canadian, who was obviously mentally ill. He sat on the floor leaning against the wall looking wild eyed and dishevelled and talking in a low voice to himself or his own personal demons. I think he was a Schizophrenic or something of that nature. You could talk rationally to him but he usually avoided starting the conversation, and so I respected that. The rest of the prisoners were Mexicans. Most of them had been working as cheap Farm Labor after coming across the Rio Grande River into the United States illegally. They had made a few hundred dollars and then given themselves up to the American authorities. When the authorities had enough prisoners, they loaded them onto a train and sent them back to Mexico where they spent their hard earned money which went a lot farther in Mexico then it did in the U.S. When the money was gone they simply came back, earned some more and repeated the whole process over again. In fact while I was there, two who had left the day I had arrived were back just before I left, a period of about a month.

A Mobile Canteen came around once a day, and sold punch cards so you could buy odds and ends, such as tobacco and candy bars. I purchased one and bought the Schizophrenic some Bull Duram Tobacco and papers. I immediately had a fair weather friend. The daily diet was monotonous mostly beans, potatoes and various vegetables. Usually hard boiled eggs or porridge for breakfast nothing fancy just very plain fair.

My time was spent just sitting around during the day listening to the Mexicans tell stories about their travels up and down the coast. Occasionally we were a captive audience for religious organizations who came and stood in the passage and preached to us about the error of our ways. Nobody paid much attention to them at all. I went to the prison chapel on Sunday just to get out of the cell block and to break the monotony.

Finally my name was called and I was transferred out of the King County Jail to the Seattle Immigration Center to stay overnight in there lockup. It was the same sort of arrangement as the King County Jail only on a much smaller scale, and there were no ramps just stairs and elevators. The dormitory was much smaller, and there were no showers just double decker bunks.

While I was there I met a couple of Ex. Cons who I had met in the Penitentiary. They had been transferred up from Los Angeles, where they had been arrested for breaking into Gas Stations and stealing the cash boxes. They had spent a few weeks in the Los Angeles County Jail, and then been deported when it was found out that they were wanted back in Canada for bad checks. All the time we spent there they schemed about escaping, and tried to get me and a young Mexican to create a diversion by starting a fight and over powering the guards. The problem with their plan, was that everyone in the dormitory, about a dozen prisoners, all Mexicans knew about it, and in no time at all one of the older prisoners called a guard. After some whispering in a corner with a guard, the Mexican was taken away. I gathered by the glances directed towards us that the old guy had told the guard everything that was planned. But when I mentioned it to the Cons they just waived it aside as a coincidence. The plan was supposed to take effect about midnight.

When zero hour rolled around I looked over to their bunks, and saw they were both sound asleep, and obviously exhausted from there long trip and incarceration. I knew that the whole thing was just a figment of their imaginations, for it didn't have a hope of succeeding. The guards I had seen were big enough to take care of any disturbance single handily with not much effort at all. The next day the three of us were hand cuffed and taken down stairs to a garage, and loaded into a car for our trip back to Canada. I noticed the Marshal, who was one of our escorts was carrying two short barrelled 38 Caliber Revolvers under his coat, and I thought, "These two jerks I'm with can run all they want, I'm not going anywhere." All the way back to the border one of them tried to get his handcuffs off by inserting a small piece of metal he had hidden in his clothing into the lock mechanism to spring the cuffs loose. The plan was, if he was able to get loose when we reached the boarder, and the car stopped. He would jump out and make a run for it. I had no idea where he thought he was going to go. What with heavily armed guards and ten foot high chain link fences on all sides not to mention American and Canadian Immigration Police all over the place. Anyway all his efforts were to no avail and in a short time the R.C.M.P. picked us up and we were back in Canada.

My erstwhile friends and I parted company in the town of Cloverdale just over the Canadian & American Border. I guessed they were being taken into Vancouver to face their bad check charges while I was being held overnight before being sent back to the Penitentiary to finish out my sentence. The Cloverdale Jail was a small building with a detachment of R.C.M.P. Officers for the area. The jail was a small room at the back of the building with a steel portable cell bolted to the floor in the middle of the room, and four bunks to sleep in. I shared the cell with a local town drunk. We were allowed to move around the room until supper which was brought in from a local restaurant. It consisted of chicken, and buns with a sundae for desert. It was the best meal I had in over a month. After I had eaten, I was locked into the steel cage in the middle of the room until the following morning. Around 9 o'clock, I was picked up and driven over to the Penitentiary in New Westminster to finish my sentence.

On arriving at the Penitentiary I went through the same procedure that I went through on my first arrival only I received the same number I had when I left, and I didn't have to go to the Fish Tier. I was taken to the bottom tier in the East Wing. I spent a few days assigned to the cleaning crew in the dome, and then I was assigned back out to the Farm Gang, and eventually I moved from the East Wing to the dormitories where I finished my time.

I put on my new Suit and Shoes, donned my Fedora, collected my ten dollars, and the money I came in with and walked out of the Penitentiary a free man. There was a mail box at the end of the Penitentiary Driveway, and as I walked by I got rid of the hat by just leaving it on top of the box. When I got into Vancouver I bought a new shirt because who had ever made the one I was wearing didn't know anything about tailoring. The collar was crooked. I got rid of the shirt. The new shirt had a sports neck and I didn't need a tie. That evening I caught the ferry back to Victoria and booked into the Lincoln Hotel, a crummy flop house, but the price was right. After a few days I left there and got a room in the Y.M.C.A. The accommodations were better. They had a restaurant and showers were available.

I was beginning to run low on funds, and I needed work. So I checked into the Unemployment Bureau, who sent me down to Doman's Plumbing and Heating. They had a large contract with the Department of National Defence, who was constructing a large Arsenal about one hour drive outside of town. Doman's were laying all the water mains for the project, and they needed laborers to help with the miles of six inch cast iron pipes that were being installed. It was very hard physical work and at the end of the day I was glad to just lay in my room and rest to be ready for the next day's grind. It wasn't long before I began to get bored with this lonely monotonous way of life.

There was a character working alongside of me on the job who I didn't like very much. He was one of these guys who knew it all, and it wasn't long before we were having an argument about the merits of all things Al. Jolson competence as a singer. It had been a long hard day and I was in no mood to listen to this guy spouting off on how good Jolsen was. It didn't matter whether he was right or wrong, I was just tired and fed up, and would have argued about whether black was white at the time. He was just as belligerent as I was and wouldn't leave it alone either. By the time we had reached town, I was determined I wouldn't be going to work with him the next day. Psychologically I was using the whole thing as an excuse to get out of the situation I was in, and become irresponsible again. The next day I counted the cash I had left from my previous pay check. I had enough for a couple of weeks, and I left on the ferry to Vancouver. I was soon making the rounds of some of Vancouver's Skid Road Hotels.

CHAPTER 7

Vancouvers East End

Arrested Again

Okalla Prison Farm

In the Stanley Hotel, (which was one of the more notorious dumps on Skid Road,) I bumped into an Ex Con, a man who would tip the scales at close to three hundred pounds and stood at least six foot four. He was a cheap petty thief who I had met in the Penitentiary. His specialty was strong arm robbery mostly drunks he'd roll after they got too drunk to protect themselves.

"Hi, how are things?"

"Hey, you are just the guy I'm looking for, you interested in helping me with a Chinese Store Heist," he growled.

"What kind of a heist?"

"We'll just go in and kick the shit out of them if they give us any trouble."

"You got a gun?"

"No I don't, hell we don't need a gun."

"Look I got a few bucks I'll buy a rifle and saw the stock off."

"Okay that ought to scare the shit out of them. I'll meet you here tomorrow night and we'll get on with it."

"Good, I'll see you tomorrow."

I went outside and noticed a sign across the street which said, "Canton Rooms." I went over and climbed up a steep flight of stairs to the second floor. I found the Chinese Manager, and rented a small room for the night. Except for a knock on the door around midnight, which was a cheap pimp trying to sell me a Skid Road Whore I wasn't disturbed, and slept fairly well until the next morning.

It didn't take me long to find a Second Hand Store. All I had to do was walk a few blocks down the street and I found what I was looking for. I picked a Remington 30 Cal. Semi- Automatic Rifle off the gun rack, paid a few dollars for it, and they even had a box of ammunition that went with it. There were no questions asked. I had the clerk wrap it so it wouldn't be conspicuous. I also bought a small second hand hacksaw to cut the stock down. So I could conceal the gun under my overcoat.

I walked back to my room and prepared the gun. It had a tubular magazine under the barrel which held seven rounds, and it would fire as fast as I could pull the trigger. It was a short carbine, so when I cut the stock down to the hand grip it was reduced to a size where I could hang it under my arm. I found a piece of sash cord in the old dresser, which when tied onto the bolt which was now showing through the end of the hand grip. I was able to tie the cord in a loop, and hang the gun under my arm from my shoulder. It was still early in the day so I pushed the gun under the bed, then I went out and found the manager and paid another nights rent. I was feeling hungry so I went out and found a cheap restaurant in the East End called the Golden. The waitress was a middle aged lady. She was very friendly. I was sitting at the bar next to an attractive woman, dressed in a knit dress which showed her charms very well. After talking to her for a while I began to notice she wasn't very clean and she had some obviously rough edges. She asked me where I was staying and I told her I didn't have any place yet. She stared at me for a while, and then very quietly asked me, "If I wanted to come over to her place." I thought I could do with a nap and a cleanup, so I said,

"Sure why not?"

She pulled a small box of pills out of her purse and made some remark about how she was having some trouble with a slight infection that some Chinese Doctor was treating her for. She took a pill and washed it down with some water from a glass on the counter. I didn't bother to ask her what kind of infection she was talking about. I didn't feel it was any of my business. She got up and asked.

"Are you coming?"

"Sure let's go."

The waitress smiled at us as we left and said out loud with a knowing look as we were going out the door.

"You-be careful now won't you?"

I just laughed and called back "Sure," as we left. We walked for about six blocks to an area of run down flats near Robson St. and up into a two story red brick building. We climbed the stairs, and she led me down a narrow hallway into a single room. A hot plate and an unmade bed were the main pieces of furniture. There were no windows, and the smell of cigarette smoke, and unwashed linen hung in the air.

"Do you want something to eat?"

She-ask as she offered me a stale sandwich that was lying on the side board. I lifted the top layer and saw that underneath was just a slice of baloney and some mustard. I told her politely that I wasn't very hungry. What I was really interested in was her.

I put my arm around her waist and pulled her close. She resisted gently and murmured, "Not now." I tried to pull her down with me onto the bed but she expertly avoided my coaxing.

"Come on relax, I'm not going to hurt you."

She sighed audibly, and said,

"Look I'm not in the mood right now besides I can't."

I thought well it must be her time of the month, and promptly forgot about it. I was feeling tired, and the bed looked inviting. I lay down, and she lay down beside me. In no time at all we were both sound asleep leaving our vacuous world behind

I awoke with a start, and found her gone. The cheap wall clock showed it was well on into the afternoon. I reached for my wallet, and quickly counted what money I had left and found I was down to five dollars. Well she hadn't bothered to roll me. She probably thought it wasn't worth the trouble. I laughed at the thought, and left for my Skid Row Room. It was getting dark by the time I got back, and I thought I had better go and meet the Con. and get this score going, or I would have to go and see if I could talk the girl into staying with her until I could make some money somewhere. I quickly hung the rifle under my arm. It was still under the bed where I had left it. The bed was made and the place was tidied up. The word was the Chinese never started trouble. They would rather mind there-own business than call the cops, and the fact that the gun was still where I had left it was proof of this. I don't see how anyone cleaning up couldn't have seen it where I had left it. I guess they felt don't make waves and it'll go away.

I wandered across the street to the Stanley Beer Parlor, which was packed with customers. It was like every dead beat and bum in Vancouver was there. I didn't know anybody, so I walked around trying to find an empty seat. Finally I saw the waitress from the Golden Restaurant sitting at a table with an empty seat. I walked over and said.

"Hi! Can I sit down?"

She looked at me for a minute, and a look of recognition came over her face.

"Sure have a seat."

Then a worried look swept over her face, and she bent forward with a look of confidentiality, and said.

"You didn't get into Maggies pants did you?"

Her abrupt crudeness took me by surprise for a second. "What!" I stammered, and then the humor of it struck me and I laughed, she didn't laugh with me. When she saw the questioning look on my face she said.

"She's got a dose and if you went to bed with her you're in trouble."

Then it hit me, the little song and dance about the pills, and why she didn't respond when I made the pass at her. The woman had done me a favor. She wasn't out to sell me a bill of goods, she just wanted some companionship, somebody to talk to, and I had missed it all.

Well I'll be damned, I was wondering what was going on. No I didn't get a thing, I'll be okay."

She smiled at me. Nodded her head in approval, and went back to talking to her friends, and enjoying her beer.

I kept a watch out for the Con. but didn't notice him around, and so after a few minutes I got up and did another walk around the parlor, checking the tables and the Wash Room. He wasn't anywhere in sight. The parlor was packed with customers, dimly lit and full of cigarette smoke. The customers were mostly down and out types, spending there few dollars on beer and companionship. The waiters were mostly big and tough guys, hired for their ability to keep order and handle the rigorous job of keeping the customers happy with a quick beer on the table.

As I was moving around among the tables, a big bruiser of a waiter suddenly appeared in front of me. He reached out and put a hand on the side of my coat where he felt the rifle hanging under my arm. He shouted above the din of noise in the parlor.

"Find a seat and sit down." In a manner which said he was used to getting his own way. When his hand touched the gun a look of surprise swept over his face, and he pulled his hand away quickly, and his tone of voice became a little more-gentle.

"You're taking up room. You better sit down before some body bumps you into a table," he said.

He then moved away heading for the beer taps at the back of the room. I knew he had felt the gun, and I quietly walked toward the door.

I reached the sidewalk and started down the street. There was nobody insight. I didn't have any idea where I was going. I heard the beer parlor door open and close behind me. I turned around and saw a big young cop standing there smiling at me.

"Hey, what's your hurry?" he said, walking slowly towards me.

"I'm in no hurry." I said.

I moved about forty feet away from the Beer Parlour door, and I was standing beside a parked car. My mind was racing over my situation, whether to run, or try and draw the gun from under my buttoned up coat, but while I was thinking of this the cop drew up to me, and at the same time he pushed me off balance up against the car, yanked my coat open and grabbed the gun. He deftly snapped the cord holding it to my shoulder with one hand, while he leaned on my chest with the other holding me off balance. While this was happening, a police car roared up behind me, and two policemen jumped out with guns drawn, and ran over to help. The whole thing had happened in seconds, and I knew I was going back to jail, and I really didn't care at all.

On the way to the Police Station, I told the arresting cop I should have blown his brains out. It was just an act of stupid bravura, but it made him mad, and that made me feel better. When we got to the station and I was booked and finger printed. The young cop took me aside and said.

"I'd like to get you into a room alone for just five minutes." His tone of voice and expression were menacing. I said.

"Listen the next time you come up on someone carrying a Semi-Automatic Rifle, and you're forty or fifty feet away, you had better draw your gun first because it might not be me."

He looked at me as what I was saying sank in, and he realized if I had been a killer he would possibly be dead now. I watched the color drain out of his face as the reality of what he had done sank in. He walked away slowly shaking his head, and I knew I had the last word.

The following day I was taken from my cell block to the Police Court, which was in the same building, and put into a holding tank with a group of other prisoner's to wait my turn in court. We were called out one at time. Most of us were remanded until another date because of bail hearings, or to obtain a lawyer etc.

When my name was called, l stepped out into the prisoners dock and was charged with possession of an offensive weapon with intent to disturb the piece. The prosecutor told the judge about my threat to the arresting officer, and my criminal record was read out to the court. This broke the air of boredom in the courtroom, and the sound of the whispering crowd stopped for a second, while all eyes turned to look me over. The judge broke the silence when he quickly ask-me what did I plead.

I said. "Guilty."

I was then asked if I wanted legal representation, and I said "No." The prosecutor got up and said.

"Your honor, I would like to point out that the defendant threatened to blow the arresting officers head off, and in the light of this vicious attitude, and his past history the Crown feels that a lengthy sentence for the protection of the public is required."

I thought, "Well I'm going back to the joint again for sure." The judge stared at me for a few moments and said.

"I'm going to ask the Okalla Prison Doctor to evaluate this man's mental attitude. You are remanded until April 2."

I did a quick calculation in my mind, and came up with a week from the day. I thought well that's not too bad. The next day a group of us was loaded into a prison van and taken to the B.C. Provincial Prison "Okalla." After the usual admission procedures, I settled in for my wait. A couple of days went by, and I was finally called up to see a Dr. Richmond, who was the Prison Doctor. I was ushered into a small clean austere office, and left alone with a slim grey haired man who smiled at me in a friendly way. He glanced through a file he had on his desk.

"I see here you have done some time at the Penitentiary." He said in a clipped British accent. I said.

"Yea, Three Years."

"Well I have been asked to send in a report on your attitude. Would you rather serve your sentence here or in New Westminster," he said.

"I'd rather do it here of course," I said.

I was surprised he even asked me a question like that, because I knew as well as he did that a sentence to Okalla meant a sentence of less than two years. That was the maximum time served in Okalla, anything over that was served at the Penitentiary

"If I recommend you serve your sentence here at Okalla you wouldn't attempt to escape, would you?" He asked

I looked up at the question, and saw he was staring at me very intently. I looked him right in the eye, and said with a chuckle.

"If you do that for me, I can assure you, I won't try to escape."

"Good," he said. How would you like to be sentenced to the Young offenders Unit?" He asked.

"Definitely not," I said.

He looked at me in surprise.

"It's a much better facility and program."

"Yea but I spent some-time on the Kazoonie Tier at the Penitentiary and I can do without any favors."

"Kazoonie Tier?" he asked.

I explained about the attempt to isolate young offenders during their off hours from the older convicts at the Penitentiary.

"I see, well I guess your mature enough and wouldn't appreciate some of the nonsense that goes on amongst the younger inmates."

"You've got that right, I said with a smile.

"I'll recommend that you be sent to Okalla to serve the sentence imposed on you by the court."

"Can you tell me how much?"

"No I don't have any control over that," he said.

"Well thank you Doctor," I said as I got up to leave.

"Good," he said as I went out the door.

The week went by quickly, and I was called to go to the Vancouver Police Courts for sentence. On arrival down town, I was put on an elevator and taken upstairs to the Police Cells. The block I was in had a row of cells on each side of the room. Each cell contained an upper and lower Steel Bunk. The doors were left open during the day and closed at night. When the doors closed a steel hook at the bottom and top of the door engaged into a slot and could not be opened until a leaver was pulled outside the cell block, which lifted the hooks enabling the door to slide open.

After lock up I could hear some noises coming from the cell next door and suddenly the clang of a cell door opening. In a few seconds a prisoner appeared at the door.

"You want out?" he asked.

I said, "How?"

"Just take off your Shoe Laces, and slip them under the hooks, and pull up at the same time."

In a few minutes the cell doors were being opened all along the cell block. I thought "what the hell," If a guard comes all he can do is put us back in again. I took out my Shoes Laces, slipped them into position and yanked upwards, the hooks disengaged and I pushed my cell door open. All it did was allow me to walk up and down, and talk more freely with the other prisoners. We managed to stay out of our cells for about another hour before we were noticed, and ordered back into our cells for the night. Nobody bothered to open the doors again, and we all settled in until the morning.

The next day, I was taken down a couple of floors to the waiting tank outside the courtroom, and was eventually called to the prisoners dock for sentencing. The Judge looked up from the papers in front of him, and said although your crime warrants a severe sentence, and quite possibly you should be incarcerated in the British Columbia Penitentiary for a lengthy

Prison sentence to protect the public. I have received Dr. Richmonds report, and he feels that because of your age you should be given a lighter sentence. On the basis of his report I sentence you to twenty months in the Okalla Prison Farm. And with that he banged his gavel on the bench in front of him, and I was hustled away to make room for the next sucker.

In the afternoon I was loaded into a Police Van. With several other prisoners, and taken on a lengthy drive to the Okalla Prison Farm in Burnaby a suburb of greater Vancouver. When we arrived, we drove down a driveway to a large portal with a Small Office for an armed guard. We drove up to the large front gate leading into the prison and stopped. I watched the driver hand the guard some papers on a clipboard, which he checked with his papers. When he appeared satisfied everything was in order he opened the gate. We drove down a narrow winding road to the front of a group of Red Brick Buildings, and backed up to the concrete steps. I thought as we were ordered out,

"Here we go again."

After going through the usual admission procedures, I was issued a uniform, and sent to a low flat roofed building with no windows, just large fire escape type doors placed at intervals along the sides with one big ventilation fan placed just above, and to the left of the door. This building had been built to ease the overcrowding in the main building. The front entrance was situated at the end of a gravel driveway, and contained the administration offices for the guards. The building was built on a sloping ground, so when you looked down the long central hallway, a series of steps were located at intervals. You could see the entire length of the building from the front gate to the back door. Branching of from the central hall were the cell blocks which were large rooms with a row of prefabricated steel cells along one side of the room. The walls of these cells did not reach to the ceiling. They stopped about four or five feet short, and the roof of the cell was made of steel bars, so you had an arrangement of three steel walls, with steel bars for a roof and bars for the front. The inside of the cell contained only a steel bunk with a mattress and a small shelf attached to the back wall. A chair was the only other piece of furniture. At the front of the cell block there was a barred window, and door. When you entered, there was one shower situated to the left, with a row of toilets in cubicles with no doors or roofs just partitions at each side, which allowed for no privacy at all. Across the room was a long stainless steel sink, with a mirror and under the front window was another general utility sink. In the middle of the room was a long heavy table used as a communal dining table and general area for writing, playing cards etc. At the far end of each cell block there was a shuffle board painted on the floor. On the end wall there was a large steel door which opened to the outside prison grounds. A large fan was situated high up on the back wall for ventilation. Every cell block had a man assigned for janitorial duties. The cell tiers were all named with letters of the alphabet.

I was assigned a cell on one of the tiers in the center of the cell block and locked up I assumed that everyone was out at work because the tier was empty at the time, later in the day I could hear the sounds of dozens of people coming up the steps, and the noise of the tiers being opened. Eventually inmates appeared in my own cell block, and my door was opened. After the initial introductions and questions about my length of stay and what I was in for, I watched the cons cleaning up at the front sink.

It wasn't long before the supper arrived. It was delivered in large Thermos Bottles to keep the hot food hot and the cold food cold. Before we sat down to eat, the utility man cleared the table and set it with steel partitioned trays and a spoon. Each inmate had his own cup. A prison guard was assigned to each tier to oversee the distribution of the food, which was done by the utility man. On most occasions it distributed fairly evenly, but even when it didn't the complaining was light because on the occasions when we occasionally received a larger allotment it broke even.

The next day after breakfast we all marched down to the end of the hall and into a large assembly hall where we were assigned our work details. The hall was also used for Floor Hockey and there was a stage built at one end for the occasional concert staged by the inmates. I reported to a guard who was standing in the hall assigning the new inmates to their gangs. When my turn came I was assigned to the Car License Plate Shop. This shop made license plates for all the cars in British Columbia. It was a large room equipped with all the metal cutting and stamping machines required for producing the provinces license plates.

The first day on the job I was assigned a machine that stamped out the holes in the plates that were used to bolt them to the car. All day I stood in front of the machine and placed the plate in a slot where two holes were punched into the plate. Directly across from where I was working was a machine which stamped the numbers on the plate. The operator had to be very quick as he placed each blank under the press because hand and eye coordination was required so that your hand wasn't caught as the press came down. The young con was very fast with the machine eventually made a mistake and his hand was caught and crushed by the machine. It happened so fast he never made a sound he just stood there and stared at his mangled hand. He walked over to the guard, and was led away. I never saw him again. After a few weeks of the constant banging of the presses and cutters and the intolerable boring job, I decided to ask for a transfer which was granted.

I found myself with a group of young teenage delinquents who were totally incorrigible. Some of them were out right psychopaths or mental misfits. The guard assigned to us was a big easy going guy, who knew these kids like the back of his hand. The kids seemed to have garnered a grudging respect for him. We were taken out into one of the fields to dig Rutabagas which I didn't mind for the weather was good and the fresh air was exhilarating. At the end of the day we were gathered and placed in twos and marched back to the assembly hall. As we were walking down the slope toward the back of the building, I felt a flash of heat on my cheek, and I smelt smoke. I glanced quickly to my right and discovered that the shoulder of my coat was on fire.

"Jesus!" I yelled and quickly took my coat off and smothered the flame which had already burned a small hole through the material. While I was struggling to get my coat off a group of cons in my gang stood around and laughed. I felt the blood rushing to my face and I glanced quickly around trying to see which one had pulled this stupid prank, but while I was struggling to get out of my coat they were all milling about and calling sarcastic remarks and thoroughly enjoying my frantic efforts. There was no way I could tell who the joker was, but I ask anyway. I looked around at the leering faces, and said, "Who's the asshole?" All I got back was a bunch of stupid giggles. While this charade was going on, our little group had stopped, and was holding up the line of cons, coming in from the fields, a guard quickly approached.

"What's going on here?" he yelled.

Nobody said anything. We just quickly got into formation, and moved off down the line. I made up my mind to be a little more vigilant with these bastards because I knew that because they had easily got away with this first attempt at goading me, whoever it was would try it again. The next morning while were lining up in the assembly room one of the group approached me and said.

"Look it wasn't me who lit your coat yesterday."

I looked at him in a disbelieving way and said.

"If I ever catch the bastard I'm going to see he never does it again, in my most menacing voice. This threw him into a quiet fury and he said

"If you make any moves on me, don't ever turn your back on me because if you do, you will be sorry you did."

The whole conversation only took a few minutes. I can only assume that this con was worried that I was going to get him when his back was turned, and he had decided to threaten me bodily harm before it happened, in the hope that I wouldn't do anything. Well he didn't know that I didn't have any idea who might have done it, and I couldn't very well start fights with a half dozen young thugs. All it would have gotten me at the least was a trip to the hole or a knife in the back. As time went by, I observed that con, had a wild temper, and was known as a scrapper over anything at all, a totally unmannered individual, but I didn't think from watching him that he was the type that would do a cowardly thing behind peoples backs, like set their clothes on fire. He wouldn't have found that funny.

The days rolled by without incident until one day we were sent out to clean some drainage ditches. The weather was very bad, Lots of rain, and fortunately our guard got tired of being soaking wet as well as we did, and took us up to the cow barns to feed some cows. When we were finished we were milling about outside the barn doors waiting for the rain to stop. I was standing quietly in the barn doorway, watching the cows eat their hay. I casually wandered farther into the barn, and began to feed one of the animals by hand. As happens when you're enjoying yourself, I forgot about my troubles, and where I was at for a minute. In the meantime, the guard decided to herd the men into the basement out of site until the rain stopped. In a few minutes I noticed the only noise was the cows chewing, and the rustling of the other animals. I looked up to find I was all alone. I stepped outside to see where the gang had gone. Just as I came out of the door, the guard came running out of the door to the basement, and almost collided with me. He was surprised and relieved all at the same time. He realized that I was not attempting to escape, but was angry that I had thrown a scare into him.

"Where the hell have you been?" He shouted. "I was just going to sound the alarm that you had escaped."

"Escaped I was just feeding old bossy over there," pointing to the cow I had just left.

"I just about had the whole prison on general alert over it." He said.

"It's not my fault you don't keep a closer eye on your men. Where's the rest of the gang?"

He looked at me for a minute and decided to drop the whole matter because he couldn't crime me without admitting he hadn't kept a close watch on his charges."

"There down stairs," he snapped.

When I joined the rest of the gang, they all looked up with expressions of disappointment and surprise on their faces. They had all thought I had made a run for it, which would have broken their humdrum routine. After I had fielded the usual twenty questions, everybody laughed but some thought I had missed a perfect opportunity when I was given a ten minute head start. Nobody had thought about where I would go with no outside help all they cared about was I would be committing an act of defiance, and showing them that not everybody was submitting to punishment without a fight. This group of course thought I was a jerk for not going. The truth of the matter was it had just not entered my head at the time. All I was doing was enjoying feeding a friendly cow. That evening I decided I had enough of these stupid bastards, and that I would ask for a change.

The next morning it was back out to the muddy rain filled drainage ditches, which were over grown with weeds and grass, and needed clearing. One of the inmates was a young kid who couldn't have been more than sixteen or seventeen years old at the most, but was obviously mentally deficient, and it was not very long before one of the most vicious of the punks found he could easily talk the kid into doing anything for him. The kid followed this asshole around like a pet dog with his master. The punk just laughed and bragged about it to the rest of his followers.

There was a storage shed located not far from where we were working which held the tools. The punk talked the guard into letting him and the kid go to the shed to exchange their shovels for hoes. I was already there picking up a wheel barrow when the two of them walked in. The punk said.

"Hey! Want to see the kid eat a worm?"

I looked at him leering at me. I thought "You sick bastard, and a feeling of rage and revulsion spread over me, I said

"You've got to be kidding," and turned away.

"Sure," he said sarcastically turning to the kid who was standing there with the dull uncomprehending look of the mentally retarded. The floor was dirt and there were one or two earthworms lying about probably knocked of shovels. The punk picked them up.

"Go ahead I dare you to eat these," he said handing them to the kid.

The kid grinned and giggled falling in to the ugly game willingly. The punk roared with laughter.

"I told you so, I told you so," he said proudly.

I just stood there watching this disgusting display, and the urge to kill this dirt, swept over me. I was holding a shovel and I felt my grip on the handle tighten. I took a few steps. His expression of triumph turned to fear as he realized I did not admire his power over the kid. I stood there for a moment and when I felt the feeling of hopelessness sweep over me again. I turned and walked back to the ditch as the rain began to fall and splash in my face like a breath of fresh air. It wasn't long before I was soaked to the skin and tired of my situation. I had to get off this gang and away from this bunch of idiots. I looked over at the guard standing there with a vacant look on his face. I thought he's probably bored with his lot in life just as I am. I laid the shovel down, climbed out of the ditch and walked over to him.

"Yeah, what do you want?" he asked.

"I'm not doing this anymore, I quit."

A look of surprise came over his face, and he suddenly became very alert.

"What the hell do you mean? You quit," he said with the surprised look still on his face.

"Just what I said, I'm not going to stand around in the rain getting soaked and digging in those bloody ditches anymore."

I guess he knew by the sound of my voice, and the determined look on my face that I meant business. He just nodded his head, and said

"Okay, it's time to go in for lunch. You think about it, and if you still feel the same way after lunch I'll have to charge you."

"I'll still feel the same way after lunch and any other time," I said.

He lined up the crew, and we stored our tools in the shed and marched back to the cell block. There were whispers and glances in my direction, but nobody said anything to me. After lunch and before going down to the assembly block I was called into the front administration office. The guard in charge of the gang and another guard who was obviously more senior were waiting. I was told to stand in the middle of the room while the charge guard told the senior guard about my insubordination.

"You don't want to go to work?" he snapped at me.

"No," I said determinedly.

"Why?" he asked.

"I don't like the gang, or the job," I said.

"You did time for armed robbery in the Penitentiary didn't you?" he asked

"Yeah," I said.

He stared at me for a few minutes and said.

"Okay your on charge for refusing to work and you'll be confined to your cell until further notice, now get out of here,"

I thought, "Well this is all right, I get a chance to dry out, and have a nap, and I don't have to put up with those assholes on the gang."

I went back to my cell smiling.

The next day I was taken up to the main building to the Deputy Warden's Office for sentencing. The guard in charge of the gang was there, and to my surprise when the deputy ask him about my attitude, and work habits, he gave a decent report, and said I was a good worker, but he didn't think I was the type to be assigned to these types of menial duties. The deputy asked me about my record and I told him about the Penitentiary time, thinking while I was doing it, that he had the information right in front of him, and already knew about it. He just smiled and closed the folder, and said

"Because of Officer MacDonalds report in your favour, and the circumstances surrounding this incident, I'm not going to confine you to solitary. But instead you will spend the rest of the day confined to your cell. In the mean time I will decide on a more suitable occupation for you that's all."

With that he opened the folder, scribbled some comment in it, and dismissed me with a glance. It was obvious that the guard and the Deputy Warden had discussed the incident before I had arrived. I still wonder what he meant by the circumstances surrounding the case and how much he knew about my dislike for the punks on his gang. I suppose after working with these people he knew who fitted the mold, and who didn't and I like to think that it showed in my attitude and actions, that I didn't.

After breakfast, I was ordered up to the front office, and told to pack my gear, I was moving along the cell block to another tier, and I was going to be that tiers utility man. This I didn't mind at all, I was going to be inside all day out of the weather, and I would be working most of the time alone, locked in the tier, and I wouldn't have to be looking over my shoulder all the time, and worrying what stupid caper I would be dragged into by these incorrigible punks on the maintenance gang.

A few weeks went by and my job changed a little bit. I was given the job of cleaning up after the guard's supper, which they ate down in the last tier of the cell block which was used as an extra auditorium and assembly area. After I had eaten my own supper and cleaned up. I would be taken down to clean up the remains of the extra Guards meal. Any food that was left over I would hand out with permission to any prisoners who wanted it. The extras usually went very fast.

On my tier there was a prisoner by the name of Loosley who worked on the Paint Gang. During a game of darts I found out he was from Victoria, and serving a year for passing bad checks. He was a middle aged man who used to be an officer in the navy. He was a very talented artist who had worked for the Government painting scenic back drops for the Provincial Museum displays. His down fall was he was an incurable alcoholic who had spent most of the past few years going in and out of prison for various stupid offences committed while trying to obtain money to satisfy his drinking problem. He was an educated man with an easy going personality, and it wasn't long before we developed a friendship. One day he told me that one of the members of the Paint Gang was due for release, and he would talk to the boss in charge if I made a request for transfer. He described the job as one where I would be sent around the prison to do various painting jobs. I decided I was due for a change so I made the request out for transfer. A week went by and I was told that I was the successful candidate.

The boss of the Paint Gang was an easy guard who had been working at the prison for a number of years, and I found that if you worked hard for him, he would leave you alone and relax his supervision, which he did for me several times in the following months.

One of the jobs we were assigned to do was the Women's Section of the prison, which was a separate building from the main men's complex. It was more like a very secure hotel than the traditional Canadian Men's Prison. The women were kept three or four to a small dormitory with double bunks, and there was the feminine look to everything. Of course while we were painting the hallways and corridors, we were assigned Women guards, who kept a close eye on us. We were not allowed to fraternize with the women prisoners at all. But they could not stop the occasional piece of conversation, or shy come on glance. When it was discovered by the male prisoners that the paint gang was in the women's prison, it wasn't long before I was approached by someone to carry kites to the women. Kites are intimate notes exchanged between the male and female inmates who used pseudonyms to avoid being caught.

The notes were folded in neat little packages and sealed with tape. The outside was marked with the recipient's pseudonym. All I had to do was pass it to the first female prisoner I could get close enough to, and they would deliver it to the right place. From time to time I would be given some kites to bring back. The guards, usually looking for larger articles during their frisks overlooked the small packets every time. I was even approached by one con, who wanted to say Hi to a female guard who he knew personally on the street. That came about easier than I thought, because while I was working in a stairwell I was in the process of moving a long extension ladder, which hit the overhead light. A piece of the glass cover came down and cut my chin when I looked up to see what had happened. It was bleeding quite a bit so I went to get a dressing for it. I was taken into their dispensary for first aid. One of the young women prisoners, and a guard were treating me, when I noticed the guard was wearing a name tag with the name I was looking for. I waited for the prisoner to leave the room for a minute, and said.

"Harry says hello."

And quickly gave her his message, which consisted of his release date, and he'd like to take her to dinner on a fixed date. The whole thing was finished in a minute. She was so surprised she just stood there staring at me for a moment, finally comprehension came to her face, but the female prisoner came into the room and we couldn't talk anymore. I took some ribbing about my little accident, and how I'd do anything to get some female attention, but the guard in charge of us didn't think anything of it, and it was soon forgotten. As we were getting things cleaned up near the end of the day I was quietly approached by the female guard and she quickly whispered.

"Tell Harry Okay."

When I saw Harry and told him he laughed and said.

"I've known her for years. She's a good role in the hay, and I see she hasn't forgotten me either."

He went away chuckling to himself.

One of the places I was sent to was the Main Kitchen. And of course when the other cons found that out, I was approached several times to smuggle various goodies back to the cell block, as a favour of course. One of these requests was for some Peanut Butter, and it came from a con on my own tier, so it was a little hard to refuse. I told him I would, but just this one time. I eventually made contact with a con in the kitchen he placed a couple of large scoops of Peanut Butter in a wax paper packet, and slipped it to me. I placed it flat against my stomach and pressed until it molded to fit flat against my body. Unfortunately when I got back to the Paint Shop we were running late, and were being rushed into getting our coveralls off, and when I took mine off, I discovered that when I had pushed on the packet it hadn't been folded tight enough and all the Peanut Butter had oozed out of the loose corners and was all over my shirt and pants. I looked like I had an accident with a young baby while changing his diapers. The Paint Boss was standing there while I was changing. His eyes just about bugged out of his head.

"Well you should know better to try and pull a stunt like that. Hurry up and clean it up we are running late, and I want to get home."

He turned around and walked out of the room smiling, and to my amazement I never heard no more about it, except the next day he moved me out of the kitchen to paint the wood frames on a greenhouse that was being built near the front entrance of the Main Cell Block.

In the afternoon we noticed some excited activity going on around the front entrance so we stopped what we were doing and watched as the Warden and the Prison Doctor, and some prison guards gathered at the foot of the prison steps. They were all looking up at the roof, which had a concrete ledge running around the edge just below the top. There was a con sitting on the ledge with his feet dangling over the edge. He had his head in his hands, and was staring at the ground below. A prison guard was trying to talk the con into coming back off the ledge and onto the roof. While this was going on the Warden was getting into his car which was parked a-long side the front steps. He then drove it to another area so if the con jumped he wouldn't land on the car and cave the roof in. An exchange of conversation went on for a few minutes. Suddenly he just leaned forward, and fell head first to the concrete steps below. There was an audible crunch as his skull fractured, and he bounced upward a few inches, and then lay still sprawled on the steps face down. The Prison Doctor quickly ran up the steps, and tried to find a pulse in the man's neck. In a few moments he looked up and shook his head, indicating to the warden that the man was dead. The Warden issued a few quick orders to the group of prison guards who were milling about, and in a few minutes a stretcher was brought in and the body was taken away. The whole incident had taken just a few minutes, the ending of a human life on a warm sunny afternoon on the concrete steps of the Prison. When something like this happens, it becomes common knowledge around the prison very quickly. But when I got back to the Cell Block that evening nobody was interested in my eye witness account, they didn't want to hear about some poor guy ending his futile life in a prison yard. The next few days I watched the obituary columns in the papers, when I could get my hands on one, but I couldn't find mention of the incident anywhere, and in a day or two it was like it had never happened, and the Wardens Car was back in its regular parking space.

A new gymnasium was being built with a stage for putting on plays and holding various indoor sporting activities. Bill Loosely was asked to paint a large mural as a stage back drop. The famous Michelangelo picture, "The Last Supper" was chosen. Bill approached me and asked me if I would like to get off the Cell Block in the evening, and come and help him set up, and paint this large picture in the new gym. I laughed and said.

"They won' let me out there with you Bill. I've got too much time left to do."

"You just keep your mouth shut and I'll do the rest. Right now I think they'll allow it. I'm the only one who can do this job, and they'll give me what I want."

"Okay," I said.

Next evening the two of us were called out, and work began on the picture. We worked for a couple of hours and Bill said.

"Are you hungry?"

I said "Yeah, I'm getting that way."

Bill called the guard over,

"Look I think we should have some tea and sandwiches brought in every evening don't you?" he said smiling in a disarming way,

The guard was taken aback for a minute by Bill's audacity, and just stared at him for a minute, thinking about it. In a moment he just smiled, and said.

"I'm going to the phone, don't leave the building."

To my surprise, he left, leaving us alone for about a half an hour. When he came back, he was carrying a tray loaded with doughnuts and coffee.

"Okay," he said, "The warden had agreed to this for the time being, Hell I don't mind this either."

Eventually the finishing touches were applied to the painting, and I was surprised at the great job that Bill had done to the detail, and his own color scheme was perfect as far as I was concerned.

A few days went by, and one evening Bill came up to me, and told me he had been called up to the Deputies Office, who told him that they were bringing in some Art Instructor from the University of British Columbia to change the faces to more closely resemble the original Michelangelo painting. He was quiet and calm while he was telling me this, but I could tell he was seething underneath and very annoyed that the Warden had decided to tamper with his work. In no time at all word had spread around the cell block about this outrage, and a general sit down was being talked up among the inmates. They felt that what Bill had created was the cons personal contribution to the new gymnasium, and they didn't like the authority trying to take that away by changing the picture to what they felt was a better product.

In the evening after super we were all taken down to the assembly block and addressed by the Warden. It seems that the prisoner's displeasure with what the administration was doing to Bill's Picture had reached the Wardens ears, and he had decided to speak to the assembled prisoners to quieten the unrest that was going through the Cell Bock. Although the whole Cell Block population was there, he made his address directly to Bill, Telling him that his work was very good, and that they had merely invited the University Artist out to see it. When the artist saw it he recommended some minor changes, which the administration felt would improve the work, and so they had accepted the experts help. There was no intended snub of Bills efforts. Bill got up, and graciously accepted the Warden's explanation, and peace was restored when the inmates saw that Bill was excepting the situation. I never did see the finished work or get to play in the new gymnasium, because a few days later I was transferred to a road camp for a change of pace.

The prison had established a road maintenance camp in the Fraser Valley, and when your prison term was getting short you could apply for a transfer. The camp was located out in the country away from any populated areas, and consisted of a Dining Hall with a kitchen, and Showers. It had two Bunkhouses for the Prisoners and a house for the Administration Staff.

When I arrived I was taken aside and offered a job in the Kitchen as a helper for the Cooks. I also had the job of seeing that the Wood Stoves in the Bunkhouses were supplied with wood, and were started in the mornings before everyone got up for breakfast, along with several other small menial chores which I did from time to time.

I accepted the job immediately because I knew that the work that the gang was doing was hard work out in the weather and besides most of the gang consisted of the young punks I didn't like from the grounds maintenance back at Okalla. Anything was better than working with that bunch.

During the day the only personnel at the camp were the two cooks, me and a guard who stayed in the house most of the time. When I finished my chores, I had the day to myself which was a far cry from laboring out in some roadside ditch somewhere, and working in the kitchen gave me access to a much better diet, even though the food was much better than back at the prison.

It wasn't long before the time I had left was up, and I was sent back to Okalla for an overnight stay, and release in the morning. During my stay I had made out my income tax return, and received a refund, so I wasn't going out of the prison broke. It wasn't much, but it was enough for boat fare and a room back in Victoria.

I walked up the road to Okalla's front gate, and found a taxi waiting in the parking lot. I asked to be taken directly into Vancouver, where I went to a Barbershop, and got a shave and a haircut. I felt a lot better afterwards.

That evening I bought a Bus Ticket to Victoria via the ferry, and booked into the Lincoln Hotel. It was a cheap hotel on the corner of Johnson and Broad Street in the center of town. I was back.

CHAPTER 8

Ducan and the Henslowes

Employment in Port Alberni

America and the Gun

The next day I went down to a small restaurant just around the corner from the hotel and had breakfast. After eating I was standing at the pin ball machine playing my change and amusing myself, when a voice asked me.

"How long have you been in town?"

I looked up and saw Len Akerman a big beat cop who I knew as a basketball player from my school days.

"I got in yesterday."

"Where are you staying?"

I nodded my head towards the hotel and said, "In the Lincoln." I just kept playing the machine only answering when spoken to. He stood there for a moment, and then turned quickly and left like he was in a hurry to get away from me. When I ran out of change I went back to my room and lay down for a nap.

I was awakened by voices outside my door. Someone said,

"He's in there alright I can see him lying on the bed."

I realized he was peeking through the keyhole, and I thought he's not only a cop but a keyhole peeper to. I laughed, and rolled out of bed and opened the door. Two big Detectives were standing there they didn't bother showing their identification. They knew I knew who they were Hell! How could you miss it, what with the Fedoras, and Overcoats, and sloppy looking Suits they had on, out of uniform, but not really, they looked like something out of a "B" movie. I realized then why Akerman was in such a big hurry to get away from me. He wanted to get to a phone and report my arrival. I didn't think I rated a visit by two of Victoria's finest.

"Yeah, what do you want?" I said, with as much boredom as I could muster.

"When did you get into town?" one of them asked.

"Akerman already asked me that question," I said with a smile.

They exchanged glances and one of them snapped back.

"Well were asking now."

I figured it was time to stop the sarcasm, and talk to these guys to avoid the trouble they could send my way. I said.

"Look I'm only going to be here today then I'm leaving town."

"Where are you going," they ask.

"I'm going up to Duncan to stay with my mom."

"You got any money?"

"Just enough for today and my bus fare tomorrow. What's this about anyway," I ask.

They looked at each other for a moment and one of them said.

"There has- been some hold-ups in town."

They both studied my reaction to this piece of information hoping for some sort of expression which would warrant further interrogation, but I didn't give it to them. I just laughed, and said.

"That lets me out. Like I said I just got in town yesterday. I just finished doing twenty months in Okalla. You guys should have known that."

I could tell by their faces that they didn't like being told their business, and I thought,

"Hell I don't like being harassed by you jerks either." One of them said.

"You be on the bus to Duncan tomorrow you hear," while pointing a beefy finger under my nose. I said "Yeah," nodded my head, and turned and walked into my room shutting the door behind me. I stood behind the door for a minute listening. In a few seconds, I could hear their footsteps disappearing down the hall, and I breathed a sigh of relief.

The next day, I bought a Bus ticket to Duncan, a small logging town approximately forty miles north of Victoria. When I arrived, I located the nearest pay phone, and looked up the Henslowes in the Phone Directory. Mom answered the phone.

Hi Mom I'm in town, and I need a place to stay for a few days."

"John! It's you?" Her surprised voice came back. "When did you get out of jail?"

"Oh, a couple of days ago, can I come over to see you?" I ask a little impatiently.

"Yes dear, come right over," she said.

I hung up the phone, and walked down the street about a block, and found a Cab Stand and went out to Herd Road where the Henslowes lived.

During my stay in the Penitentiary my Mother had gotten lonely, and struck up an old acquaintance with the Henslowes, who my Father had worked for as a handyman before I was born. Mr. Henslowe who was long dead owned fifty acres of land three miles north of Duncan on Herd Road. He was a comfortably well off English man who ran a kind of Hobby Farm, raising a few head of cattle and various other farm animals. From the looks of the place when I arrived, it was probably a very nice well- kept small country estate in its day. When he died his wife and one of his three son's "Lawrence" were the only ones still living on the property, one son had moved to California and the other who owned some adjoining property had settled in Duncan, and didn't associate with Lawrence at all due to some sort of family feud.

Mrs. Henslowe was in her eighties and almost totally deaf and Lawrence was a simpleton with some very strange outlooks on life. He seemed to be living fifty years behind time and was very eccentric. Mrs. Henslowe was extremely religious and during the weeks her main source of pleasure was to listen to the Sunday Church Services on a large cabinet radio which was located in the front living room of the house. She would come downstairs from her bedroom about ten o'clock in the morning, and tune into her favorite church service, and relax in a comfortable chair placed directly in front of the radio. The station was turned up as high as the dial could go, and of course the radio was so loud that nobody could understand anything being broadcast. She would sit there listening to this roar of sound coming at her, as if she could understand everything that was being said. Maybe she could? I'll never know, because the minute she came down, and turned up the radio I would just leave, and go for a walk around the property, or visit the next door neighbours for an hour.

When I first arrived, I made the mistake of taking Lawrence and his mother out to the town's local movie theater on a Saturday Night. The feature was a very popular one at the time, and so the theater was packed. When the feature started and the audience became quiet, and totally immersed in the plot, Mrs. Henslowe, being totally deaf couldn't hear what was going on, and every once in a while she would ask Lawrence in a very loud, and clear English accent, "What's happening now Lawrence?" And he would reply at the top of his voice, because she was deaf, and describe what the dialogue was. Well after a few loud and descriptive explanations from Lawrence, the Movie Patrons were ready to throw them both out on the street. Through all the commotion both of them failed to understand what the commotion was about, and sat there, totally ignoring the verbal threats coming their way. Finally I managed to get both of them back out into the lobby of the theatre by telling them I wasn't feeling well, and that we had to leave. I didn't have the heart to tell them that if we didn't leave some of the patrons were going to break every bone in their bodies.

To make up for the spoiled movie, I thought it would be nice to walk down the street to a small restaurant called the "Green Haven," and buy each of them a dish of ice cream. When it was time to leave, and I had finished paying the bill, Lawrence who was standing beside me had taken an interest in a display of Ball Point Pens and proceeded to get into a long drawn out discussion with the store clerk about the merits of how to hold the pen to get it to write properly. While this was going on, a line of patrons was beginning to form behind him waiting to pay their bills. The fact that the Store Clerk, and the people waiting in line were getting very annoyed with Lawrence's complete indifference to anything but whether a Ball Point Pen had to held straight up and down or on an angle before it would write properly didn't mean a thing to him. "Lawrence people are waiting," I said, trying to draw his attention to the situation.

"These pens are totally inadequate, they won't write unless you hold them like this," and he proceeded to scribble on the counter top while holding the pen in a perpendicular position. While this was going on the clerk was looking at me with an annoyed and beseeching look. I looked at the long cue of impatient customers, and realized if I didn't do something pretty soon Lawrence was going to get thrown out onto the street bodily. I gently helped Mrs. Henslowe out of the booth she was in, and walked over and took the pen out of Lawrence's hand, placing it on the counter. I then took hold of Lawrence's arm and hustled him out of the restaurant onto the side walk, and held him firmly until Mrs. Henslowe arrived helped by the Store Clerk. He thanked me with a relieved look on his face and hurried back to his impatient customers.

"There were customers lining up to pay their bills Lawrence, and they were getting a little annoyed waiting," I said.

"Oh, he said, well I felt the public shouldn't be subjected to inferior merchandise, and those pens are not the answer the manufacturers try to make out. The Fountain Pen is still the more comfortable writing instrument," he said, complete assurance that he knew what he was talking about in his voice. Changing the subject I turned to Mrs. Henslowe and said as loud as I could.

"Did you enjoy the Ice Cream?"

"Oh yes, she said in her clipped English accent.

"Well shall we go home?"

I didn't get any objection, so I hailed a taxi, and vowed never to take them out into the populous again.

It wasn't long before I began to run out of money. Lawrence and my mother were both on welfare, and I couldn't ask them for anything. You can't get water out of a stone. After a few days I realized I was going to have to go job hunting, and when I mentioned it to Mom she suggested I apply to the Human Resources Department of the Government for welfare. I didn't like the idea of this at all. It was a feeling of being a beggar, and I felt a feeling of humiliation just discussing it with her. I guess she sensed this and told me she would talk to the Social Worker who was looking after them. I said, "I didn't like it," but to go ahead anyway.

Two or three days went by, and finally a young attractive woman came out to talk to me. I told her my situation, and she said I wouldn't have any trouble getting help, and my first cheque would arrive at the end of the month. It was easy money, and I gave half of it to Mom to help them out. I still didn't like it. It seemed like all my life was in a state of welfare dependence, and object poverty.

Mom's next door neighbours the "Darcey's were probably her only social contacts in the neighbourhood. Harold Darcey was a retired postman for the area who suffered from chronic lung disease brought on by years of mining before he became a rural postman in the Duncan area. His wife was a friendly and kind woman, who never said an unkind word about anybody as long as I knew her. They lived in a very small house with two teenage sons, and a daughter, and supplemented Harold's pensions by tending a large vegetable garden and keeping a couple of cows out back on the few acres of land they owned.

Over the years as a postman, Harold had made a lot of friends, and even though he had retired he still kept up contact with them by the occasional trip to town, and a stop in at the Green Haven for a cup of coffee and a chat. On one of these excursions he had bumped into an old friend who was a member of the local Carpenters Union, and during their conversation he found out that there was a large pulp mill being built at Port Alberni, a small Mill Community centrally located on the Island. Harold remembered I was looking for work and asked if there might be any openings. He told him that the work had just begun and that they were hiring on a regular basis. Harold told him about me, and how I needed work, and was there any chance I might pick up a labourers job of some type.

"Look. I'm going up on Monday tell the kid I'll pick him up on Hersey's Corner at about five o'clock in the morning and not to be late,"

"Thanks, he'll appreciate it."

"Glad to do it, by the way he'll have to pay into the Car Pool to help with the gas. I'm driving a couple of other carpenters up to."

"I'll tell him," Harold said with a smile.

After supper I received a telephone call from Harold to come over, he wanted to talk to me. When I arrived his wife made us a cup of tea, and Harold told me about the offer to take me up to the mill in Port Alberni for a chance at a job. I didn't know while we sat there drinking our tea, and discussing my chances of getting a job that a new and darker phase of my life was about to begin.

The next morning I was up and ready to go. I walked out to Hersey's Corner. It was really the corner of Herd Road, and the Island Highway, but there was a large Chipper Truck garage, and gas pump on the corner called Hersey's Trucking, so everybody in the area called it Hersey's Corner. It was pouring with rain and still dark, so I stood under the gas pump canopy and waited. It wasn't long before a large Pontiac Sedan pulled up and honked its horn. I walked over as a short heavily built man got out from behind the wheel wearing a matching khaki shirt and pants with heavy work boots.

"You John?" he asked "Hi, I'm Albert Dawes, Just call me Turk."

He shook my hand without waiting for a reply.

"Here we'll put your bag in the back," he said opening the Car Trunk. I was carrying a large brown duffel bag, Mom had found somewhere. It held a change of underwear, and some work clothes, Mom had bought for me.

I still had my prison made shoes and I was going to use them as my work shoes. They were good for something after all. I still had some clothes left from before I went to prison so I had enough gear to get by on until I got my first pay check. I was introduced to the three other carpenters in the car, and I settled down in the back seat as we headed toward Port Alberni.

We arrived at the construction site in the afternoon, and we drove directly to the administration offices, which consisted of an outside Time Clock area, and a single floor wooden building. Immediately on entering I found myself in a large room, with a long counter at one end with cues of men all applying for work. It was very noisy. Everybody was talking loudly to be heard above the din. I picked a line up, and waited for my turn at the counter. When I finally arrived, a young obviously harassed girl snapped at me.

"Yes, what-a-ya want?"

I couldn't resist snapping back.

"I'm looking for work."

"What kind of work?" The labor Pool is all filled."

"Look!" I said with a low growl in my voice, "I just came up from Duncan, and I need a job any job and I was told you were hiring here."

Her eyes came up from the paper work in front of her, and stared at me for a moment. I guess my voice had invoked interest from the people in the room, because I noticed it was suddenly a lot quieter. I could feel the heat of anger in my face as I stared back defiantly.

"You see that man over there with the yellow Hard Hat on?"

"Yeah."

"Go see him, he's the Job Superintendent maybe he's got something because I don't," she said with finality.

"Thanks," I said and turned my back on her, and walked over to the Superintendent.

"Yes?" He said.

"I just got up from down Island with some Duncan Carpenters and they told me I could find some work here.

"What's your name?" he asked.

I told him.

"And you came up with Turk from Duncan, are you a carpenter?" He asked.

"No!" I said, surprised that he knew Turk. I'm not a carpenter, but I did come up from Duncan with Turk.

"Laboring okay?" He smiled.

I felt a weight lifting off my shoulders when I realized he was going to hire me.

"Sure" I said.

He pulled a small scratch pad from his breast pocket, and wrote a few words on it. He tore of the page, and handed it me.

"Take this to the counter, and they'll fix you up," he said.

Before I could thank him, he had turned his attention to someone else. The same girl at the counter served me, and when she saw the note I was quickly hired and processed through the system. I found Turk and his friends waiting for me outside.

"Come on, were going over to the camp, nodding towards the Construction Camp situated across the street from the building site, to get a room."

We quickly found the Administration Building, and in no time at all, I was registered and given a room in one of the large H huts. The rooms were furnished with two cots, and a locker for each cot. The Bathroom facilities were situated down the hall in the center of the H. My roommate was a large burley Czech who was a laborer the same as I was. He didn't speak very good English, but I gathered that he was a Police Detective in the Czech Republic before the communists took over, and when they came, he was a political non entity, and so he fled the country, and eventually came to Canada. During the time I worked at the camp, he spoke very little to me, and I to him, so we never became friends, just acquaintances.

The next day I reported to the Administration Office, and was told where to punch in, and then I was sent out on the site with a group of five other laborers to begin work. It had rained heavily overnight, and the foundation site I was working on was knee deep in mud, and we were struggling through this carrying twelve ft. 2x12 for the carpenters. The weight of the planks caused us to sink over our boots in the mud and with every step we had to pull our feet out with tremendous effort, because of the suction of the clinging mud. After a few hours of this I was nearing exhaustion. I had just dropped my end of the plank, and was struggling in the mud to bring it up again, when I heard Turks voice.

"Hey, John how are you doing?"

I looked up, and saw him standing with the Yard Superintendent grinning down at me from the edge of the excavation. I put on a brave smile, and yelled back.

"Well, I'm telling you I'm getting a pretty wet ass down here."

"How would you like to get out of there, he called back?"

I stared at the supervisor thinking to myself Turk must have some clout here.

"Would I ever," I yelled.

Turk and the supervisor engaged in some low conversation which I couldn't hear very well. The supervisor called down.

"Come on up outa there, you are going to be a runner."

I didn't know what a runner was, but anything was better than what I was doing. So I was quick to hop out of the mud and up the excavation's bank.

The supervisor took me over to another project, where the framing was more advanced, and the carpenters were working on a dry deck. I was introduced to a large heavy set man with a European accent.

"This is John Henry. He's going to be one of our site runners."

He turned to me and said.

"Henry is a Yard Foreman, you'll work for him, he' will tell you what to do, by the way get a Hard Hat. You can't work on the site without one. Be sure you have one by tomorrow morning."

The first week on the job went by without incident. It was the following week when things began to get interesting. One of the carpenters approached me one morning and asked me to get a Fork Lift and driver to bring his crew some lumber he needed. He was working as a Carpenter Foreman in charge of a crew. As I was walking away to do his bidding, he nonchalantly said.

"You know most of the drivers around here don't you?"

"Yes."

Wondering what his interest was.

"You know where the Carpenters Office is don' you?" he asked.

"Yes."

There's a couple of bars of lead piled at the rear, ask one of the drivers to pick it up, and drop it off under the steps of number 5 H hut, he'll find a case of beer there waiting."

I was a bit surprised at this, because I thought this was a nice family guy, but then I knew a lot of temptation on these large construction jobs passed by every day, and I knew they were hard to resist. I said. "I need my job and walked away." I wasn't worried about any repercussions, because he probably needed his job to. I later found out that petty thievery was going on at a tremendous pace. I wasn't the only runner assigned to my job-site, a young teenage kid was working with me, one evening when the whistle blew and everyone was picking up their tools to call it a day. I noticed that the kid had forgotten his lunch pail. I picked it up, and called after him at the same time I noticed how heavy it was. He heard me, and hurried back with a worried look on his face.

"What have you got in this thing, an anvil?" I said.

He looked at me for an instant, and then smiled.

"Nuts and Bolts," he said.

I laughed, and said, "You have got to be kidding?" "O no," he said and flicked the latches on the pail to show me what he had got, and sure as hell what he had was a pail full of various size screws, bolts, and nuts and washers. I looked at him, and he was smiling with a satisfied look on his face.

"For Christ sakes, if you got caught with that you'll lose your job, maybe even go to jail." He just laughed, and said.

"I take this home every-night. They'll never look in my lunch pail."

"Hell! You showed it to me didn't you? How do you know I won't turn you in?"

"You wouldn't do that," he said and walked away

Well I guess he had me pegged, and I went back to camp, for a shower and some supper.

The Camp Mess Hall was a large building, containing the kitchens and a large room lined with tables and benches for eating. You checked in and told them who you were at the door, and your name was ticked off the list of camp occupants. After you went through a door you picked up a tray and selected your food cafeteria style as you walked down the line up. There were usually two or three choices of the main dish, with a separate table for deserts. The cooks and helpers stood behind a counter, and filled your requests as you went by, a simple and efficient method of quickly feeding hundreds of hungry Construction Workers.

"Hi kid."

I looked up at who was addressing me, and found myself staring at Pat, an ex con who had been in the B.C.P. Boiler House on the plumping gang when I was shoveling coal in the Boilers

"Hi Pat, long time no see," I said.

"Hut 4, room7," he said. Come on over about 8, I've got a couple of beer. We can shoot the breeze for a little while.

Kazoonie

"Okay," I said, I'll be there."

Small world I thought as I headed for a table.

A week later the Job Supervisor came up to me, and the French Kid, and asked us if we wanted to be laborers for the Iron Workers with a chance of learning the trade. I saw a chance for more money, so I said yes. We were put carrying the iron reinforcing rods commonly known as rebar and used for reinforcing concrete. The job was far and away heavier, and harder than being a runner, but I stuck it out, and eventually I was granted a work permit by the Iron Workers Union to be a Rodman, whose job is to tie the rebar into position before the concrete is poured into the walls, and foundations of the various new buildings being built on the job site.

I worked with the permit for a couple of months, and when the Union thought that the apprentices were proficient enough in the trade, we were told we would all have to go to Vancouver B.C. to the Main Union Office to take a test to become full members of the union. So on Friday evening, we all went down to Nanaimo and boarded the ferry for the trip across the Georgia Straight to Vancouver. During the trip over, I spent the time watching a big Black Jack Game that had started up on the saloon deck. I think two or three players had lost their wages before the ship docked, and I wondered if any of them were married, and if so, how they were going to explain to their wife's what happened to their money. Every big construction job has its card games, and it's Card Sharks, and there always seemed to be a game going on somewhere.

When we got to Vancouver, the apprentices who were staying overnight just to write the test the next day, and return home, went looking for a cheap room up in the east end of the city, an area of Cheap Hotels and Beer Parlors. That night a couple of us went up to Pender Street in China Town to a cheap night club, and had a couple of beers before calling it a night.

In the morning while walking along Hasting Street, just window shopping. I heard the French Kids voice calling to me from the other side of the street.

"Hey, John I got a piece of tail."

For a minute I thought my ears were playing tricks on me, but when I finally located where the shouts were coming from, I laughed and shrugged it off to a sixteen year old kid's enthusiasm. When he saw that I had seen him, he ran over yelling at the top of his voice, something about a Girl and a piece of tail. I said.

"Hold it. Do you want the whole town to hear you?"

He went a bit red in the face, and glanced around sheepishly, but no one was paying any attention to him at all. A lot worse things had happened on the Mean Streets of Vancouver in the past, than a skinny kid yelling about a piece of tail at the top of his voice.

"What are you talking about?" I said.

"I went up to my room in the hotel, and was just getting cleaned up, when I heard a knock on the door. I opened the door, and this girls standing there. I said what do you want, and she says do I want a piece of tail for twenty dollars. But I said No, ten dollars, and she says okay. I got a piece of tail." He was smiling like a Cheshire Cat. I thought, I wonder if this was his first bit, and then I thought if he can stand there with a Cheap Hooker, and negotiate a price, it probably wasn't.

"You got the time?" I said, changing the subject.

"Sure, Eleven o'clock," he said.

"Well, let's share the cost of a taxi that is if you can still afford it." I said with a grin.

"Ah, come on," he said, and we went in search of a cab

The test was simple enough a few verbal questions about different bends in the rebar and the color codes painted on the rods for blue print identification. Then we paid the sixty five dollars initiation fee, and were congratulated for becoming members of the union. I don't know if anyone was failed or not, for there were at least twenty or more men waiting in line to take the test, and to pay the fee. That evening I boarded the Nanaimo ferry for the trip back to camp.

A year had gone by since I had taken the Union Test to become a Rodman, and during that time I had opened a Bank Account and bought a car, a l947 Buick Road master, so I was no longer relying on my carpenter friend for transportation back and forth from Duncan. Things were looking up.

I had made a few friends in the camp, mostly ex-convicts I had met in prison. It never occurred to me to settle down, and change my life with decent friends, and begin building a future. With the money I was making, and a big car, I was heading down to Victoria on the weekends, and just stopping off in Duncan on the way to give Mom a few dollars. The bank account was soon dry, and any money I was making went for gas, and booze with the boys in Victoria.

My youngest brother "Billy" who had joined the army when I was in jail the first time, decided to come out and visit with a couple of his buddies in a Chevrolet bought down east in Manitoba. When he arrived in Duncan, Mom gave me a call at camp, and told me. I decided without hesitation to give my notice, and go and visit with him for a few days not giving any thought to what I would do when he had gone back to Manitoba.

We had a fun filled week together, and it was time for him to return back to the army. He had spent all of his money, and didn't have enough for his gas or ferry fare to the main land, so he borrowed what he needed from me, and like a fool I believed him when he said he would send it to me as soon as he got back. I never heard from him for over ten years after that.

There was no more hiring going on at Port Alberni, so I went down to Victoria and stayed at the Y.M.C.A. I managed to pick up a job laboring for Farmer Construction. In the mean -time, I traveled to the Union Office in Vancouver, but there was a line up right out to the street with guys looking for work, and I just received the brush off when I got to the desk.

On the way back to Duncan, I decided to use the Horseshoe Bay Ferry, and the deckhand directed me to close to the side of the ship and when we arrived at Nanaimo in the evening it was dark, so when it became my turn to drive off the ship, the side of the car was badly damaged when it came into contact with the ship's hull as I was unable to turn inward enough because of the line of cars on my left, and as I was at the head of the line I just kept driving off the ship. It was the last trip of the day and by the time I got clear of traffic, and located the Administration Offices the compound was clear of employees and the offices were closed. I drove my wrecked car down to Duncan and went to bed.

In the morning after examining the damage to the car, I realized it was beyond my ability to pay for any repairs or to meet my payments on the vehicle so I just abandoned it in my Moms front yard I learned later that the car dealership eventually repossessed the wreck.

When I got home from the job one night, a phone message was waiting for me from one of the Rodmen I had made friends with at Port Alberni. He was working for Farmer Construction as a laborer, and I would have a beer with him occasionally in the evening after work. He was a nice guy with a wife and kids, and didn't know anything about my past at all. And I didn't tell him anything. The note had his name and a phone number on it, and asked me to give him a call at his home. So after super I called him up. He was excited with the news he had for me, that he had heard they were building a new pulp mill at Croften, a small community north of Duncan, and were looking for Rodmen to help reinforce the foundations. It was a chance to get away from the dirty work we were doing for poor wages, and make some real money for a change. So I made arrangements to have him pick me up and we would go to Croften, which was about ten miles on the other side of my Moms place altogether about forty Miles from Victoria, to look for work. When we arrived we were hired immediately, and we donned are Hard Hats, picked up our tools, and went to work. I didn't stay in the Construction Camp, I stayed with Mom, and Lawrence in Duncan because the accommodations were much more comfortable, and it gave me an opportunity to help them out occasionally financially. I bought a small phonograph and some records, and I could play some of my favorite music which I couldn't in camp, and I also had considerably more privacy.

A couple of months went by, and the foundations for the mill were finished and the work slowed down, and I was laid off and soon the little bit of money I had put aside was gone. I went down to Duncan's

Unemployment Bureau, and applied for work, and was given a job as a laborer on a construction job at Bamberton Cement Works. The plant was located about fifteen miles south of Duncan on the highway. The first day on the job who should I find working there but the carpenters from Duncan who had left Port Alberni to work closer to home, so at least I was with familiar company. The construction site was a miserable place to work for everything was covered with at least a half inch of cement dust which made working conditions intolerable. The dust covered your clothing and penetrated every orifice of your body.

I was getting pretty fed up with the working conditions at Bamfield, and was contemplating looking for cleaner work, when I received a phone call from a con from the past.

"How did you know where I was?" I asked.

"Oh, I remembered you talking about staying in Duncan at the Henslowes, so I just ran through the phone book. I'm in town, are you interested in coming down for a coffee?"

"Sure, where are you?" I ask.

"I'm at the Green Haven."

"Okay, I'll hitch a ride down and be there in about a half hour."

As soon as I walked in the door, I saw him sitting at the counter. He stood out for he was not dressed like a local at all. He was wearing an overcoat, and a Fedora, and his shoes were carefully cleaned. He had a weasel like face, with a cold look to his eyes.

"Sit down have a coffee," he said before I could greet him.

"Thanks, how are you doing?"

"Not bad, I bumped into some guys I know, and we took a safe out in Chemainus, last night," he said.

"You're kidding?" I laughed.

"No we got a truck and a hydraulic jack with wheels. We cranked it up under the safe, and rolled it off the front step into the back of a pickup truck, and I just drove away. I got a few bucks out of the deal. You still got a car?" he asked.

"No" I said.

"Ya wanna go down to the States for a few days?" he asked.

"I don't have any money,"

"That's okay, I want the company, two work better than one any way. I figured we'd go down to Los Angeles, and pass a few bad cheques, and make some real money,"

"Sounds good to me, I'm getting tired of Duncan these days any way."

"Okay, let's go."

It wasn't long before we were across the American Border on a bus and heading for Seattle. Along the way Pat decided it would be more practical to buy a cheap car so we could stop and go when we wanted. He was paying the bills so I just agreed with anything he suggested. We left the bus in Seattle and wandered around until we found a small used car dealership which had a very cheap 1949 ford Sedan. It had almost new tires on it and a very clean engine. We made a quick purchase and drove it off the lot. It was dark out, and I noticed as I was driving it down one of Seattle's brightly lit main Streets, that cars kept blinking their lights at us. Finally we came to the conclusion that there was something wrong with the vehicle. I pulled over to the side of the road and walked around the car and found we had no tail lights and very little headlights showing. I got back into the car and worked the light switch until I managed to get a little more- light showing. As we proceeded out of town it started to rain, and so I switched on the windshield wipers only they didn't work either. So every once in a while when the rain built up on the windshield Pat would lean out the side window with a cloth on a piece of wood and try and clear it a little for me, or occasionally I would stop and wipe it clean. We continued down through Oregon that way until we reached Nevada where it began to snow and the situation turned to where I couldn't see anything at all and I finally hit a sheet of ice in the middle of the Highway, the car spun around twice and went off the road. There we were with the rear wheels stuck in the sand in the middle of Northern Nevada with no traction at all. The more we gunned the car trying to get up onto the highway the deeper the wheels sank in the sand, in the meantime the temperature was falling it was the last part of November and it was getting colder because the car heater didn't work either. In frustration I was feeling around under the dash when I found that the line for the windshield wipers wasn't connected so I managed to hook it up, a Small Victory. Finally after two or three hours of cold and worry a large sedan appeared and immediately stopped. Three very large young men got out and without even asking just told me to get behind the wheel and they would have us out in no time. I gunned the car and they pushed and we were back on the road. They left as quickly as they had come, one of them wished us good luck as they drove off.

Eventually we arrived in Reno Nevada, and while we were walking around town, we stopped in front of a pawn shop which had a few guns in the window.

"Let's buy a gun, I said.

"No, I don't think so," Pat said.

"We can use it if we get in a tight situation," I said.

"What sort of a situation?"

"Well one where we need to scare someone to get away. You know?"

"I robbed a bank in Calgary once, Pat said.

"You're kidding me?" I said.

"No four of us robbed a bank, and got caught. I did eight years for it in Stoney Mountain Penitentiary, and I don't want to be involved with guns again."

"Hell, you don't have to, I'll look after it. Let's just go in and take a look."

"Okay, we can take a look."

It was a small store with the usual assortment of guitars and stereos on the shelves. A man in his thirty's came to the counter and with a smile asked

"Canadian?"

"How can you tell?" I said.

"It's the Indian Sweater," he said.

"You don't see sweaters like that around here too much." I was wearing a Wool Indian Sweater, which Mom had made for me, and the pattern was done in red wool instead of the usual black so it stood out more.

"Well! What can I do for you today?" The salesman asked in a friendly manner.

"Were interested in a gun," I said.

He walked over to the display in the window and picked up a couple of revolvers and brought them out to the counter to show them to us.

"What do you want it for?" He asked casually.

"We have a small business in Vancouver B.C." I lied, and I thought it might be a good idea to have a gun around for protection, and to do a little target practice."

"Well this little 22 revolver is in good shape, holds nine rounds probably just what you need." He held up an H&R long barrelled revolver, and handed it to me. It felt very light, and comfortable in my hand.

"How much is it?" I ask.

"I can let you have it for twenty three dollars," he said.

I looked at Pat, and he just nodded in agreement, and said nothing.

"Okay we'll take it."

"Good," the salesman said, as he pulled a form from below the counter top.

"I need some personal information for the police, he said.

As casually as I could I said.

"Oh, what's that?"

"You know, like description, age, color, stuff like that."

"Okay," I said.

Kazoonie

"What is the color of your eyes?"

"Grey," I said.

We went through the listed questions on the sheet, and I lied about my name and address. I thought I detected a flicker of disbelief come from the salesman but he didn't say anything. Finally he said.

"That should do it," and slipped the gun into a brown paper bag and we left. Pat hid the gun under the front seat of the car and we didn't discuss it anymore. We left Reno and headed across the border into California and stopped in a town called Eureka Just north of San Francisco.

That evening, Pat told me we were short of money, and had just enough to get back to the Canadian Border. As he was footing the bill, I didn't say anything, and so the next morning we headed back to Seattle. When we arrived he said.

Pull over in a side street, and we'll leave the car and take a bus back to Vancouver."

"Leave the car?" I questioned.

"Yeah, we can't pay the customs on it, so we take the loss. Just leave the keys in it and walk away."

I realized there wasn't anything we could do about it if we wanted to go back to Canada, so I agreed.

"Okay, it's just a pile of junk anyway," I said.

We found the bus depot in short order, and made our way to the wash rooms. Against the wall just inside the door was a scale for weighing yourself after depositing a coin. Pat said.

"I'm going to hit this scale, when the joints empty, keep watch outside."

I stepped outside the washroom door and waited. I thought what the hell, if someone came. I didn't have the gun Pat did. Suddenly there was a loud crash, and in a few moments Pat came rushing out of the room, with an excited look on his face.

"Quick!" he said, as he grabbed me by the arm, and yanked me back into the washroom. I looked down and saw that the floor was covered with pennies, nickels, and dimes.

"Grab as much as you can, and let's get the hell out of here," he said excitedly. I quickly went to my hands and knees, and started scooping up handfuls of coins, and stuffing them into my pockets. He was laughing as he did the same thing. I found it was contagious, and started to laugh to, realizing how ridiculous we must look down on our hands and knees scrambling to pick up the nickels and dimes scattered on the Washroom floor. Suddenly, Pat jumped up and said.

"That it, let's get out of here before someone comes."

We quickly walked out, and up the stairs to the waiting area, found a ticket desk, and bought two one-way tickets to Vancouver. We found a place to sit, and wait for our departure time.

"Don't you think we should get out of here," I said.

"Na, there not going to frisk everyone in the depot, and no one saw us, besides they'll think whoever did it is long gone."

I realized he was right, but I couldn't help watching the door nervously.

"Relax, nothing is going to happen," Pat said.

And sure enough in approximately an hour while we waited, nothing did happen, although I felt a great deal of relief when we boarded the bus for Canada. I found out from Pat later, that when he jimmied the front of the scale and pried open the coin box lid, the coins were above the lid and not below it as he had thought. The system was set up for quick removing of the coins by gravity release, and Pat not knowing this did not have anything in place to catch the coins when he pried open the lid, and the coins just cascaded out onto the floor leaving him ankle deep in nickels and dimes. After counting the coins, we discovered that we had picked up a little over sixty dollars. The cash box was undoubtedly full. I guess who ever walked in on the mess just helped them-selves, a washroom in a bus stop is always very busy and someone must have found the break in very quickly, but in at least an hour while we waited, watching the depots front door, nothing happened. There's a little bit of larceny in everyone, so the saying goes.

We arrived in Vancouver, and took the Nanaimo Ferry to Vancouver Island, where we caught another bus to Duncan, and booked a room in a cheap hotel. The next day we hitched a ride into Victoria,

"I'll go up to Ma James place and stay there. When you think the heats off, give me a call, it's in the book, James at Carlton Place," I said.

Pat looked at me for a minute as if thinking it over, and then he said.

"Look you take the gun with you."

"Why?" I said surprised.

"I'm going into town, and if I should get picked up for questioning a gun is the last thing I want them to find on me."

"Yeah, you're right, I'll hide it at James's and if we need it we'll know where we can pick it up."

"I'll see you later," he said, as he handed me the gun, and walked away without a backward glance. I stuffed the gun in my belt, and headed for James's.

Ma James lived in a large wooden frame house, with approximately six or seven large rooms. The house was situated at the top end of a small side street, called Carlton Place which was near the junction of Yates and Fort Street, two of Victoria's main through fares. In its prime the house was used as a rooming house run by Mrs. James. She was a large heavy set middle aged woman, who had had her share of bad luck. I don't know what happened to her husband, but her daughter had contracted a fatal disease and died in the U.S.A. after a two year battle. During that time, Mrs. James spent every nickel she owned on her Daughters medical bills and neglected her property, and eventually she lost the house for failure to pay her taxes. Two local business men picked up the house for a song from the local municipality, but took pity on her, and let her stay on as caretaker so she would have a place to live. She also had a son who was a Heroin Addict. A tall drink of water with big ears who was a petty thief, and would do anything to support his habit, which he felt was his undeniable right to engage in, and would argue to great length about the subject if given half a chance. He was doing time in the B.C. Penitentiary at the same time as I was, when I met him, and I had bumped into him on occasion at the Kings Hotel, a local hang out for some of Victoria's nor do well citizens. Occasionally he would invite me and some of the local punks up to Carlton Place, and we'd pool are meagre resources, buy some beer and go and sit in Ma James kitchen and talk about better times, and commiserate with Mrs. James about the loss of her daughter, and how she'd been cheated out of her house. It was pretty obvious that the shock of losing her daughter had reduced her to a shell of what she once was mentally. She tried to talk the street people that her son invited to stay awhile into fixing up the house in turn for a roof over their heads, but there were no materials or tools. Here and there you could see half-finished projects that had been started but never finished. This only made the house more run down in appearance, but Mrs. James never gave up trying.

When I arrived at the house, I walked around to the back kitchen door and found Mrs. James sitting in the kitchen listening to the radio and knitting.

"Hello, Mrs. James is your son around?" I asked.

"Hello, she said with the look of suspicion she always gave everybody. "No I haven't seen him in a few days I think he's in Vancouver. Jeans up stairs though."

Jean was his Wife. She wasn't a dope addict but she wasn't much good for anything, just a hanger on who I found out later on was getting laid by her husband's best friend, so much for the sanctity of marriage.

"Oh! Is she staying here now?" I asked.

She shrugged and said.

"Just for a few days until Harold gets back."

"Can you put me up for a few days I'm a little short right now, but when I get some money I'll make it right."

She looked at me with a resigned look on her face like she'd heard this all before. I gave her my best smile.

"Oh, all right, she said, but no loud parties.

"No, nothing-like that, I said. I'll be out most of the day looking for work, I lied. I just need a place to sleep."

"Well take your pick, she pointed towards the stairs. The rooms are all empty. Jean's down here beside me."

"Thanks," I said, and headed up the stairs. I picked a room with a sofa and a bed. I found some blankets and sheets in the closet, and made up a half decent bed for myself, and was soon sleeping the sleep of the exhausted.

In the morning I stuffed the gun down behind the cushions of the sofa, and thought I had better get some money from somewhere, and buy some ammunition for it. After I had cleaned up, I went down stairs and made some idol conversation with Mrs. James. Jean wasn't up yet. Later on in the morning I asked Mrs. James if I could use her phone.

"No long distance calls." She said.

"I want to phone my mother in Duncan, I'll reverse the charges," I said.

"Well, all right as long as you reverse the charges," emphasizing the reverse part by jabbing her forefinger at me.

"Sure no problem," I said.

I phoned Mom in Duncan, and told her where I was, and asked her to send me twenty dollars so I could come home. When she heard I needed the money to come home, she agreed right away. The fact that twenty dollars was a financial burden to her didn't enter my mind I just didn't care.

"Thanks Mom just send-it by the C.P.R. Telegraph Office. I'll get it today and come up to-morrow," I lied. Be seeing you," I hung up.

That afternoon I went down to the telegraph Office and picked up four five dollar bills. A short distance down the street in a sporting goods store I bought a box of 22 Calibre Bullets for the revolver. I spent a couple of days between the beer parlors in town and Ma James and soon the few dollars I had were gone.

Sometimes during the evening a few of the locals from the beer parlor would come up and sit around in my room or kept Mrs. James company, and gossiped about the day's events and drink Mrs. James coffee and eat anything they could get their hands on. One evening while I was down stairs one of them was looking for loose change I guess behind the sofa cushions in my room, and found the gun. One of the guys with him, who had just lost his job as a carpenter and still had a few dollars left, promptly bought it from him for ten dollars. No one who was present at the time even questioned the fact that it might belong to me, because it was in my room. The gun was stolen, and sold in a matter of minutes no questions ask.

The next day I was sitting in the Kings Beer Parlor drinking a bummed beer when the Carpenter who was sitting at the tables paying for the beer leaned over the table and said in a low voice.

"I've got your gun."

Of course he had my full attention instantly.

"What are you talking about?" I said.

He quickly told me about the past quick transaction made at James's. I stared at him a minute, and said.

"Of course you know I want it back, and I don' give a damn about the ten bucks you paid. It wasn't his to sell to you in the first place."

"I know that, he said. I want to get back to Winnipeg, but I don't have enough money to make the trip. I've got an idea we can use the gun and rob the Excalibur in Esquimalt."

"I take it you've got a plan on how to do this." I said sarcastically.

"Of course," he replied.

"Look, bring the gun up to James tonight, and we'll talk it over."

"What time?" he asked.

"Any time, I'm not going anywhere," I said.

Kazoonie

I felt his eye's on my back as I got up to leave. That evening he arrived, and we went up to my room, after we were comfortable on the sofa. I ask him.

"What's the plan?"

"You know the Excaliber Beer Parlor don't you?" he asked.

"Yeah, I know it."

"Well when the navy yard gets paid, a lot of them go in there after work, to have a few beers, and cash their cheques.

"What's the set up-?" I asked.

"There's an office in the back, with a counter and window in the wall." They keep the money in a safe, and the navy yard guys line up in a hall outside the office to cash their cheques. All we have to do is be there a few minutes before quitting time at the yard, walk through the office door, and help ourselves from the safe,"

"The trouble with your plan is you've got a beer parlor full of drunks and you always get Hero's when you got drunks," I said.

"Well you didn't get me up here to tell me that," he said sounding a little annoyed."

"Take it easy, I said. We can take a bank I've got in mind instead."

"A bank?" he said incredulously.

"Yeah, there's one in James Bay on Sequoa Street. It should be a snap. Banks tell their employees not to resist. We won't have any trouble with it at all."

He sat there for a minute staring at me and then slowly broke into a grin.

"I like it, he said let's do it."

"We'll have to steal a car, and get another gun for you. What are you going to do stand there and beg for the money?"

"No I see what you mean, he said, I'll just drive the car," he exclaimed, with a bright look on his face.

I shook my head in disgust.

"I guess you want me to steal the car to?" I thought, I wonder if he can drive a car.

"Can you drive?" I ask.

"Sure I haven't driven for a while but I'll be okay," he said smiling weakly.

"Did you bring the gun with you?" I ask.

"Yeah, I have it here."

He reached into his belt and pulled it out, and handed it to me. I got up and walked over and got the ammunition out of the dresser.

"We'll go down to the cellar, and fire a few rounds nobody will hear anything down there."

The cellar was a large room dug out underneath the back of the kitchen. It contained a large Wood and Coal Furnace which hadn't been used in years. It was reached through a trap door in the floor and a flight of stairs which went down well below ground level. I found the lid of a Jam Jar and tacked it up on one of the kitchen floor support posts.

The H&R Revolver could be loaded slowly by putting the ammunition one bullet at a time through a slot in the back of the cylinder while you revolved it by hand or you could take the whole cylinder out by pulling the cylinder pin out and putting the rounds in their slots without having to rotate the cylinder. When the cylinder was loaded you replaced it in the gun, inserted the pin, and you were ready to fire. The gun had a six inch barrel, and held 9 rounds, but being a 22 calibre weapon it was light and not very bulky.

We stood back and fired a few rounds from about fifteen feet. Even at that close range are accuracy had a lot to be desired. After a while the post showed a lot more holes than the jam lid. The gun even misfired a few times, but after examining the dud bullets, I think the cap didn't work because the hammer indentation where it had struck home with considerable force was clearly visible but had not exploded the charge. The noise of the guns discharge was muffled by the dirt walls of the cellar as I thought because there was no sign of any curious neighbours, and no police came knocking at the door. After a while with only a few rounds left, I decided target practice was over, and we went upstairs. Mrs. James was in the kitchen, but didn't ask what we had been doing even though she obviously knew from the disapproving looks she threw our way. Upstairs we got back to business.

"Okay now we know the gun works," I said laughing.

"Yeah, he said looking very serious, I hope nothing goes wrong."

"Cold feet all ready?" I laughed.

"No" he said, shrugging, but the worried look didn't leave his face.

"I'll steal the car, and take the bank all you'll have to do is drive. It'll take a day or two to find a car. I'll get in touch with you when I'm ready," I said. He seemed to brighten up a bit when he found out he wasn't going to be taking a major role in the robbery. He gave me his address, and left without a backward glance. I thought I wouldn't be seeing him again, and I would have to do this by myself, for I had made up my mind with him or without him the job was on.

CHAPTER 9

Stealing a Car

Robbing the Bank

Capture, Trial, and Back to Jail

The next day I walked slowly around Victoria's side streets, casually looking in car windows, looking for one with the keys still in the ignition. It wasn't long before I found a l950 ford Mercury, parked on Cook Street. I had found a pair of gloves among some old clothes at Ma James which I had brought along, so I put them on, and casually tried the car door. It opened without any difficulty. I eased behind the wheel, and turned the key in the ignition, nothing happened. I checked the floor for a foot starter, and didn't find anything. It was a moment before I noticed the small button to the left of the steering wheel. The car's engine roared to life as soon as I pushed it. A great feeling of relief swept over me. I quickly looked around to see if I had attracted any attention. The few people walking by remained intent on what they were doing. I slipped the car into gear and drove the required thirty miles an hour to the address the Carpenter had given me. I knocked on the door and a Young man answered, I explained who I was looking for and he said,

"He's in Number 5 at the top of the stairs."

I knocked, and the Carpenter opened the door. When he saw me standing there he knew what I had come for, and his face changed from a smile to a pale sickly worry.

"Take it easy, I said, every things all right. Aren't you going to ask me in?"

He hurriedly glanced over my shoulder as if expecting the police to be right behind me at the same time he grabbed my arm and hustled me inside.

"I wasn't expecting you so soon," he said.

Beads of sweat had appeared on his upper lip as if by magic. I laughed, and said.

"You don't look as if you want to see me at all. You know if you want out now's the time to say so."

"It's okay, it's okay, he stammered. You got a car?"

I nodded.

"It's about a block away, all we have to do is hop in, and go down and get the job done."

"Okay let's go."

"Wait a minute, you got any gloves?"

"Gloves" He asked.

"Yeah, you don't want to leave any finger prints in the car?"

"Well, I don't have a record."

"That's got nothing to do with it. It's after the job that it starts getting tricky you don't want the cops finding any prints to connect you to the job, If you should get picked up do you?" I thought, Jesus what a dumb bastard. He wants to rob a bank, but he doesn't want to rob a bank, what the hell does he want? I know, I thought the money. He thought about it for a minute and finally he said.

"I think I got an old pair of work gloves around here somewhere." "Well, get them, and let's go, the damn bank will be closed before we get there." I said, getting more frustrated with his stalling.

"Besides they could be looking for the car now."

Kazoonie

After rummaging around in a couple of drawers, he finally found them, and ran out of excuses. We left the house and walked over to the car. I handed him the keys.

"You better drive it, I haven't driven for a long time," he said.

"For Christ sakes, you better get used to the car now, because you aren't going to have time after the jobs done. Come on get behind the wheel and let's get going."

With an audible sigh he finally gets in.

"The ignitions here and the starter to your left just put your foot on the clutch turn the key on and push the button."

He nervously followed my instructions, and was surprised when everything went according to plan.

"Okay let out the clutch slowly, and let's go," I said.

I could see the whites of his knuckles he was gripping the wheel so hard.

"Come on," he said.

Suddenly the car leaped forward mounted the curb, and threw me into the dash board with a resounding thud. The engine immediately stalled, and the car stopped. Fortunately I had managed to get one of my hands up, and deflected my forward motion enough to keep my head from banging into the wind shield. I quickly gathered my composure, and glanced around. There was nobody on the street.

"Look, I haven't got time to give you lessons, I'll drive it down to the bank, and you watch. When I come out, you drive us away. Do you think you can do that?" I said sarcastically.

"Sure, sure," he muttered.

I changed places and carefully backed us out onto the street again.

The bank was a small branch on Sequoa Street which serviced the public in the area. I circled the block so I could come up on the right side of the street and park directly in the front of the bank.

"When I get out, you get behind the wheel, and keep the car running," I said. "Relax I'll be back in a minute."

I got out of the car, and watched to make sure he got behind the wheel. He looked pale, and the sweat on his upper lip was more apparent than ever. I felt totally relaxed and in charge, and realized I was enjoying the whole situation tremendously. The pressure of the gun stuck in my belt gave me a feeling of invincibility. I nodded at him casually and walked over to the banks front door and pushed it open. I had been here before, years ago, to cash a construction check, I had earned when working as a laborer on a job nearby, and it had entered my mind at that time what an easy bank to rob.

As I stepped through the door I noticed nothing had changed. The Managers Office was still to my left, followed by the administration Area, with the staff busy at their desks, and directly in front of me was four teller's cages. There were a few customers, one at the teller's cage' and two busy with a transaction at the Administration Desk. I stepped up behind the customer at the teller's wicket and waited. When the customer had finished his business, and my turn came, I stood there waiting for the teller to acknowledge me. He was counting a large bundle of twenty dollar bills. He was young with neatly combed hair, and had the look of a man who knew his job, and did it very well. He finally looked up, but before he could say anything, I acted,

""I'll take that," I said as I reached over the counter and snatched the twenty's out of his hands and stuck them in my pocket. A look of total surprise swept over his bored face. At the same time as I grabbed the money, I pulled the twenty two out of my waist band and levelled it at his chest. A look of fear swept over his face, and his hands came up to the level of his chest as if to ward me off. I quickly vaulted to the top of the counter and looked around. The two customers at the administration counter who were obviously man and wife froze when they saw me astride the counter. The husband was telling his wife not to panic as they tried not to look at me. The Staff was all staring in surprise with their mouths open. Suddenly a large woman who was nearest to the vault made a move toward it. I quickly pointed the gun at her and she stopped in her tracks.

I then dropped into the Teller's Cage, and shoved the young teller into a corner and rammed the gun barrel into his stomach and snarled.

"Don't move."

A look of total terror was on his face, and I realized I had everything under control. I quickly yanked open the cash drawer and stuffed as much money as I could into my pockets, and then vaulted over the counter, and began backing out toward the front door. As I passed the Manager's Office, I noticed he was standing at his desk, bent over a little with one hand on a drawer trying to open it. A customer was sitting in a chair to one side. I pointed my gun in his direction with a menacing gesture, and he quickly straightened up. I backed through the front door, and hurried to the car. The carpenter looked at me and said.

"Where the hells the money, did you chicken out?"

I pointed the gun at him with one hand and dumped a hand full of bills on the seat with the other hand,

"Drive for Christ's sakes," I yelled.

"Jesus," he said, and shot the car out into the traffic with a tremendous jerk. The first intersection with a light we came to, I told him to take it easy, and slow down and stop, but when he brought the car to a sudden stop, he stalled it by not putting his foot on the clutch. There we were, one block away from the bank stalled on the main approach to the bank which was certainly the way any police would be coming in response to the banks alarm.

"Shit!" I shouted, Get this god damn car moving."

I hurriedly glanced through the rear window to see if we were being followed, but I didn't see any unusual attention being paid to us. The Carpenter was in a total panic by now, and was pushing the starter button as hard as he could, but obviously he had flooded the car with gas when he jumped the clutch at the light. I could feel the blood rushing to my face as I got madder and madder at his ineffectual attempts to get the motor started. I pointed the gun at his head and spoke in as menacing a voice as I could.

"Put your foot on the clutch, and get moving or I'll leave you here."

He paused in his efforts, and stared at the gun in surprise, and then he calmed down and started the engine in his next try. A feeling of elation swept over me, at the same time the light changed to go and we sped away. I directed him to a side street in the Theater District.

"Get out and leave the keys," I said.

He jumped out of the car, and hurried around to the passenger side.

"Take it easy don't attract any un-do attention, we'll walk over a block and go to the movies for a couple of hours. We have to get off the street quickly."

"Okay let's go," he said, as he started to walk away hurriedly.

"Slow down, just walk normally." I snapped at him

After watching a movie for a couple of hours I whispered, "You leave first I'll follow a few minutes behind." He nodded, got up slowly, and left. I followed. I could see him walking ahead of me heading for Ma James. As we walked up the street a Motorcycle Cop came cruising slowly by checking the license numbers on parked cars. I realized he was looking for the Mercury. I laughed to myself, and thought they haven't found it yet.

It wasn't long before I reached James, and found the Carpenter in my room waiting eagerly for his share. I emptied the contents of my pockets on the floor. The carpenter was all smiles. I picked up a bundle of twenties and started counting, suddenly my hands began to shake, and I lost all powers of concentration. I looked up and found the Carpenter staring at me with a surprised look on his face.

"What the hells the matter," he said.

"I don't know shock I guess. I was wound up and the come down is hitting me now." I said.

"Here I'll count it," he said.

"You better, I can't think anyway,"

I laughed nervously. The take was thirty-eight Hundred dollars. We divided it evenly.

"What are you going to do with yours," I asked.

"Hide it for a few days, and then I'm going to get out of town. You know, I could have gotten more, but we forgot to take a bag with us."

He looked a little nonplused over that, but nodded and said.

"I've got enough to get out of here, and go home, and that's all I care about, how about you."

"Well back to business, I've got to get a change of clothes and a haircut and then I'm leaving town for a few days myself. At least until it quiets down a little. There are some clothes stored in a trunk in the front room that will fit me. I'll help myself to them. I'll see you later."

A few blocks away I found a small Barber Shop, where I got a haircut and had a bite to eat in the corner Hamburger Joint. When I was finished, I went back to the house. I had been gone about an hour or two at the most. I was met at the door by a very excited Carpenter, who quickly told me a couple of R.C.M.P. investigators had been there looking for Mrs. James son.

"What did you tell them?" I asked.

"I told them I was living here, just a quest, and Ma. James backed me up."

"She did?" I exclaimed in surprise.

"Yeah, they weren't interested in me, just in her son. I don't think they'll be back today."

"Lucky I wasn't here, they might have put two and two together with the both of us together.

"No doubt at all," he said.

"I'm going to get rid of the gun, and leave first thing in the morning," I said. "Take care of yourself." I called as he went out the door.

I slept well that night, and left for the Bus Depot early in the morning, and purchased a ticket for Nanaimo. I thought that it would be safer to take the Nanaimo Ferry to Vancouver than the Swartz Bay Ferry, because the police would more than likely be watching the closes exit route than one that was seventy miles away. The trip to Vancouver was uneventful. I spent most of the crossing in the ships bar, and felt quite relaxed and comfortable when the ship tied up in Vancouver.

A few blocks up from the Canadian Pacific docks, across the street from the C.N.R. Train Station, I found the St. Francis Hotel, situated just down from the center of the city on the water front. It was a small lower class hotel, with a restaurant and clean rooms. I walked into the lobby, and up to the front desk a clean cut young man ask me if I needed any help.

"Yes, I would like a room, and I want to deposit some money in your safe for safekeeping." I said.

"How long are you staying?" he inquired.

"Oh, just for the night."

He handed me the register and pointed to where I should sign. At the same time he produced a brown envelope from behind the counter. I pulled out my share of the Bank Money, and peeled of a couple of hundred, and gave the rest to the clerk. He stared with a startled look on his face, as if he had never seen that much money before. I realized I might have made a mistake giving him the money, but I thought it couldn't have been that unusual. Hotels must handle this kind of a request all the time, and pushed the worry out of my mind, besides it was too late, he had already seen the money. I watched him count it.

"Six-Hundred and Eighty- Dollar's would you please sign here?" pointing to a line on the form he had laid on the counter.

"Sign, I asked.

"Yes it's standard procedure for large sums of money."

I signed on the dotted line, and he pushed the money into the envelope and handed me my room key. I noticed he seemed a lot more nervous, and his face was a little flushed but I didn't make anything of it. I went up to my room to clean up. After a rest I decided to go up to the east end, to the Balmoral Hotel and have a few beers. I thought the money was much safer where it was, and I would be a lot safer without it in my pocket, because where I was going was no place for anyone carrying large sums of money. If anyone got wind of it, chances are you would wind up in an alley with your head split open, and your pockets empty.

The Balmoral was a small hotel with a beer parlor located in the East End. The area was surrounded by cheap hotels, and restaurants, and if you stayed in the area on a Saturday Night you would see all the ex-convicts I had met at the Penitentiary at one time or another during the night. The place was thick with dope fiends, prostitutes and thugs of every description. It wasn't an area for anyone with a gentile upbringing.

The beer parlor was busy with the usual going and coming of the dope fiends, searching for a connection to buy their evening's heroin fix, and the local street hookers trying to pick up a john. I sat down at a table against the wall, and had just started on my first beer, when I felt somebody's presents at my shoulder. I looked up quickly into the face of a tall thin red head, wearing a black overcoat and white dress shirt open at the neck. His pale blue eyes looked into mine without blinking.

"This seat taken?" he asked.

"No, help yourself.

"You been working?" he asked.

"No let me buy you a beer. I just got into town from Victoria. Are you working?"

"No," he said shaking his head. I'm staying at home it's cheaper that way," he said smiling for the first time since he'd sat down.

"He was a Bank Robber I had met in the Penitentiary. He and two others had held up a bank in Vancouver just before I had held up the corner grocery in Victoria, and had gotten caught and sentenced to three years. A rounder came over to our table, and without even making time for small talk he was trying to connect me to a hooker. He told him to cut it out, and to beat it.

"Come on let's get out of here, we'll go next door to the Golden and get a coffee."

The Golden was a small restaurant and Coffee Shop, which picked up the late night trade from the Balmoral, and the other joints in the area. We sat at the bar, and ordered are coffee. I noticed a woman in her forties plus, sitting next to me nursing her coffee. She was a little shop worn but not unattractive, and she was fairly well dressed. Every so often a man would come over to her and whisper in her ear and laugh leeringly, and she would shake her head and laugh. These little moments never led to any lengthy conversation, just a quick few words which I couldn't hear over the din of the patrons, and the music from the juke box in the corner. I didn't have anything to say to Rusty who was just staring into his coffee cup, so I amused myself by watching the goings on around me. I turned to look at the woman, and found her staring at me.

"You're very popular tonight," I said.

Her eyes were dark, and hard, without any warning she said.

"If you want conversation and my time, it'll cost you. The rate is twenty an hour."

I turned and looked at my companion, who had suddenly taken an interest in what was happening around him. He grinned, and said.

"There you are, there's your chance."

"You have got to be kidding." I whispered back.

He laughed, and said.

"Look, I've got to meet a guy, and I'm late all ready, I'll see you later."

He quickly got up from the counter, walked away without giving me a chance to say good bye. I turned back to the woman. This was all new to me being propositioned by a street hooker in such a blunt manner had left me speechless for a change.

"Well make up your mind I haven't got all night she snapped. My curiosity was aroused, but I remembered my narrow escape from before so I said.

"Look some other time I'm a little tired tonight."

An annoyed look came over her face and she reached for her purse and got up and walked towards the door.

After leaving the restaurant I noticed the streets were becoming deserted, so I decided to call it a night. I walked down to the St. Frances, and when I arrived and stepped into the deserted lobby, I suddenly had an uneasy feeling. I glanced around and the only person in sight was the female hotel clerk behind the front desk. I stopped short of the counter and stared at her for a few seconds. She looked nervous, and her face was a little flushed, I said.

"Good evening," as I continued up to the desk. "Could I have my key please? Room 340".

I had just stopped in front of the desk, when I was suddenly confronted by a big burly man pointing a snub nosed thirty-eight at my stomach. At the same time my arms were pinned by a second man from behind and I was given a quick frisk by an expert.

"He's clean," he said in a rough voice.

The big cop in front of me holding the gun, was staring straight into my eyes with a hard mean look on his face, just daring me to make a wrong move. I said nothing. I just stared back unflinchingly, and all the time I was thinking, what the hell difference does it make. They were obviously staking the lobby out waiting for me. One behind the counter, the other in the small foyer of the side door, and I had walked right into it. I should have obeyed my instincts and walked away, but somehow I just didn't care. The cop behind me yanked my hands back and put a pair of handcuffs on me.

"Are you named Diener?" The one in front ask.

"Yeah that's the name," I said.

"Did you deposit some money here in the hotel for safe keeping?"

I didn't answer.

"Come on you signed the envelope, and we'll be able to match the handwriting of the signatures."

"Yeah I put some money in so what?" I snapped.

"Some of the serial numbers check with some money from a bank robbery in Victoria." Where did you get it?"

"Oh, I picked it up in a poker game at the Lincoln Hotel in Victoria. I lied feebly.

"Well, we will see about that, come on," he said getting to his feet.

While all this was going on, neither of the cops had bothered to identify themselves. The mean looking one who was the younger and more fit looking of the two said,

"I'm Detective Sergeant Portier, and this is my partner Detective Harris Vancouver police."

I said nothing. They were dressed like something out of a Dime Store Novel. They both had on rumbled Suites and Ties, with Overcoats and Fedoras, and Black Oxford Shoes. They were big and burly, and would stand out as tough middle age cops from a mile away.

I was led out of the hotel and walked about a block to an older model Pontiac, which didn't look like a Police Car at all, except for a large aerial attached to the bumper. My head was unceremoniously shoved down, and I was pushed into the back seat. In a few minutes I was at the admitting desk of the Vancouver Police Department. In the upper floors of the station, I was told to empty my pockets, and then a young harness cop gave me a thorough search to see if I was carrying any weapons. After this I was loaded onto an elevator and taken upstairs to the cells for the night. Nothing had changed since the last time I was here. I curled up on my mattress and went to sleep

The next morning I was let out of my tier to walk around with the other prisoners in the corridor facing the rows of cell blocks. In the center of the corridor was an elevator, and sitting at a small desk just to the left of the elevator door was a young unarmed Police guard. I assume he was stationed there to prevent any possible disturbance if it should arise. I thought the whole thing was a futile gesture. There were at least twenty prisoners on the tier walking around with free access to the guard. If any two decided to attack him he would be at their mercy before he knew what hit him. He just sat there, looking very stiff and nervous never taking his eyes off of us. I felt kind of sorry for him.

While I was leaning against the wall watching what was going on a tall dark young guy approached me. He was wearing a black overcoat and shining black Italian style shoes. His thick black oily hair was combed straight back, and his eyes were a deep brown which blended in nicely with his olive complexion. He was a very handsome person.

"Have you got a Cigarette?" he asked.

I noticed there was a slight lisp to his speech.

"I haven't had a cigarette all morning," he complained waiving a limp hand at me in an effeminate manner. I thought, Oh Christ another faggot.

"No I don't smoke," I snapped.

"Okay, I just asked." He said, rolling his eyes upward. "What are you in for?" he ask, with a quizzical look on his face.

"Robbery, and you, I inquired.

"Well, I'd hang out in the local queer bars, and wait for some well healed Fagot to try and pick me up. I'd go up to a room with him, and when he was looking the other way, kick his teeth in, and help myself to his wallet. They seldom blew the whistle, but I guess I did one to many. I've been waiting trial for a couple of weeks now, you?" He asked.

"I just got here."

The elevator door opened, and a Harness Cop got out, and started reading names out loud from a clip board he was carrying. My name was last. About seven or eight of us were taken on the elevator to a long narrow room which sloped from one end to the other. We were lined up at the low end. I looked up and saw the bank clerk from Victoria sitting on a chair surrounded by uniformed and plain clothes cops. They were all whispering, and staring intently at the lineup. The cop with the clip board yelled out.

"Number one, step forward,"

And the first man in line took a couple of steps forward. This procedure was repeated until they got to me. I was number six. I was kept standing a little longer than the others. A couple of the others were asked again to step forward, and finally I was called for the last time. Then we were hustled out, and back to the same cell block we had left.

In a couple of hours, two plain clothes cops different than the arresting cops came up and ask to see me. I was told that I had been positively identified by the Bank Clerk, and asked if I wanted to make a statement. I said, "No," and I told them that I thought he had made a mistake, and I didn't want to talk to them at all. They just shrugged, and said.

"Suit yourself," and walked away to the elevator.

Later on in the day, Detective Smith and Evens came over from Victoria to take me back to stand trial. I was taken downstairs to a large room which looked like the parade or muster area and introduced to the Victoria cops who told me my rights, and took me to a small interrogation room in a corner of the hall.

"Cigarette," Detective Smith asked holding out an opened package.

"No, I don't smoke," I said.

Immediately their eyes went to my hands, I laughed.

"No, there's no nicotine stains,"

I held up my fingers so they could see for themselves. A sheepish look came over their faces, when they saw I had noticed their obvious doubt of my ability to tell the truth.

"Don't play that game of good cop bad cop with me. I've been around long enough that all it's going to do is waste both are time."

"Okay, we'll get right to the point. Who's the other guy?" Evens asked.

"Other guy," I laughed.

"Yeah you know the guy who drove the car."

"You've got to be kidding."

"Look, It' will go a lot easier on you if you tell us his name, and where we can pick him up."

"I don't know what you're talking about." I grinned.

"Okay have it your way." Evens shrugged.

Smith got up and left the room for a minute, when he came back, I was taken out to the parking lot beside the station. Another Vancouver plain clothes cop came with us, and I was shoved into what looked like the old Pontiac I was first driven to the station in. After a lengthy drive, we arrived at the Horseshoe Bay ferry terminal for the trip back to Victoria via Nanaimo.

While we were waiting for the ferry we sat in the local coffee shop and had coffee and doughnuts on them. When we had finished, I was asked if I wanted to use the washroom. I said sure. Nobody in the coffee shop was alerted I was a prisoner because they had taken my handcuffs off, when the Vancouver Cop dropped us off.

"Don't get any ideas. If you run I won't hesitate to shoot you." Evens said.

I had traveled on the Horseshoe Bay Ferry in the past, and I knew that the Mainland Terminal was situated in a difficult area to escape from on foot. There was one road coming in and one road going out. I realized I wouldn't get very far before being picked up, so I put the idea out of my mind.

During the trip to Nanaimo, we sat in the ships lounge near the confectionary. I was allowed to use the wash rooms and handcuffs were not applied. One of the officers noticed me looking at Victoria's local newspaper on the Confectionary Counter.

"You looking for news of your capture?" he asked with a smile.

"Well the less publicity I get the better," I said.

"If you were smart, you'd plead guilty in front of Judge Hall, and get it over with," he said.

"Hell no, the last time I co-operated with you, and Judge Hall, I got three years as a first offender. There were guys doing time with me, who were my age, and had committed worst crimes, and had records as long as my arm with only two years. I don't want anything to do with Judge Hall, besides I'm not guilty," I smiled. He tried to pump me with more conversation but I realized I had said too much all ready and shut up.

When we arrived at Departure Bay terminal in Nanaimo, we walked off the ship, and were met by a Victoria Police Car and driver. The weather was cold and it snowed steadily on are trip down the island to Victoria. When we passed through Duncan I glanced out the Car Window, and saw that there was about six centimeters of snow on the ground. I noticed the detective sitting beside me had fallen asleep and the two in the front seat were not paying any attention to me. I weighed my chances of jumping clear of the car at the next intersection if the car had to come to a stop. The Henslowes place was at least three miles away and the only routes were by the highway or by a long circular route around the town, and along several back country roads. The other way was just straight through farmland and woods, but in this weather, I would not have got very far. While I was contemplating all this, the car had passed through Duncan and never stopped until we reached Victoria's Police Station.

The next day, in the afternoon, the two cops who had picked me up in Vancouver came into the cell block and picked five prisoners for a line up. They were taken out and told to stand in line in front of the Police Desk.

"Okay, Diener stand in line with the others." They said.

Then I realized the lineup was for me. The three of us were standing just inside the open cell block door arguing about the inadequacies of their system, but they were holding the cards, and I realized the futility of arguing about it. When I turned to walk over to the lineup, I could see through an open hall way door. There were three or four people sitting on a bench straining mightily to see and hear what was going on. I knew then that the lineup had been compromised, and the Bank Employers knew who they were to pick out even before they were asked to. I went through the obvious charade, and of course I was picked out immediately by everybody who was asked to look.

That evening I received a visit from a young girl and her friend who had read about me in the papers. She was a friend of the family since childhood, and had probably been overcome by curiosity. I hadn't seen her in years and she was wondering what had happened to get me into this mess, and she could show off to her friend as well. During are chat, she expressed surprise that I had been arrested because she had read in the papers that another man had been picked up who fitted the description of the robber, and had been identified by the bank employees as the culprit.

I found this piece of information very interesting. She told me that the police had showed the Bank Employees some photographs of various suspects and they had picked out this man by mistake, leading to his arrest. The only thing that had probably saved him from a long prison term was my arrest, with some of the banks marked money.

The next day I made my first appearance in court and was asked by Judge Hall how I pled guilty or not guilty. I pled not guilty. The Judge then asked, who I assumed was the prosecutor, whether I had legal representation, and when he found out I didn't and was unable to afford one, he stated the court would appoint someone to represent me.

A couple of days went by and I was called out of the cell block to meet my lawyer, who identified himself as Mr. Murphy a beefy blond young man. He asked me a few questions about where I was at the time of the robbery. I told him I was at Ma. James. He asked me if Ma James could verify that, and I told him she wasn't home at the time. I could see he didn't believe anything I was telling him. Finally he looked me in the eye and said.

"As your lawyer I'm bound to keep anything you tell me in strict confidence. Do you understand that?"

I said, "I did."

"Did you rob the bank?"

I realized there was no point in lying to him. He was supposed to be representing me, and I wasn't helping him by telling him a bunch of lies. I laughed and said.

"Yea, I knocked it off."

He just nodded his head, and said.

"Well that's enough for today I'll see you in court."

The rest of the day I thought about my chances, and I realized the only thing that might help me was the fact that all the bank employees, except one, had made a mistake and identified the wrong man. Everything else pointed to me. My possession of the marked money, the teller's positive identification, and the subsequent changing of the rest of the bank staffs minds about the original wrong identification they had made. I knew I didn't have a chance of beating the beef, but I wasn't going to admit to a thing.

The next day I was taken upstairs to the courtroom again, and told by Judge Hall that sufficient evidence had been presented, and that I was to be remanded and held for a jury trial. A few days went by, and I was taken to the city's Federal Courthouse to watch the selection of the jury take place.

The Federal Courthouse was a very old building situated in Bastion Square near the city's water front, because the case was now transferred to Federal jurisdiction the Mounted Police became involved, and I was assigned a big R.C.M.P officer to guard me. The day's proceedings consisted of the prosecution presenting various prospective jurors who were asked various questions about their back grounds and were either accepted or rejected by the defence and prosecution. After the proper amount of jurors was selected, the Judge set the case to be started the next day, and I was taken back to the City Jail.

The next day, Murphy took me aside, and told me a lawyer by the name of Proudfoot was going to give him a hand with my defence. I found out later that Proudfoot was the ex-Chief Prosecutor for the city of Victoria, and he had fallen on hard times due to his drinking. He had been caught behind the wheel of his car drunk, and been convicted of driving while intoxicated, because of this he had lost his appointment as City Prosecutor. During his school years he had become a friend of my sister and when he found out who I was he volunteered to help in my defence.

The trial lasted the day, and my defence was mostly about the wrong identification by the Bank Employees. The bank employees were all apologetic about their error, but they all said they were sure this time it was me. Of course the teller who had to confront me in the bank was the damaging witness. He never wavered when cross examined about his identification. And then of course the bills with the identical serial numbers found on the bills I deposited in the hotel safe, and my signature on the deposit envelope made an air tight case for the prosecution. My lawyers went through a waste of time by bring in the guy who was wrongly accused in the hope that it might help damage the identification evidence, but when I saw the close resemblance between myself and the man, I realized his presence at the trial only confirmed it was an easy mistake to make. He was tall and slim and dressed very similar with the same color hair and eyes. I recognized him as an ex-convict I had seen in the Penitentiary. That would explain why the police had his picture to show to the Bank Employers. The only thing that didn't fit was he was a known Check Forger, and had never been convicted of a crime of potential violence. The jury was never told this fact at the time of the trial. He was just brought in to show the differences in appearance, which as I mentioned earlier probably did more harm than good.

After the lawyers had made their closing summations to the jury, and the jury had left to decide my fate, the lawyers made a few half-hearted attempts to cheer me up, and tried to sound like it had gone very well for me, but I knew what they were trying to do. I just laughed and told them that I appreciated their efforts, but I didn't think we had a hope in hell.

I fully expected to be sent back to the City Police Cell's to await the verdict, thinking that they would take at least a couple of hours to make up their minds, they were back in an hour with a verdict of guilty, which I fully expected. The judge didn't make any statements he just stated the jury's verdict and then sentenced me to twenty years. I heard an audible gasp come from the spectator's gallery, and I found out later that Mom was there and had performed a spectacular fainting spell, and had been taken to hospital, but recovered quickly. Detective Smith came up to me as I was being led from the courtroom, and shook my hand with a big grin on his face.

"Tough luck eh John he said.

I just looked at him and smiled back and said.

"I'll be back," as I was being led away.

The very next day, I was hand cuffed to another prisoner and taken by the R.C.M.P. to the airport. I noticed that we were being followed out to the airport by another police car with three plain clothed officers in it. I guess they were being cautious because my partner hadn't been caught, and were worried about a possible attempt to help me escape.

When we arrived at the airport, we were placed on an R.C.M.P. plane instead of a commercial flight. The usual procedure, is when you're in the plane the handcuffs are removed, but the key didn't fit so I had to fly to the mainland with the cuffs still in place.

When we arrived the prisoner I was with who was handcuffed to another officer before boarding the plane, left for Okalla, and I was taken to a local R.C.M.P. detachment to find a key that would fit. As we drove through the Vancouver suburbs, I gazed out the windows of the car watching the activities of the people, knowing it would be a long time before I stepped foot on the streets again. A melancholy feeling swept over me for a second. I pushed it aside and forced myself to think about an appeal.

The admitting procedure at Okalla hadn't changed much and I was soon locked up in the Remand Wing. I was asked if I was going to appeal my case and I said yes. I was then given the appropriate appeal papers which I made out and turned in for mailing.

My cell mate was a Homosexual, who was waiting for trial on a charge of indecent Exposure, and committing an indecent act. He had been caught naked in a parked car with another man while performing a blow job on him.

When we were herded down to the wing's shower room, which was a room on the bottom floor able to shower five or six at a time, he would show signs of extreme shyness and cower in a corner. I noticed he didn't have any body hair at all during the short time he was my cell mate, he didn't cause me any trouble or make any advances. He was obviously not an aggressive Homosexual. He was just a pathetic little man caught in a world of evil men who took advantage of his feminism.

The weekends were family visiting days, and from our cell we could look over the yard fence, and see part of the path leading down to the front gate. He was watching eagerly for expected visitors and when he saw them he exclaimed excitedly.

"Look, here comes my wife with my lover."

At first I didn't get what the hell he was talking about. I stood there staring at him in surprise, and all I could say was.

"Your wife with your lover,"

"Yes over there the girl with the blue coat on."

From where I was standing I could see a reasonably attractive woman, and a good looking man walking down the path.

"Your wife and your lover, what the hell are you talking about."

"I was under the care of a psychiatrist a few years back, and was leading a normal life. I met my wife and we were married, I even have a son."

"What happened?"

"Well everything was going fine, when I met my lover, who was a friend of my wife. She invited him over for lunch one day, and one thing led to another and I had a relapse."

"Does your wife know?"

"Oh, yes she's living with my lover now."

"How come he's not in jail with you?"

"No, no, the man I was charged with is down on the tier below us."

I just shook my head, and stopped asking him questions. I thought I had problems. This guy was so totally perverted and turned around that I realized he was beyond changing for any length of time, and he should be in an institution where he could get some lasting help. Either that or just leave him alone and release him into his own little hell.

A few days went by and I received a visit from Proudfoot, who expressed his condolences for my long sentence, and offered to help me with a parole application in seven years. I didn't tell him I was appealing the sentence. I had the feeling he was just going through the motions, and I didn't believe he would be of much help anyway. I thanked him for the offer and he quickly walked away.

A week later I received another visitor a man who I had met only once, "Bill Smith." He had been approached by my mother who had asked him to come to Okalla to find out if I needed any help. "Bill Smith, known as the Light House Philosopher, was one of Victoria's most famous eccentrics. I had met him years earlier when he was operating a combination Second Hand Store and Pawn Shop. He didn't remember me, I was just browsing in his store at the time, and he had tried to sell me on his merchandise. He was tall and slim, with a cultured English accent a very well-spoken man. He was famous for his forays into local politics. He had run for Mayor of Victoria two or three times, and dropped out for various reasons, one of which was during a vigorous argument with one of his political opponents, he had struck him on the head with a claw hammer, luckily inflicting only a minor wound, of course he was charged with assault and fined. He was also known to bring his various causes to the public's attention by performing outrageous stunts such as marching through the streets of Victoria carrying a small Black Coffin to bring his arguments to the public attention through the local news media. He had at one time been a Light House Keeper in China and had occasionally come in contact with pirates and had other adventures. He had spent the Second World War as a prisoner of the Japanese. I don' know how my mother met him, but he agreed to help her. He expressed amazement at all the armed guards surrounding the exercise yard as he came in and disgust at the difficulties he had in getting permission to visit me, as he wasn't a relative, and he had come at off visiting hours. He offered to help me with my appeal, and ask me questions about anybody who might he considered a good character witness. I couldn't think of anybody who could or would want to speak on my behalf. He told me not to worry about it, and he would arrange something. After about a fifteen minute visit he left.

A month went by and I was taken back to Victoria to face the appeal court which was held in the federal Court House where I was originally sentenced. Bill Scott was there, and he had brought my mother. The court consisted of three Judges and a lawyer who was the representative of the crown, who was contesting the appeal. Bill Scott made a rambling speech emphasizing my age and the length of sentence. My mother talked about the family's hard times over the years, and how I had been helpful to her financially when I had been working. When I was given a chance to speak I didn't have much to say except that the length of sentence didn't offer much hope for rehabilitation after being incarcerated for so long. The Crown Attorney merely read my prison record and stated the facts speak for themselves and that the maximum sentence was life in prison for the crime I was convicted of. When it was over the Judges remanded me for another two weeks, and said their decision would be brought down in Vancouver. The next day I was taken back to Okalla.

When the two weeks were up, I was taken along with several other prisoners to the Vancouver Federal Courthouse. After sitting in a holding cell for a couple of hours, I was taken upstairs by two very large older R.C.M.P. Officers dressed in their Dress Red Tunics. I was ushered into a large courtroom filled with court officials and spectators. I sat in a Prisoners box flanked on both sides by the Mounties and listened to several Corporation Lawyers arguing points of law for their very wealthy clients. After a while my name was called almost as an afterthought. The Prosecutor who represented the Crown at my original trial was there, and he was asked by the five Judges on the bench if he had any statement to make. He rose with a knowing grin on his face and glanced contemptuously over at me and said.

"No, you're Honor."

And with that, the judge said.

"The appeal of John Diener of the sentence of twenty years for Bank Robbery is hereby dismissed. The whole procedure hadn't taken more than five minutes, if that. I looked at the Mounties and said.

"Is that it?"

They nodded their heads and one of them said.

"Yeah, that's it lad, let's go."

The decision had really been a foregone conclusion, a waste of the Tax Payers Money.

In a few days I was back in the Sheep Dip Bath at the Penitentiary and down to B7 and the Fish Tier. New prisoners were coming in so fast I was only kept on the Fish Tier for five days. During that time I didn't shine any bars. I spent my time keeping the tier I was assigned to, supplied with clean linen and clothes for the inmates on bath day and I dropped off the library books to the cells. An old time forger, who I had made friends with on my previous jolt, sent me down a tube of tooth paste when he found out I was back. I appreciated the kind gesture because I knew how hard it was to get your hands on contraband like that.

I wasn't given a choice of work assignment this time. The senior dome guard informed me I was moving to B7 Tier G cell six, and I was to report to the Shoe Shop for work in the morning.

CHAPTER 10

20 Years a Long Jolt

Appendicitis, Admission to Hospital

Music and a Few Incidents

The next morning after breakfast, I reported to the main dome assembly area and lined up with the convicts for the Shoe Shop. When everyone was present we marched out a door situated in the corner of the dome which led outside the main cell block to the back of the prison, where most of the work shops were situated in a long two story building. This building held the laundry which included the shower and change area for the North and East Wings. These wings did not have individual showers on each tier. The prisoners had to take their weekly shower on assigned days during the week. This was done by sending individual shops to the showers on certain days during the week. The Shower Room was nicknamed the Race Track. When you arrived you lined up at a door which led into the laundry. Another convict called out your number to the workers in the back who brought your clothes rolled up in a tight bundle with a towel, you then lined up alongside a row of benches, and stripped naked. At one end of the room was a door with the bottom half closed and the top half open. When everybody was ready we filed by the door and handed our dirty clothes to a convict on the other side who dropped them into a laundry basket. From there we stepped under a row of showers and soaped ourselves down as fast as we could. A guard stood on the outside of a low wall, and prodded the cons along with a short stick to keep the line moving. When you got to the end of the first row of showers, you rounded a corner and started down the other side under another row of showers, where you rinsed yourself off as quickly as you could, and dried yourself off and picked up your clean change of clothes at another half door.

In front of the building alongside the shower room was the Barbershop, and about once a month you got a haircut whether you needed it or not. The whole thing was conducted the same as the shower system. You filed in and sat on a bench and waited your turn for a quick haircut, a half inch on the top and a quarter inch on the sides, shorter if you wanted it. No one was allowed long hair.

Above the Laundry was the Tailor shop. All the Prison Uniforms including the guards were made in the tailor Shop. Off course the con's working there were the best dressed in the prison. There was a small entrance foyer alongside the laundry wall. In this foyer was a small room, which held a supply of used and repaired boots for distribution to the New Cons when they came in, or for a change when you're old ones wore out. Nobody received anything new when they first arrived. It was up to the individual to make deals and hustle anything new if he wanted it.

On the other side of the foyer was the Carpenter shop which made anything the prison needed in wood. They also built and repaired furniture for the Federal Government in the area.

Above the Carpenter Shop was the Blacksmith Shop, and next to that was the shoe Shop, and below that was the Canvas shop. At the north end of the building was a wing which held a School of Carpentry, and a School for typing and Shorthand. A smaller building a short distance from this wing held the Machine Shop, and a little distance away another building held the garage and Automotive Building. In this building was the Boiler House with the Engineers Department and all the related trades such as Electrical and Plumbing Departments. Below the School of typing was the Paint Shop. All of these shops were fully equipped and performed the functions they were required to do efficiently, except for one thing. I never heard of any of the trade's shops producing any tradesmen, who made a successful career of what they learned.

The Shoe Shop was equipped with everything required to repair and make shoes and boots. There were stitching and sanding and polishing machines. Each Convict had a bench and all the tools he needed to build an oxford or boot. The one Prison guard who ran the shop took the foot measurements and saw to the orderly running of the shop. He also made the Black Jacks which each guard carried for protection. A separate bench which was equipped with sewing Machines made the Shoe Tops.

The first day, I was assigned to a bench with a big over weight man who was introduced to me as Bill. After the initial introductions he asked.

"Where are you from?"

"Victoria," I said.

"So am I, he smiled.

I noticed his number was considerably lower than mine, at least as low as Sailor Mac's.

"What ya in for?"

"Bank Robbery, they gave me twenty years."

"Well it looks like we are going to see a lot of each other." He smiled.

"I'm doing an indefinite term for rape," he said.

I then knew why he had a low number an indefinite sentence was given to repeat, offenders who were considered to be Habitual criminals, and were beyond reform. The prisoner's sentence was reviewed periodically to see if he had changed enough for possible release, but he was doing what was considered a life sentence, and the few convicts who had been sentenced to this type of incarceration usually spent upwards of ten years before being considered for release. I listened to the usual protests and complaints about what a raw deal he'd gotten, and commiserated with him a little. I really didn't care at all. I had enough troubles of my own.

The guard came over with a half dozen pairs of worn out boots.

"Bill, show him the ropes and teach him how to repair these."

Without a back ward glance he walked away.

"How's he for a boss?" I asked.

"Oh, he's all right as far as screws go. You know, mind our own business and do your job and he'll leave you alone."

Most of the conversation was done out of the corners of our mouths in a subdued tone. We didn't have to worry about being over heard. The roar of the stitching and sanding machines and the banging of hammers were deafening.

At one end of the shop was the guard office. At the other end were two open toilet cubicles. The guard had a clear few of all the work benches and prisoners, and there was-not any real areas of concealment. I also noticed he didn't mingle with the convict's for any length of time, and during the few incidents of trouble amongst the cons he kept his distance, and used the phone in his office to call for help. Immediately below the steel staircase leading to the shop, was a guard kiosk. The guard stationed there during working hours had a clear view of the front of the buildings. Anybody breaking out of the front of the shops would be seen almost immediately. The back of the building was covered by the guard towers on the back wall and anybody wanting in or out had to depend on the guard in the kiosk to bring up the key and open the door. The guards in the shops were locked in with the inmates, and had to depend on the outer guard also.

Each work bench was equipped with a hammer a very sharp knife for trimming leather, and a long sharp pointed awl for making holes. All of these tools could be used as deadly weapons, and some of the prisoners were operating on half a deck, and were quite capable of using them for cold bloody murder. Fortunately the few incidents that occurred only got as far as threats and by the next day cooler thoughts prevailed.

The Shoe Shop had one of the best Soccer Teams in the Penitentiary. Most of the players worked in the shop, and the rest came from the shops around the prison. The team manager and star player worked in the shop, so the team took the name of the shop and the other teams were named after the bigger shops in the prison. The was the Laundry, Shoe Shop, Tailor Shop, Kitchen, and so on, with regular scheduled games which took place during the afternoon exercise period.

The other sports such as Basketball, Softball and Volleyball were played at appropriate times of the year with organized teams and managers. I played in every sport for a number of years. I even refereed the Basketball games for a season. For the soccer I played goalie, but in the second season I was kicked in my right side directly over the appendix while I was lying on the ground holding the ball to my side. I don't know whether it was a deliberate attempt to hurt me or not. The action was very fast at the time, and I assume somebody on the opposing team tried to kick the ball loose from my grip, missed it and hit me instead. At the time it didn't hurt very much and I managed to clear the ball away from the goal mouth, but l when I got to my feet and walked back to cover the goal again I was suddenly bent over with an excruciating pain directly over my appendix. It hurt so much I could hardly move. I managed to attract the attention of a fullback, and told him to cover the goal. He saw I was in extreme pain and came over. A guard standing nearby was watching what was going on, but didn't approach or offer any aid. I managed to limp over to him, and tell him what had happened. He could see by the expression on my face that I wasn't kidding, so he took me over to the gate in the wall leading to the Cell Block. He got the attention of the guard on the corner tower who lowered the key on a line so he could open the gate. After the gate was opened the key was pulled up by the Tower Guard. I could hardly walk but I managed to make it to the South Wing and up the stairs to the Prison Hospital. A guard who was a paramedic grinned at me as I staggered in. He asked me what was wrong, and I explained the situation to him. He said.

"Well, I guess you got a nasty bruise when you were kicked, you'll be all right after a night's rest."

I thought it was a bit strange that he never asked me to strip off my shirt or made any attempt at an examination at all. He just dismissed me back to my cell on B7. After a couple of hours the pain slowly subsided, and in the morning I was able to go back to work.

During the following year I was not to feel up to my usual level of fitness, and finally in the middle of the night I woke up to excruciating pain in my lower right side. I was in so much pain I couldn't move. I lay on my back trying to put some of my weight on to my left side hoping to ease the pain. The guard walked by on his rounds but I didn't say anything hoping the pain would go away even though I knew he wouldn't be back for another hour. Finally for what seemed an eternity the pain began to subside, and eventually I went back to sleep.

In the morning I decided to report for sick parade. This was done by reporting to the guard in the dome on your way to breakfast, and explaining what your problem was. After I explained what had happened during the night he decided to let me report to the Hospital on my way out to work. I felt relieved that I had been believed as being sick rather than a malingerer. Usually a big percentage of the cons who reported in sick were drug addicts trying to get their hands on prescription drugs or just to get out of work for a few days. Because of this it was very hard to get accepted as sick. You had to look and feel sick and be very convincing before you were allowed up to the Prison Hospital. I assumed this problem was created by the fact that at least half of the prison population was involved with drugs at one time or another in their lives.

After breakfast I reported outside the South Wing Hospital Gate. There was a small group of cons waiting to be checked out. Most of them looked legitimately sick to me. I noticed the con I gave the tobacco to when I was a Kazoonie. I walked over and said.

"What's the matter with you?"

"Nothing," he said, nervously.

He stared at me for a minute, and I noticed he was jittery and wild eyed.

"You look a little crazy to me," I said and laughed.

"There's nothing wrong with me, I'm fine," he muttered, forcefully, taking a quick threatening step towards me.

"Hey, I'm only kidding," I said throwing up my hands in mock surrender. He calmed down as fast as he had flared up.

"I have to go and talk to the shrink. I stabbed my partner in the side down in the Kitchen Butcher Shop yesterday afternoon, and they want me to see the shrink before I go to Wardens Court."

"He isn't dead is he?" I asked.

"No, no, I just grazed him." He shrugged.

"What happened?" I asked.

He stared at me suspiciously for a second, and turned abruptly, and walked away. I thought, Jesus he's gone nutty as a Fruit Cake, and made a mental note to keep my distance.

By the time my number was called, I was feeling nauseated, and ready to lie down. After I explained what had happened the night before, the medical attendant decided to keep me in the Hospital until the following morning for observation. There were several cells for this purpose and I was assigned to one. After I was given lunch I couldn't hold it down and every time I wretched I would get a sharp stabbing pain in my lower right side. I refused supper.

The next day I was let out of my cell and taken into the treatment room. A guard Paramedic was there with a con attendant.

"I've been told you were throwing up last night," the guard said.

"Yeah, I felt lousy after lunch. I didn't feel like eating any supper."

He reached for the phone and dialled a number.

"Hello doctor, it's Harry Rhodes over at the Penitentiary. I've got a prisoner here who says he's got a pain in his right side. Yes, he says he's been throwing up, Okay I'll do that." He said.

After a few minutes listening to the doctor's instructions, he said.

The doctor wants to send you out to Shaunesy Hospital for a checkup. Your symptoms resemble Appendicitis. I knew that when you came in." He said, with a know-it-all smile.

I thought, hell why the hell didn't you do something then, instead of keeping me waiting all bloody night. I was taken back to my cell, and in about an hour I was escorted out of my cell to the front entrance, placed in hand cuffs and driven by car to the Hospital in Vancouver. Shaunesy Hospital was the city's Veterans Hospital. It was run by the Federal

Government, so all the Federal Penitentiary Prisoners who became ill were taken there for treatment.

On arrival at the hospital I was ushered into the Emergency Department and placed on a stretcher in a treatment room and the hand cuffs removed. In a few minutes a doctor arrived. "Undo you're belt, and slide your pants down to your hips please." I complied with his request. The guard had disappeared. I assumed he had just stepped outside the door.

"Relax. I'm going to check your abdomen."

I felt a sharp pain every time he probed my side insensitively, and naturally I tightened up my stomach muscles.

"Come on relax, I can't feel anything if you don't loosen up," he said in an annoyed tone of voice.

"Look, I don't know what you're feeling for, but it hurts," I shot back with a cold stare. He stepped away from me quickly and said.

"You have Appendicitis and you'll be going up to the operating room right away." And with that he turned and walked away. I never saw him again.

In a short while an orderly came in and I was taken up to another treatment room next to the operating theater. The orderly helped me undress.

"Lay down on the stretcher, I'm going to give you a pubic shave," he said it wasn't a complete shave of the area just a quick shave and wash of the operating site over the lower right hand side of my Abdomen. When he was finished he handed me a hospital gown and told me to put it on. After a few minutes another Doctor came in dressed in white and proceeded to give me a rectal examination without any explanation of what it was for. He made a mess of the sheets with fecal matter and lubricant which the orderly grudgingly cleaned up.

"What the hell was that for," I asked.

The orderly laughed, and said, "Just another intern practicing his technique."

"Christ, that's all I need," I said disgustedly.

The orderly laughed uproariously at his little joke, and then he pushed me into the operating room where two doctors were waiting to perform the operation.

I was helped onto the operating table, and told by one of the doctors to lie on my side and bring my knees up to my chest.

"You're from the Penitentiary aren't you?" He asked in a friendly manner.

"Yeah," I grunted.

"How long is your sentence?" he asked.

"Twenty years," I said.

He let out a little whistle between his teeth.

"Twenty years," he exclaimed loudly, "What for?"

"Bank robbery," I said.

"Anybody hurt?"

"No, nobody was hurt,"

While the conversation was going on, the other doctor was hooking up an intravenous line to my arm. When he was finished he said.

"I'm going to give you a needle in your back now. There how was that?" he asked.

"Like I've just been stung by a large bee," I said.

"Oh," he chuckled, as everything went black.

When I woke up, the room I was in was in total darkness. I could feel a bandage and some discomfort on my right side. My Hospital gown was soaked in sweat, and I felt as weak as a kitten. I glanced around, and when my eyes became accustomed to the dark I noticed I was in a two bed room, and the bed next to me was occupied.

After what seemed like an eternity, a nurse came into the room.

"Well you're awake. How do you feel?"

"Lousy! I'm covered in sweat and weak as hell."

She felt my gown and bed clothes.

"I see what you mean, she said. We'll get you a change, back in a minute," she said, as she hurried out the door.

In a few minutes she was back with three other nurses. They quickly removed my gown and the beds top linen, leaving me covered with only a sheet. In a few minutes the bed linen was changed, and I was dressed in dry pyjamas. I was given a shot in the hip and settled comfortably for the night.

In the morning after breakfast, a young attractive nurse came in and started changing the linen on the patient's bed next to me. When she was through she came over and asked me to get out of bed.

"You've got to be kidding," I said. I've just had my Appendix out."

"So! You'll be all right, come on roll out of bed and sit in the chair."

She bent over and put her arm under my shoulders to help me sit up and I smelled the perfume she was wearing, and the freshness of her suddenly made me remember I hadn't spoken to or been near a woman in four long years. She noticed how intensely I was staring at her and pulled back as her face became slightly flushed with embarrassment. When she was finished she left me sitting in the chair for a while and my side began to get very sore, so I gingerly struggled back to bed by myself.

In the afternoon an orderly came in and checked a metal bottle hanging in a cloth bag on the edge of my side table.

"I see you haven't voided to day."

"No, I don't have to."

"When was the last time you went?" He asked.

"I don't remember, sometime yesterday I guess."

He rolled the blankets down and gently pushed on my lower abdomen.

"I see you're a little distended he said, I'll have to measure you're out put, so don't use the Toilet, use this bottle.

Later on the young nurse who had made the beds in the morning came.

"I have a shot for you, It will help you void," she said.

I carefully rolled over on my side, fully expecting to receive the injection in the hip.

"I think you can sit in the chair for a while, and I'll make up your bed."

I gingerly rolled over and sat on the edge of the bed and stood up.

"Okay, loosen your pyjamas, and bend over. I'll give you your shot now."

I loosened the draw strings on my pants and carefully bent over, but when I did this I was a little off balance and I let go of my pants which slipped down to my ankles leaving me naked from the waist down. I tried to reach my pants but found it very uncomfortable.

The nurse walked slowly around the bed and stood staring at me with a flushed look on her face. She stood there for a minute and began to giggle and laugh. I couldn't believe my eyes she thought it was funny, well I didn't and I felt anger welling up inside me, and embarrassment.

"It's not funny, help me with my pants will you I'm having trouble reaching them," I growled.

She came back around the bed and helped me get a hold of the pants and at the same time giving me my shot. When she was finished she left and I could hear her laughing as she walked down the hall. I received another shot that evening, but their attempts to get me to void in the bottle that day failed, and so I was given a catheterization the next morning. It wasn't long after that that everything returned to normal.

In a couple of days I was moved to a three bed ward that was occupied by a couple of other cons. The bed to the left of me contained a large powerfully built man who was doing two years for assaulting a Police Officer. He had just had some varicose veins stripped from both his legs. In the bed directly across from me was a young East Indian who was doing five years for rape. He had just had all his teeth extracted. The ward was provided with a Penitentiary Guard to see we kept out of trouble.

One afternoon a nurse came in to give me my daily Penicillin shot, which I was receiving to get rid of any abdominal infection I had built up before I had the Appendix out. About fifteen minutes after she was finished the young nurse who had taken an interest in my bare bottom came in and began pulling bed curtains. "What are you doing?" I asked.

"It's time for your Penicillin shot," she smiled.

"Oh no, I just had it."

She began to pull the bed clothes down, and giggle again. I grabbed the blankets and yanked them up.

"Look I just had the damn shot and I'm not taking another one so close together, besides my ass is beginning to look like a pin cushion," I snarled at her.

"I just checked your chart and there's no record of you having your shot this afternoon," she said indignantly.

"Hey did somebody just give me a shot a few minutes ago or not?" I yelled to the other two in the room.

The East Indian looked up and nodded at the nurse. "Yeah he just had his shot," he confirmed. The big guy just grunted.

"Well I guess who ever gave it to you forgot to write it in the book."

She sounded disappointed that she wasn't going to have another look when she gave me the needle.

"You are our favorite patient you know." She lied as she pulled the curtains into place.

"Yeah sure," I said.

The next day an Intern came in and took my stitches out and told me I could go back to the Penitentiary the next day, but if I wanted he could fix it so I could stay in over the weekend. I thanked him and declined the offer. The place wasn't much better, and I just wanted to get on with doing my time. He showed some surprise at this and left. I thought about it for a while and realized I was becoming institutionalized. I was losing my ability to communicate in the outside world. In the Penitentiary I could retreat to my cell for eighteen hours a day and not have to make any really important decisions at all or be bothered by anybody although the six hours I was forced to mix with the other convicts was a living hell. Everything you did or said was an exercise in survival mentally and physically, mostly mentally. What you didn't have you soon learned not to miss, and so what was wrong with the Penitentiary, and what made it a living hell was the prisoners, and guards that were in it. When I could retreat to my locked cell, I was away from it and in my own little world.

I had been working for about a year in the Shoe Shop, and I was getting a little tired of the monotony and noise. So I decided to ask for a transfer to a new project that was being developed in a room above the Paint Shop. It was a School of Typing and Short Hand. I had taken typing when I was in grade nine, and so I was ahead of the game with more knowledge than the other cons in the class.

After about six months, I was asked to get up a filing system with a folder for each con working in an industrial shop which meant anybody who was supposed to be learning a trade. The various Trades Instructors would make out a report each month on their progress report. The report would then be collected and put in their folder.

The guard, who was looking after the cons in the Typing School, was responsible for this filing system. The problem was, he couldn't leave the school and the cons alone while he went about to the various shops and collected the reports although the school was virtually a self-taught system. You were handed a book on Pitman Shorthand, and a manual on touch typing, and told to get on with it. Some took the whole thing seriously and worked hard, where some of the others did nothing but loll about and did their best to distract the rest. Alongside the school in the same wing, was a large open room, which was being used as a Carpenter School. The area was big enough to build framing mock ups of house's and to hold a tool shed and a small class room for follow up lectures. Some of the cons were doing lengthy sentences. There was a young prisoner doing life for murder. The rumor was he smothered his girlfriend but nobody really knew what happened. Some said she choked on his sperm while performing oral sex on him. Because he was only sixteen the girl's parents asked for leniency, and they gave him life instead of hanging him. There was myself along with two or three others doing twenty years or more.

There were only three guards watching, and trying to instruct ten times as many prisoners including a few aggressive homosexuals as well. Because of this they decided to trust one of the cons to go around the prison picking up the progress reports from the instructors, and filing them properly. I was called into the office and told I was to be given a pass which would allow me to move freely throughout the prison and my prison pay would be increased to twenty cents a day which was as high as you could get. The only catch to all this was I was not to tell any cons what was written in the progress reports. This put me behind the proverbial eight ball. It wouldn't take long for the cons to find out about the progress reports or to begin to wonder. "How did I get such a plum job?" and "How they were doing in the reports?" It could only lead to trouble. The guard didn't ask me if I wanted the job, he just told me I was to do it and that was it. I figured I had better keep my mouth shut, and let them think whatever they wanted. For the next few months I told who ever asked me about their reports that they were doing just fine and they didn't have a thing to worry about, although some of the reports I saw were disasters. Only once did my new position bring me trouble. I can't think of any other reason for what happened.

In the cell next to me was a con a short stocky individual who worked in the Electrical Shop, and had a penchant for breaking the rules and was constantly in and out of the hole for various reasons. He was doing twenty-five years for bank robbery. There were four of them who were attempting to rob a bank in the Fraser Valley when two Mountie's answered a silent alarm. One went into the bank while the other one waited outside in the police car. Thinking it was just a fake alarm, he didn't go into the bank with his gun drawn. He stepped up to the counter and was shot by one of the bandits. He fell to the floor. Another bandit who was holding a sawed off Shot Gun and hiding behind the counter in front of him stood up, but before he could get off a shot the Mountie drew his gun and shot him in the arm. The bandit who had fired first ran by him on his way out of the bank the Mountie shot him through the heart dropping him in his tracks.

In the meantime the con, who was in the vault, heard the shots and came running out holding an empty cash box against his chest. The Mountie took aim and fired, the bullet entered the cash box and ricochet across the room. He raised the automatic he was carrying in his other hand and began to fire rapidly at the Mountie, wounding him at least six or seven times, but none of the bullets were fatal. The fourth bandit who was sitting in the getaway car, panicked when he heard the shots and roared out of the bank's parking lot. The second Mountie immediately sized up the situation and realizing what was happening, set out in pursuit. A short distance away from the bank the bandit lost control of the car and crashed off the road. He was immediately arrested by the pursuing Mountie, Later when the getaway vehicle was searched a Russian Submachine gun was discovered with a hundred Round Magazine also found was a short army submachine gun which was fully loaded. If these weapons had been brought into the bank and used, the carnage among the employees and customers would have been terrible. I don't think the Mountie would have survived. The three bandits were sentenced to twenty-five years a piece. The young getaway driver received an early parole. The shot gun wielder kept his nose clean.

There was one serious incident which came up while we were standing in line waiting for our lunch trays on a weekend. My next door neighbor flushed around the face and a bit wild eyed when he came out of his cell. He didn't say anything until we stopped outside the kitchen tray wickets.

"I hear you're a Stool Pigeon," he said.

I stared at him for a second in disbelief. To accuse someone of being a Stool Pigeon in front of several other cons without any kind of proof was a dangerous and rotten thing to do. For nobody is hated more amongst the prison population than Stool Pigeons. I realized I would have to react to this accusation and fast. He was staring wild eyed at me with a wicked curl to his lip a totally sick grin. I realized he was going through some sort of paranoid attack. I could feel the heat rising to my face as I lost my temper and rage took over. I reached out with both hands and grabbed him by the front of his shirt and jerked him toward me, until I was staring directly into his eyes.

"What the hell are you talking about?"

I snarled into his face. I had caught him by surprise and sudden fear swept over his face. I shoved him back in disgust. The group of cons who were standing with us melted back out of the way in case of trouble. They had looks of surprise and anticipation on their faces I just turned my back on him and he did nothing. He just stood there looking flustered and angry at my reaction to his stupid accusation. The rest of the cons sensed it was over and nothing was going to happen, and the ranks closed again around us. In a few minutes the line began to move and I was soon- back in the solitude and safety of my cell.

That evening as we waited in line again for our supper trays, he appeared beside me. He opened his hand and showed me a small Jack Knife with about a two inch blade. I immediately tensed myself for a possible attack.

"The next time you lay a hand on me, I'll shove this up your ass and break it off," he snarled.

"Look, what the hell did you expect me to do stand there and take a stupid accusation like that? I should have knocked your teeth down your throat. As for that piddling little Jack Knife, I think you're losing it and you'd better get a hold of yourself. I'm telling you right now you picked the wrong guy to fuck with. Now layoff, and do your own time." I had kept my voice down so I couldn't be heard above the noise of the line. He slipped the knife into his pocket and shrugged his shoulders and turned away from me. From that time on for at least two more years the incidents were never mentioned again and our relationship remained cordial. I was thankful for this, because during this time he remained in the cell beside me.

My new position had a great many advantages. I got tired of filing and fending of aggressive cons inquiring about their progress reports. I'd use my pass and wander around the prison picking up delinquent reports. The extra ten cents a day I was being paid came in handy for a little extra from the Canteen, which was opened once a week so the cons could buy a little extra tobacco or the occasional soft drink and toilet articles. I would save my money for a month and buy as much tobacco as I could and use it for barter. Soon the cons were coming to me with money that had been smuggled into the prison and buying articles they needed from me. I found out from a member of the Paint Gang that one of their guards if approached right would bring in contraband articles from outside. I ask him what his end was and he told me the guard took half and all he wanted was a first look at any Pornographic Books the guard brought in. I wasn't into Pornographic Books, but when I told him that he shrugged his shoulders and said.

"I guess we don't have a deal then."

"Wait a minute. I didn't say that did I?"

I knew that without him, I wouldn't make the connection I also knew I had the money and he didn't.

The prison supplied most of the basic necessities. I had plenty to read and enough money in my canteen fund to get what I needed as far as confectionary items were concerned. I also had to be careful, because I could only hide a very small quantity of contraband in my sparse cell. We were subject to the occasional search of our cells by the guards and I didn't want to lose any of my hard earned good time (good time was earned for good behaviour.) Magazines, Shaving Soap Toilet Soap, and Tailor Made Cigarettes were prime contraband. What I was interested in was the better brands and not the institutional issue. The Magazines never changed. Taylor made cigarettes were available in the Canteen but were just too expensive, and didn't last as long as the McDonalds roll your own tobacco. A Package of Tailor Made given away to the right people could get you what you needed from the department he worked in, Pressed Clothes, New Shoes, and even a little extra food from the Kitchen.

I found out later after I'd been using the con from the Paint Gang for a while that he was a Sexual Deviate who was doing four years for rape. He had flagged down a woman Taxi Driver in Vancouver and asked her to take him to an empty house. When they arrived he lured her inside by telling her he was a little short on the fair and could she come in for a minute. As soon as she stepped through the door he grabbed her, beat her senseless and raped her. She gave an excellent description to the police, who alerted all the taxi companies in town, and it wasn't long before he tried it again and got caught. After a while I began to be sorry I had to use him as ago between with the guard, and I needed a good excuse to break it off. The reason for this was for every so called legitimate item I ordered from outside he was making his own orders for Pornographic Material and was getting a reputation as a connection by the cons as a source of this sexual fantasy material. Fortunately a little scam being worked by the drug addicts to get one of the guards to bring in heroin went wrong.

One of the Trades Instructors for the Carpenter School was also engaged in smuggling articles for some of the cons and one of them decided he could get him to bring in some dope by threatening to expose him as a smuggler of contraband to the warden. He had been working at the prison for years, and exposure would have meant instant dismissal, loss of his cheap housing in the Officers Town House complex just outside the prison walls and his pension would probably be forfeited. Like a damn fool that he was, he broke down and agreed to do it, thereby putting his life in the hands of some of the meanest and unimaginably vicious people that he could ever know.

He was told where to go and who to get in touch with. Unknown to the cons in the Penitentiary the people who they were sending their sucker to were under surveillance by the police. When he arrived the next day for work he was asked to go up to the Administration Office where he was met by the R.C.M.P. who searched him and found the heroin. He was immediately charged with possession of heroin for the purpose of trafficking. I later learned he was convicted and sentenced to nine and a half years to be served at a Penitentiary down east in New Brunswick. The cons responsible for his down fall denied everything and as there was no cooperating evidence he was let off with a reprimand by the warden, and sent to work in the dome as a cleaner. I heard later on he had asked for a transfer to another Penitentiary down east because of his inability to get even the smallest of privileges from the prisons management and their constant harassment in regards to prison rules. His request was denied.

A new programme was opened up after I had served about two years. Anybody who could get a musical instrument sent in from outside, and had a reasonable good behaviour record, could go to the Protestant Chapel in the afternoon and teach themselves how to play. This was done from Monday to Friday. Weekends and holidays were omitted. When I learned of this, I wrote a letter to Mom and ask her to speak to Bill Scott about letting her buy me a Clarinet cheap from his second hand shop. A month went by and I was told to report to the Chapel in the afternoon for the music programme. When I arrived I reported to the guard who was in charge of the programme. He handed me an Old Battered Clarinet Case. I eagerly opened it and found a Metal Clarinet it was obviously a beginner's instrument from some school programme. There was a Beginners Book on how to play it called the E.Z.Y. to the B flat Clarinet. In a small compartment in the case was a packet of Clarinet Reeds. I had seen a Clarinet before. Billy my brother was learning how to play one in school, and occasionally brought it home for practice. I had never seen a metal one and I was a little surprised that I had received something that wasn't black and made of ebony or plastic.

The guard who was in charge of the group was one of the better screws in the place. He did the best he could about getting repairs for the instruments, and buying any necessary equipment the cons ask for. There was no money allotted for the program, if you wanted anything you had to have money of your own on account in the prison, or relatives willing to help you out with funds.

"Do you know how to play that thing?"

The guard ask.

"No, but I got a book on it," I said.

"Okay, pick yourself a spot and get started," he said, with a smile.

I looked around and saw several cons playing a variety of instruments scattered around the church. There was a couple of Accordions several Saxophones and Guitars, a Piano which belonged to the prison, and a set of Drums. I didn't see anybody playing a Clarinet, so I picked out a pew and sat down and started reading my book.

After about six months I wrote home and ask for a better Clarinet and Bill Scott came through again, and sent me a quality Clarinet which had been made in France. It was second hand but in good condition and had a far better tone than the metal one.

As time went by, I learned the basic fundamentals of Clarinet playing, and how to read music. The group had picked up another Clarinet Student and a couple of Trumpet Players. But a most important new acquisition was a man who could compose music for a small band which was composed of mostly dope addicts and pushers with the occasional burglar and armed robber like myself. The band leader couldn't play an instrument because he only had one arm. I never did find out how he lost it. He wrote simple Dixie land pieces for us, but mostly arrangements of old classics like, Dark Town Strutter's Ball, or when the Saints Came Marching in. To start with we were terrible, but after a few months, we could beat out a tune fairly well. The leader was a volatile man with a nasty temper, and at first there was the occasional fight between him and individual band members on how a piece was being played.

There was one instant where hot words were exchanged and he slapped one of the trumpet players across the mouth. Before he could retaliate a small knife was at his throat and he was being told if he moved he would have his throat cut. The guard was at the other end of the church and didn't see what was going on. I don't know how he could have missed it. The voices of the two combatants were at a screaming pitch as well as the other members of the group trying to calm them down. Finally after what seemed like an eternity, someone said.

"Put the stupid knife down you're going to screw it up for everybody here,"

The leader quickly glanced around at all the hard eyes staring at him and the knife disappeared as quickly as it had arrived. It was not to soon either. The guard's voice broke into the urgent conversation.

"What's going on here?"

"Nothing," the leader said ingratiatingly smiling at the guard, just a little misunderstanding that's all."

The guard stared intently at us for a minute, and sensed the tension in the air, and wasn't fooled by the weak attempt at cajoling him into thinking everything was all right.

"All right, break it up and go back to individual practice for the rest of the session," he said.

There were a few moans of disgust as they picked up their gear and wandered off to practice by themselves because we all enjoyed playing in our little group together. All in all the above incidents were few and far between. As well as the band a Dixie land group was organized and I was asked to play the Clarinet. The group consisted of a Trumpet, Trombone, Clarinet and Drums.

One of the sporting activities allowed in the yard was boxing, and some of the cons got together and with permission from the warden organized a boxing tournament to be held in the dome. Our Dixie Land group was asked to perform during intermission. The leader wrote some arrangements for standard Dixie Land favorites and after a little practice we didn't sound too bad so we agreed to do it.

The ring was set up in the middle of the dome and the cons brought out their chairs from their cells and sat wherever they could find space. Our group was situated in the corner of the third tier deck overlooking the dome. When the intermission came around the ring announcer, who was a con announced that we were going to play, and introduced us by name. I was nervous at the start. By the time he was finished, I didn't think I could play a note. Each one of us had a short solo section we were required to play, if it wasn't for this I wouldn't have worried about my performance so much. A missed note here and there when you're playing as a group would hardly be noticed by a bunch of worked up cons at a boxing match.

Our one armed leader was there to start the beat and we got away to a rousing rendition of" When the Saints Come Marching In." To my amazement a great roar of approval came up from the four or five hundred cons. This lifted my spirits and I wasn't nervous anymore. I played my solo as loud and vigorously as I could, and when the Trumpeter cut into his section to my surprise I was given an enthusiastic round of applause. The

Trumpet Player and Trombonist were better musicians than I was by far, and I'm sure that the success of our efforts was due to them. When the match was over we serenaded the cons back to their cells with a rousing rendition of Dark Town Strutter's Ball. I could see them yelling and singing in time to the music, which gave me a great lift and dispelled my fears of making a mess of it entirely.

One of the cons approached me in the yard one day and told me he was being sent to help establish a new Minimum Security Prison on Vancouver Island. He had done quite a bit of time and I figured he was being slowly prepared for release. I congratulated him and suggested this might be a good thing. Only a few cons had done more time than him, a few murderers and Habitual Criminals. He was doing life for murder, and as far as I knew he was the only con going with that length of sentence to a Minimum security prison. Later I found out that they had combed the records for prisoners with past construction ability, and good behaviour records.

The prison was situated on a peninsula of land which jutted out into the Strait of Juan de Fuca, and was surrounded on three sides by water. There were some old wooden and stone buildings still there, the remains of a Government Fumigation and Isolation Station. Ships that had passengers with communicable diseases were sent there to be fumigated. There was a small hospital building where the patients were kept who had Typhoid etc. A large dock was situated on the lee ward side of the peninsula, and the remains of an old Leper Colony. Various other smaller buildings were scattered about. These buildings were to be renovated into dormitories and workshops, for the future transfer of prisoners from the main Penitentiary in New Westminster to relieve the overcrowding. When I heard about this I was pleased and excited. I might be able to get a transfer after a few years and move to a better environment.

In a few weeks Frank the kid who was the first accused murderer was back in the Penitentiary for trying to escape. He had just walked away from the prison because there were no fences or bars to keep him in. They had not been installed yet. He walked up to the front door of a house not too far away from the prison and gave himself up to the occupants who put him in the bathroom until the Mounties arrived to take him back to the prison. I don't know what went wrong, but something caused him to bolt for freedom, and then to just give himself up to be sent back to a small cell and the monotony of a completely controlled life. I just put it down to be that he was completely institutionalized and couldn't stand the responsibility of a little less organized existence. I ignored the suspicion in my mind and applied for a transfer anyway.

CHAPTER 11

Williams Head Medium Security Penitentiary

Back to the Maximum Security Pententiary

A Few Escapes that Didn't Last Long

A Few More Incidences and My Final Parole

It wasn't long before my transfer was approved, and I arrived at what was called William Head Minimum Security Penitentiary. There were a few long timers with me. A drug trafficker doing twenty years for attempted murder and another man doing fifteen years for bank robbery, who had also beat a charge for murder when his girl-friends best friend was found in a ditch with several bullets in his body.

There was little formality about our arrival. We were assigned sleeping quarters, and the following day work assignments. I was given a job as a helper in the kitchen which consisted of delivering the food to the dining hall and serving the prisoners when they filed by with their food trays. My bed consisted of the bottom half of a double decker bunk in a dormitory situated in an old red brick building shaped like a war time H. hut One Dining Hall and three dormitories in the wings. The center section was the kitchen and a room with benches and a television set. The building was two stories high with four rooms in the top floor. These rooms held about four single beds a piece which gave the appearance of being a little more comfortable. They also had individual washrooms while the dormitories each had wash rooms, but a far greater number of cons used them. One advantage over the main Penitentiary was you could use the showers in the evenings and weekends whenever you wanted.

The job of dishing out food to the cons as they filed by was terrible. As in every situation in life when you deal with a group of people there is always a few who are never satisfied, and are looking for trouble. One young half breed Indian would come down the line and when I served him he was never satisfied with the amount.

"Come on ass hole it's not your food you know." He'd say.

I never replied because there was always a guard standing nearby watching for any real trouble. I knew it wouldn't make much of a difference if I countered with a threat, because the only thing he would understand was physical violence, and if I did that I would be the big looser so I left him alone. Fortunately I only had to tolerate the food line for about a week when I was called to the administration offices. The warden and another guard who was wearing a crown on his sleeve designating him as a supervisor or an instructor were waiting for me.

"Were trying to organize a school of drafting and basic engineering," the warden said. "This is the officer who is going to be the instructor." I nodded in his direction at the same time trying to size him up. He had a neat clipped mustache and I guessed he was approximately fifty years old. He was wearing some campaign ribbons from the Second World War on his chest. I thought another army type, good at throwing his weight around and nothing else.

"I see in your record that you can type," the Warden said.

"Yeah," I replied.

"Good you will report to this officer in the morning, and act as his secretary until further notice," the Warden ordered.

"Where's the school?" I asked.

"It's in the last building out on the point," he replied.

Kazoonie

I was to find out later that the guard had been an officer in the British core of Engineers during the Second World War.

"I'll fill you in on your duties tomorrow." He said.

The next day I wandered out to the point and entered a wooden single story building. There were two class rooms separated by a smaller room which was being used as an office. As you entered the front door there was a room about the size of the office as well.

I spent the next few weeks typing up requisitions for Gardiner which is the name I'll give him for the rest of this narrative. Gardiner was trying to set up a budget, and organize a school curriculum for his new students. It wasn't long before I realized there was something wrong with William Head. There seemed to be a favouritism given to prisoners, particularly the ones who had been there a little while. In the middle of the prison grounds was a dormitory which was new and had individual rooms which were set up much more comfortable than the abominable conditions of the old dormitory. Each convict had his own room which was set up with adequate shelving and cupboards and painted in pleasant pastel colours. Even the eating arrangement was different you could eat in your own room if you wanted to. I felt the cons were being played against each other for the privilege of getting out of the dormitory and into this much more comfortable facility.

I enjoyed the sea air and the quiet walks around the peninsula on my time off during weekends and during the evenings in the summer.

Nobody was allowed out after dark so we were all confined to our crowded barracks with very little to do. No more than we had at the main penitentiary. The worst of it was we had no privacy at all where at least in your penitentiary cell you could with draw away from being disturbed by anyone. The only interruption was the passing by of the night watch every hour on the hour like clockwork. Here in the barracks there was a constant din of noise going on. Occasionally a fight would break out over some petty annoyance and for a few minutes the monotony would be broken.

I found soon after my arrival that nobody was interested in the hustle for material things. There wasn't any Shoe Shop to make new shoes, just a repair shop with two cons keeping shoes wearable. There was no Tailor Shop at all so nobody seemed to be interested in hustling to improve their appearance at all. Those who were interested in fishing, and had managed to get some fishing tackle, could fish of the dock or shore for a variety of fish, and some were fairly successful.

I wasn't the only con assigned to Gardiners so called Drafting School. There was also Jim who was doing fifteen for Bank Robbery. At the time of his transfer to William Head he was trying to get a High School Education through the British Columbia Correspondence School Branch. For as long as I had known him which was at least four years he had never let very much get in the way of his doing these courses. He had angled and applied only for jobs that gave him the time he needed. He couldn't do his courses while working in the Tailor shop. So he had got management to send him to the Tool shed in the Carpenter Shop, where all he had to do was hand out tools between course assignments. This fit into his requirements nicely. While he worked with me at Williams Head especially during the time setting the school up, he didn't have much to do. He couldn't type and there wasn't any equipment purchased so he just spent his time at his assigned table and worked on his correspondence courses. Later on he ran the camera for educational films and learned how to print large blue prints on presses Gardiner had scrounged from somewhere. I learned years later that he had managed to completely educate himself.

I was typing requisitions out constantly, making ten or twelve copies of each request all day long. This went on for several weeks. During this time nothing changed, and no equipment arrived. Gardiner had changed and was getting impatient for I'm sure he wanted to get his programme off to a good start, but the usual red tape was holding things up. He was working on something at his desk one day, and I was pounding away at my typewriter producing the endless requests for the elusive equipment, when I ran into some problems on form layout so I ask him what I should do. He was bent over, intently studying some papers and he just ignored me. So I ask him again. He suddenly looked up with an angry look on his face.

"Will you shut up?" he snapped.

I was completely taken by surprise. Up until this time we had had a good relationship. I had co-operated with him in everything he had wanted me to do. Arriving for work early, and going back to the dorm late, and I was just as tired of it as he was. This verbal attack was uncalled for and it put me and him back in our proper places. Convict and Prison guard.

I got up from my desk quietly and looked over at Jim who was staring at me intently, but he made no effort to say anything to ease the situation. I walked towards Gardiner's desk. He sat there watching me come toward him slowly. I could feel the anger and frustration in every fibre of my being. His face changed an expression of anger to one of wide eyed fear. I think he thought I was going to attack him. I stood over him staring with my eyes narrowed to slits into his face.

"You bastard who do you think you're talking to? I worked hard for you, and when I ask a question I get shut up for an answer, Bull Shit." I growled at him.

"Get yourself another secretary I'm not working for you anymore."

He didn't respond, just sat there gripping the edge of the desk with both hands.

"I'll be getting out of here one day, and if I see you on the street I'll have your ass." With that I turned and walked out of the building. He still hadn't said a word to me, and when I glanced back he was still sitting there staring straight ahead.

I knew I was in trouble, and I would be crimed for my insubordination, but I didn't give a damn. The whole thing had brought me back to earth, and made me realize that I was just another con which I had forgotten for a while. William Head as a rehabilitation center was just a joke, another long line of nonsense. Now I realized what had happened to Frank. He had probably fallen into the deceit that we were human beings and then yanked back into his cage, and scolded, reminding him that we were still animals after all.

I walked into the dormitory and lay down on my bunk and waited for the guard who would take me to administration for my inevitable scolding and punishment. As sure as hell a guard appeared in about a half hour and escorted me to the Wardens Office. There was no sign of Gardiner. The Warden was all congeniality.

"Well now, what seems to be the trouble?" I understand you don't want to work anymore."

"No I never said I wouldn't work anymore, I just won't work for that ass hole Gardiner."

His face reddened slightly at my slanderous reference to Gardiner.

"I don't like it here, I have the feeling, that were all being played against each other and it's all a big con game. I want a transfer back to the Penitentiary where I know exactly where I stand."

The Warden stared at me for a few minutes as if he was surprised at my outburst.

"You will work around the grounds until I can give your request further consideration. You're dismissed." He mumbled.

I was escorted back to the Dorm, and told to remain inside. I was to report to the duty officer in the morning. I couldn't believe how lucky I had been. Back at the New Westminster Penitentiary I would have lost good time, and been thrown into the hole on bread and water for at least a week for what I had done. Insubordination and refusing to work, was a very serious offence, not to mention threatening an officer. I think what had saved me from a more severe punishment was my prison record. I hadn't been in any real trouble for five years, and I was on top of the pay scale. If I was suddenly punished severely for my transgressions, and sent back to the Penitentiary right away it wouldn't look good on their so called rehabilitation record, so shortly after what had happened to Frank.

The next morning, I reported to the duty officer in the dorm, who just happened to be Tom Craycroft. Tom and I had been friends for years. I went to school with him. My mother and his were the best of friends. I had seen Tom at the New Westminster Penitentiary during what I assumed was his orientation period. I had said "hello," and informally called him Tom which he acknowledged. I didn't go out of my way to approach him, because I knew we were as far apart as any two people could get. I only addressed him, out of our passed friendship as two kids on the street, and when I had too.

"Good morning Tom," I said making sure nobody was in hearing distance in case the wrong Idea was assumed by the cons or even the other prison guards. He looked at me with a cold expression on his face and said very softly so nobody could over hear.

"Don't call me Tom."

I was instantly jolted into reality by the tone of his voice. I could feel the dislike for me in its tone. I just stood there slowly rocking on the balls of my feet the blood rushed to my face in anger. I felt like making him eat his words. But I realized it was a losing cause, so I just smiled into his face and said quietly.

"Sure Tom."

I was expecting an immediate reprimand, but I guess he realized I would never call him anything else. Mr. Craycroft or sir was simply out of the question. He just didn't deserve it from me. I knew him to well. At that moment I had decided I would never address him by any kind of name again. He also decided by the look on his face, that to push the issue would be futile, and snapped at me.

"What is it?"

The exasperation in his voice was apparent.

"I was told to report to you for assignment to the grounds keeper," I said, still grinning at him coldly. He looked at a list he had on his clip board, and pointed over to another young con, coming down the hall. "You go with Stevens over there he'll tell you what to do." Without a word I walked away from him and never spoke to him again.

"I've been transferred to the grounds, Craycroft told me to go with you."

Stevens looked a little surprised when I told him I was being transferred.

"What the hell is going on?" he asked.

I told him about the events leading up to my quitting my job, and asking for a transfer out of there.

"You know I've only got six months left on a deuce. If I wasn't so short, I'd go back to the joint too," he said. "This place is really chicken shit."

I had noticed Stevens wandering around the grounds, but I had made a point of avoiding him, because he was the embodiment of the punks I used to know on the Kazoonie tier. A wise cracking hustler, but I didn't care any ambition or desire to work had left me. I just wasn't interested. I had a good partner for doing nothing, and he was an expert at it. The next couple of weeks, I puttered about the grounds, doing menial tasks, like raking leafs and cleaning up the green house.

In the evening everyone was confined to their quarters. Card games and watching television in the television room was the main activity for the prisoners until lights out. One evening I was in the television room watching the fights. Sitting in front of me was the obnoxious half breed as loud and stupid as ever. I noticed another inmate who had the reputation of not standing for any nonsense from other inmates at all, and at any perceived offense he would wait his chance and ambush you when you were least expecting it, and you usually wound up badly beaten up if you weren't on your guard. He quietly walked down the row of seats in front of me and sat down beside his quarry. The lights were out and the place was dimly lit by the television set. When the next commercial started on the set he suddenly grabbed the Half Breed around the neck in a strangle hold with one arm and proceeded to beat him unmercifully around the face with his other fist. It all happened so fast that the Half Breed was unconscious and bleeding from the nose and mouth before he knew what hit him. The brief scuffle was hardly noticed over the din of the boxing match on the set. The cons to the right and left of the combatants quietly got up and filed out of the room. I noticed nobody came to his aid. He was not worth the trouble, and it was obvious he had given the wrong person a bad time and paid the price for it. I got up and left the room. I waited outside in the hall a few minutes to see what would happen and in no time at all the Half Breed came out with his head tilted back and blood dripping from his nose onto his prison shirt. One of his eyes was swollen shut and he was a pretty sorry sight to behold. I grinned at him, and walked away without saying a word. Later in the month I witnessed two more fights in my dormitory one of them was an ambush by the con who took out the Half Breed, evidently he didn't like the captain of his soccer team giving him a bad time over some play that had went wrong on the field. The results were the same. The other fight was between the occupants of a double bunk, the lower occupant didn't like the upper occupant's descending methods and finally the whole stupid thing blew up into a toe to toe slugging match. For a while it was interesting, because they both had some fighting skills, but soon a guard came in and broke it up, and took them away for a reprimand. Nothing more came of it.

Finally one morning I was told to pack up my gear and get ready to be transferred back to the Penitentiary in the afternoon. I was just as pleased to be going back as I was when I arrived. At least I would know exactly where I stood. And I would have the quiet and privacy of my cell only the walk by of the guard every hour.

I was loaded into the back of a van, and driven out to the ferry. On my arrival at the mainland, I was met by another van, and driven to the Penitentiary. The guards were surprised to see me coming back because there hadn't been any voluntary requests to come back up until now. When they ask me why, I told them I thought it was a Chicken Shit place, and as far as I was concerned I didn't want any part of it. The hard line guards smiled at this reply, and nodded their heads in agreement, but didn't agree verbally. The dedicated reform minded types didn't say anything but I could see they weren't very happy with me for not going along with their experimental programme. The cons didn't say anything to me at all, just whispered amongst them-selves.

To my surprise, I was sent back to my old cell in B7 next door to the con who had accused me of being a stool pigeon. It was like I had never left. In the morning I reported to the Dome Supervisor, and was put to work sweeping one of the tiers. After a few days I was called out of line going for breakfast, and told to report to the Kitchen Office on my way to work. I didn't really care if I worked in the kitchen or not, except it was a chance to get my hands on some extra food.

The kitchen was on the first floor directly below the Protestant Chapel. The Administrative Office was situated high up on the right wall as you entered. You had to climb a flight of stairs to gain access to the office which consisted of two rooms. One wall had a row of large windows which allowed the guards a clear field of vision of most of the working area. The first room contained a few filing cabinets and two desks. One was equipped with a type writer. The other room was the office of the senior administrator of the kitchen. The back of the kitchen consisted mostly of the Bake Shop and ovens. Along the left side were the Kitchen ranges and the front wall contained the tray lines. The center held the usual equipment needed to run a large institutional kitchen. Under the offices was a room containing a couple of showers which the cons could use when they had time, In the basement was the Storage Area, and the Butcher Shop and the docking and Loading area for trucks bringing in the supply's.

The Kitchen on the whole was an efficiently run part of the prison feeding approximately 700 prisoners three meals a day, with the farm and piggery at the back of the prison supplying meat and vegetables to augment the kitchen larder.

The Taylor Shop and Shoe Shop producing shoes and clothing and the entire maintenance of the prison being performed by the prisoners the whole prison was self-sufficient.

I was directed up to the Kitchen Offices and introduced to the Kitchen Supervisor. A tall balding man who took me out to the first office and introduced me to the Kitchen Clerk, who was a guard who didn't participate in much security work, except to help supervise and line us up for the count when coming, and going in the morning and at lunch time, and in the evening when the night lock up was being done. He spent most of his time doing clerical work in the office than being a turn Key. He was a quiet young man who I was to find to be very easy to get along with. My job was to be the best position I had held in prison as far as work was concerned yet. All they wanted me to do was type up the Kitchen Menu for the day, making a copy for each department in the Kitchen. I also had to type up a few recipes from time to time to break the boring routine of the same thing every day during the week. This took me about a half hour in the morning, and the rest of the time I spent wandering around the kitchen scrounging extra milk, and the occasional goody from the bakery. During my stay in the kitchen, I put on an extra twenty pounds of weight, and I had to work at keeping it down out in the exercise yard, so I was playing a lot of hand ball and volley ball. In the kitchen we were issued two changes of clothes a week and allowed to shower whenever we could fit it in. Hygiene was practised because of the area as best we could. To bath whenever we wanted was a very welcome privilege. Any extra food I could get on my tray at night I gave to the Cons in the cells to the left and right of me, which they appreciated. Extra milk and the occasional juice broke the monotony of Prison diet.

I found out from the con on my left who was called Hansen that he was doing six years for manslaughter. We were let out of our cells on Saturday morning so we could take showers, and the ones who were waiting their turns would lounge against the tier railing and tell tall stories, or just gaze out of the window over the wall at the traffic on the Frazer River spread out before them and dream nostalgically of the past.

"I hear you're from Victoria."

A quiet voice broke my reverie. I found a tall slim con with a few pock marks on his face leaning on the rail next to me.

"Yeah, I lived there all my life," I said.

"I was stationed there when I was in the navy." He volunteered.

"How much time you doing?" He asked.

"Double sawbuck," I said.

"Phew," he whistled between his teeth. "You kill somebody?" he asked.

"No just robbed a bank."

"Oh, he nodded knowingly. "I only got six years for killing a guy. It's really murder taking banks these days."

He laughed, and began to talk more freely when he found out I was receptive to his conversation.

"I was invited to a party at this guy's house. I had a few drinks and dosed of, when I woke up, the party was over, and I found this guy trying to get into my pants. He made me so mad I strangled him with his tie." He laughed, and said he won't be doing that again. I guess the judge didn't like faggots either." I used to be in business with a guy in Penticton. I left town for a few days, and he cheated me out of my share. I knew he walked to work every day through the woods, so I took my hunting rifle and laid in wait for him along the route he took. I figured if I shot him in the head the bullet would go right through, and they wouldn't be able to match it up with my gun. Well it was a nice hot sunny day and while I was laying there alongside the trail I fell asleep. The local game warden was out doing his rounds and found me there. He stepped on my rifle so I couldn't bring it to bear on him. He asked me what I was doing out there at that time of the morning with a loaded gun. It wasn't hunting season. I told him I was just doing a little target practice and fell asleep before I could get started. He didn't believe me because he confiscated the gun. It took me a week to get it back. That bastard partner of mine doesn't know how lucky he was." He chuckled over the memory of it. "I couldn't kill him now because the Game Warden would be sure to remember me on the trail with the rifle."

He actually looked disappointed that he hadn't been able to get his revenge, and he stood there for a moment shaking his head as he remembered his bad luck. I thought to myself this guy is very dangerous. It wasn't so much that he had deliberately planned to murder someone in cold blood. It was the way he described it like he didn't see anything wrong with getting even at all. I immediately made up my mind that I wasn't going to get him mad at me in anyway shape or form besides he lived right next door. I found during the next two years he would turn out to be a quiet friendly person who minded his own business. You would never have believed that he was a cold blooded killer at all. There were other inmates who had this cold detachment about them in regards to human suffering. Some of them were serving time for terrible crimes and never showed any compassion towards their victims at all when talking about it. One of these was the drug trafficker who was at William Head with me. I was playing on the same Volley ball team as him, and when one of the players on the team badly twisted his ankle and couldn't play or even walk, had to be carried off the court in considerable pain, the trafficker was very upset that this punk had ruined his game, and he couldn't get a replacement player right away. For a moment I thought he was going to start kicking him when he was down. His whole demeanor was as cold as ice, no sympathy at all he just walked over to him as he lay on the court and very quietly began to berate him.

"Get up, Ass Hole, if you can't play, get somebody who can, you're ruining my game."

I thought for a moment he was going to kill him. Malevolence was written all over his face. He didn't care about the fact the man could have a broken ankle or at the very least a severe sprain. He was only interested in the delay his injury was causing to his game. Finally he stalked away in disgust. I thought I had better be very careful around this guy, and find a very good excuse for not playing on his team.

Along with the tough psychopaths, there were several weird types in the prison. One who comes to mind was Nicknamed Bladder Ass. He picked up this name by stealing a football bladder out of the equipment shed in the Exercise Yard and smuggling it back to his cell. He managed this because the old procedure of frisking the cons in the dome before they were returned to their cells had been discontinued. The reason I think was because of the huge prison population it would just take too long. Bladder Ass was some sort of a sexual deviate who stuffed the rubber bladder up his rectum and then tried to inflate it. Somehow it got stuck he couldn't just leave it there so he reported to the sick parade in the morning to get it removed. It wasn't long before everyone in the prison knew about it. He instantly became the butt of a hundred crude jokes such as, "Hey Bladder Ass what ya doing trying to float over the wall?" Those remarks didn't faze him a bit, he just wallowed in his knew found fame, and grinned vacuously. He probably had never had so much attention in his life. He was a really pitiful example of the short comings of the penal system.

There were several Transvestites, and aggressive homosexuals. One of the more famous was called Gloria. All the Transvestites were given names by the inmates. Gloria was more female than male in everything he did. He talked the cons in the Tailor Shop into making him female under wear. He even managed to get his hands on some women's makeup and appeared for morning breakfast parade wearing eye shadow and lip stick. The cons cheered loudly when he was dragged away for a cleanup and three days solitaire. He was constantly getting his hands on makeup after that, so the guards gave up and just made him wash it off in the morning before appearing for breakfast. He agreed to this and kept from being constantly thrown in the hole. Some of the homosexuals and sexual perverts were very aggressive and didn't think anything of propositioning anyone they took a fancy to. There were those who solicited there favors all the time. They made my flesh crawl, and I tried to avoid them whenever possible. Fortunately after a while they sensed I wasn't interested and left me alone.

A new gymnasium was built where the old exercise yard was situated alongside the East Wing. It was equipped with a stage and a projection booth for weekend movies, and was large enough to hold most of the inmates at one time. Inmate labour was used in its construction, and it wasn't long before two inmates escaped. During an evening exercise period they managed to get out of sight behind the stage, and remove a steel grill over one of the outside windows. They scaled the wall with the use of an electrical extension cord, which was strong enough to bear their weight. The cord had been hidden previously during the construction for just such a purpose.

The gun towers situated on each corner of the wall were not manned at night and there was no patrol around the inside grounds. These precautions were not needed after the day shift. In the days before the prisoners were let out to watch the T.V. in the domes and to use the Gymnasium. The small amount of freedom from their cells and the overcrowding provided the opportunity for the two Cons to disappear during these small lapses of security. Nobody noticed they were gone until the count, when you were back in your cell which was plenty of time to get away.

Another instance of the use of these lapses of time to escape was between the moving of several hundred convicts from the outside exercise yard back to their cells after a week end afternoon. A Con climbed into the chimney of the stone barbecue. He used some of the other inmates to screen his movements and crawled into the large barbecue pit and then up into the chimney. At the end of the exercise period the Convicts were herded back to their cells and counted. As soon as the yard was emptied, the guards in the gun towers would come down and leave the area unsecured. The con just came out of his hiding place and climbed over the chain link fence. The tops of these fences were lined with three or four rows of barbed wire which was not enough to prevent anybody from clearing these obstacles with a little effort. By the time the prison population was counted and it was determined that they were a prisoner short, and had counted again, the prisoner was well away from the prison. This prisoner was only doing three years, and he only had about a year left in his sentence. The trouble was he had received a letter from his girlfriend, telling him she had met someone else, and this had put him into a depression, and he was determined to get home to straighten his problems out. He was caught in downtown Vancouver shortly after his escape, and returned to the Penitentiary, which meant a stretch in solitary, and an additional amount added to his time for escaping custody, which is a criminal offence.

There were other escape attempts which failed before the prisoner could get out of prison. One of the inmates worked in the Automotive Department. Somehow he managed to smuggle a Pneumatic Jack into his cell. His cell was situated on the ground floor of B7 facing the Fish Tiers Exercise Yard. Due to overcrowding the prisoners with just a few months left in their sentences, or ones not considered high risks for escape were bunking on the lower landings of each cell block. The arrangement was similar to the H Huts. One night after lights out, he used the powerful jack to snap one of his cell bars. He was a small thin man so he managed to squeeze himself out through the hole and was proceeding to set the jack to bend the bars in the windows facing out onto the back yard where he could make his way to the wall and use a rope he had made to get over the wall to freedom. He had asked one of the Cons bunking on the landing to listen for the guard, who would be making his rounds, and to tell him when he heard him coming. But instead of being vigilant he spent more time worrying about the trouble he could be getting into and not enough doing his job. The guard suddenly appeared in the cage at the end of the tier, saw what was going on, and sounded the alarm. The jig was up.

It was this same Con who threatened to kill one of the prisoners at William Head, because he suspected him of being a Stool Pigeon for the Warden. The Stool Pigeon happened to be the painter who was the middle man for me, with the guard who was bringing in contraband for a cut of the money. He had been transferred to Williams Head before me, and had got assigned to the Paint Gang there. He had managed to ingratiate himself with the Wardens wife when he was painting there house. He had the best living quarters in the prison with plenty of privacy in a newer part of the prisons accommodations. It seems he was telling the Wardens Wife what was going on behind the scenes with the other prisoners. And when they found out they threatened to kill him. Four long term prisoners all of them drug traffickers. The group consisted of the Con who had attempted to escape with the Car Jack, and the one who demonstrated his utter disregard for the prisoner who injured himself on the Volley Ball Court, they were among the group returned for security reasons. They also returned the Stool Pigeon, who was thrown into a cell in the East Wing and assigned to the Janitor Gang in the dome. Here the guards could always keep him in sight and away from the cons who wanted to harm him. I learned he never went to the exercise yard or the evening entertainment time. He remained in his cell in constant fear for his life. Finally after a couple of weeks he was transferred to another Penitentiary in another province.

The total collapse of William Head's reputation as a veritable vacation establishment compared to the main prison was soon spread around amongst the cons and the applications for transfer fell to almost zero. The vast majority of the prisoners were from the mainland which of course made it easier for visitors and for the smuggling of dope and contraband. The failure of myself and the young lifer, and the three other prisoners to adapt to Williams Heads so called rehabilitation programme removed all the most well-known and the longest serving Cons there. So for a while the screening process became tougher, and most of the con's, who were transferred were serving less than ten years and had a lot more to lose if they screwed up.

As the years went by, William Head was to obtain the reputation as one of the best and easiest places to serve time, and long term prisoners from across the country vied for a chance to be transferred there to serve the remainder of their long term sentences.

Even though I had been sent back to the main prison, I was still allowed the top wage. Once a month I had to donate one day's pay to what is called the Inmate recreation fund. This fund was augmented by the sale of hobby articles to visitors, who attended the occasional bazaar, staged for the public in the guard's dining room. A percentage of each sale was donated to the fund. This fund paid for week end films and other pieces of equipment which made the Cons life a little easier.

Once a year an election was held, Inmates were allowed to campaign by word of mouth and the placing of posters around the prison walls. The successful candidates would represent the inmates by forming a committee and presenting suggestions to the Prison administration on the use of the prisoner's entertainment fund as well as the organization of sporting events. Once a year a track meet was held with a barbeque which was always a success, with approximately seven hundred prisoners donating to this fund it always had a balance for the occasional purchase of large pieces of equipment, such as a modern movie projector or a new television set. There were television sets in B7 and the Main Prison dome.

One evening the prisoners were let out of their cells to watch television in the domes and selected tiers were let into the Prison gymnasium to play badminton and other sports. Two of the worst Psychopath's had gotten together, and had planned an escape from the gymnasium. Somehow they managed to get through a door leading to the prisons inside yard, but ran into the guard who had been assigned to patrol the inside grounds after the first escape from the gym. This guard had a large German Shepherd Guard Dog on a long lead. He proceeded to force the pair back into the gym. As soon as they slammed the door into the dogs face they immediately pulled homemade knives and took the first prison guard they came across hostage. They herded him into a small room used as an office, put him into a chair, and held a knife to his throat. The minute the alarm was sounded the staff began trying to get the rest of the prisoners back to their cells. This not only consisted of the prisoners in the gymnasium, but all the prisoners watching television in the two domes.

The prisoner who was assigned to the Radio Room and had control of the intercom was one of the first cons to realize what was happening when several cons began shouting "Don't go back to your cells." He used the intercom to spread the message. There were at least four hundred men out of their cells. This included B7, as B7 was a separate cell block, a considerable distance away from the mounting disturbance in the main cell block, the prisoners did not realize what was happening, and merely grumbled when they were swiftly ushered back to their cells and locked up. The barred gates leading into B7 were quickly shut and locked, effectively sealing off most of the long term prisoners from the rest of the inmates. The H Huts, the East Wing and the North Wing were out of control in a matter of minutes. The regimentation and the monotony of spending eighteen hours a day in a cell five and half ft. wide by eleven ft. long broken only by a little television and athletics had brought the smoldering prison population to a boil, and the escape attempt was the fuse that had set the volcano off.

The few guards assigned to locking up the prisoners tried to obtain some order but quickly realized if they didn't get behind locked doors that they would be in peril for their lives, and they quickly retreated out of the prisoner's confinement area.

The Con in the Radio Room took over the intercom and began to tell the prisoners to not go back to their cells. He also advised everyone who was listening over their receivers what was happening.

The two so called escapers were still holding a knife to the Guards throat and threatening to kill him if they weren't granted immunity from punishment. They also wanted to immediately be transferred to another Federal Penitentiary back East.

While this was going on the Prisoners had begun to smash up their own cells and hurl trash from the landings to the floor below. The Canteen was broken into and looted. The Television Set in the dome was smashed. The frustrations of their miserable lot in life had risen to the surface and they went on a rampage.

Kazoonie

It wasn't long before some of the cons in B7 were infected by the excitement of what was happening in the main section of the prison, and began shouting encouragement to the other prisoners to smash up their cells and create as much disturbance as they could. Surprisingly, the majority of prisoners on B7 ignored the whole thing and did nothing.

B7 was built in sections, every two tiers were sealed into a unit and what was going on in one section couldn't reach another section, even if one section were out of their cells if the main door was closed, the disturbance couldn't carry over to any of the other sections. Nothing happened, and I think because of this B7 was spared what followed next. In what seemed like a very short time, we suddenly heard above the screams and smashing sounds coming from the main prison a dull thumping sound followed by the sounds of breaking glass. The voice of Beaver the Radio Man came on my receiver advising everybody to soak their towels in water and to place it over their nose and eyes to help ward of the effects of the tear gas. In the middle of his advice he was cut off, and I guessed someone threw the switch against his will. After a while the shouting died down, and I fell asleep.

In the morning when B7 was finally let out to pick up their breakfast trays, it was done in a very slow manner. Each tier was let out after the previous tier was back and locked up. The passage way between the kitchen and B7 still reeked of Tear Gas and the lower landings of the North & East Wings were littered with smashed cell Cupboards and torn paper which was soaked in water from broken sinks and toilets. By the time I had returned to my cell my eyes were stinging from the effects of the gas so I bathed them in cold water.

The ring leaders of the revolt were rounded up, and the prisoners in the lower tiers of B7 were moved and shuffled around to other parts of the prison so their cells could be used to confine the trouble makers. They weren't allowed to pick up their trays at the kitchen. The food was brought down to the tier and distributed to one prisoner at a time. They tried to keep their rebellion going by yelling and screaming for a couple of nights but the close confinement soon dampened their ardor, and after a few days they were released into the regular population and sent back to their regular cells and duties. It all happened quickly the opportunity to rebel came like a flash and ended in just a few hours. Nobody was seriously hurt and except for the canteen and personal items very little damage was accomplished. All that happened was the prisoners lost their canteen privileges until the unit could be restocked and their T.V. viewing until the sets could be replaced. B7 fared much better our privileges were restored more promptly because we had caused little or no damage at all. B7 confined the biggest percentage of long term prisoners. Amongst us lurked some of British Columbia's most dangerous men. The fact that the riot did not cause more property damage, and the fact nobody was killed was probably due to the quick confinement of these prisoners before the riot could spread, and that it was a spontaneous act and not planned. Some of the B7 prisoners were organizers and very intelligent men. Most of the middle men in the drug trade along with the few murderers, and armed robbers who were all doing more than ten years in prison were confined in B7.

The two cons who had accidently triggered the riot were talked into releasing the guard. The futility of their situation was apparent, and rather than be killed by the police or the prison guards they gave up and were thrown into solitary confinement. After a couple of weeks they were tried and convicted of attempted escape and an additional sentence was added to their time. They requested a transfer to another prison down east and it was granted.

In the years to follow after my release there were far more serious incidents causing considerable destruction and even a death, but this was after I was gone from the scene to never return.

Previously to the riot, I had decided to make my first attempt to obtain a parole. I had asked for an application form, and was waiting for the administration to bring it to my cell. After a few days a guard came by and pushed the envelope through the bars of my cell. The application was just a printed document with an area for requesting a parole, and an area asking me why I should be given one etc. I wrote that I had completed approximately six years of my sentence and I had some money given to me by my Mother. She had sold the property after my Step Father had died and the proceeds she was living on was coming to an end. When she went to apply for social assistants she was turned down because she still had two thousand dollars remaining in the bank. Apparently she had to be broke before she could obtain any assistance from the Government social Assistance Department. So she sent me a cheque for the remaining money in her Bank account. She then reapplied for help which was granted. I received a generous wind fall and she obtained a small steady income.

One bright sunny morning, I received an order from a guard in the Prison Kitchen to go down to one of the Prison Administration Offices, which were in a temporary Quonset hut just inside the front prison wall. I ask what for but the guard didn't know. He opened the kitchens back door, and I strolled down to the office enjoying the beautiful weather on the way. When I arrived I was ushered into the Senior Administrators Office. He told me to sit down and abruptly told me that the National Parole Board had granted my Parole Application, and I was to be released in the morning. It had been a month at least since I had made my application, and I had given up on getting out on the first try, thinking I had barely served a third of my sentence and I had been granted a parole in my first jolt, which I had violated. I was completely taken by surprise and my expression probably gave that away. The Administration Officer was staring at me with a look which said "You'll be back." He said with a sneer on his face.

"I hope I don't see you again."

I replied loud and clear.

"You Won't."

I got up without being dismissed, and walked out into the sunshine.

On the way back to the kitchen I thought I'm not going to have a new Suit or Shoes realizing that there was no time to make them. Besides I had a very good Suit and Shoes in storage so I didn't give a damn. I decided not to say anything about my pending release to anybody, they would find out soon enough, I figured I could do without the twenty questions. I had enough on my mind as it was, without the inevitable request to make phone calls etc. for a bunch of people I didn't even know.

When the bell rang in the morning, I just hung back while everyone filed out to work nobody even noticed I didn't follow. A guard came by to check the cells to see if everyone was out. When he questioned what I was doing there. I told him and he just nodded and left. A couple of hours went by and finally a guard came by and I picked up my meagre belongings which were the same things I was issued when I came in. The rest a few knick-knacks I had collected over the years, I put in the wall cupboard, and shut the door. The new occupant might find some use for them. I was rushed up to the Main Admittance area, given my old Suit and Shoes and told to get changed. I was then taken down to the main Admission Offices, and issued the money I had earned over the six years I had been incarcerated. I saw that the money I had had when I came in was there to. I signed for it and the guard took me through the front gate to a waiting car. During these events I never ask where I was going or inquired about what was happening, for years conversation with the guards was always at a minimum, and you knew you always did as you were told without an argument or you were punished, and so from day to day you never thought much about what was happening, you just did as you were told because it was all laid out for you, and it soon became an monotonous routine. The guard said he was going to take me into Vancouver because he had an errand to perform, and then he would take me to see a Parole Officer for further instruction. When we arrived at our first destination, the guard told me I could get out and stretch my legs, and he would be back in a minute. He walked away and entered a building across the street. It was the first time I had been left alone on the street in six years. I looked around and thought I was in an industrial area on the out skirts of Vancouver. I could have just walked away if I had wanted to, but I had too much to lose by doing that. In a few minutes the guard came back with a parcel, he threw it into the back of the car, and we continued on towards Vancouver. Eventually we arrived at our destination, a Government Building in Vancouver. I was taken in and escorted into an office and introduced to a young man who didn't bother introducing himself, he just smiled and handed me a brown envelope and a ticket for the bus to Victoria. He explained that I would be met at the ferry by my Parole Officer. He shook my hand and said

"Good luck."

I looked around for my escort and he was already gone. I stood there feeling rather surprised that they were allowing me to just walk away, and follow there instructions to the letter. I picked up the envelope and my Bus Ticket, and walked out on to the sidewalk. Then I remembered I had been to the Vancouver Bus Station several times in the past. I smiled to myself and my day brightened up. I thought smarten up, It's time you made some decisions for yourself. It wasn't long before I found my way to the station. I found out what time the bus left for Victoria, and I was on my way.

When I arrived at the Victoria Dock, I walked off the ship to the front pickup area, and stood waiting for my Parole Officer who I had never met. I assumed he had my file with a picture, so there wouldn't be any foul ups. A half an hour went by and nothing happened nobody arrived. I thought I had better phone the Parole Board Office. So I found a phone with a phone book, and gave them a call. A woman answered, and I explained who I was, and where I was. She sounded surprised, and worried. She explained that my Parole Officer "A Mr. Gaw," had gone to the Victoria Bus depot to pick me up. I told her that I was told I would be picked up at the ferry Terminal in Victoria. She said.

"Thank you for giving us a call. I'll get in touch with him, and tell him where you are. Don't move."

I thought "Jesus Christ here I am a fugitive all ready, Oh, well what's new." I picked out a seat in the reception area and sat down to wait. In about an hour, a tall man with light brown hair strolled into the room, and came directly over to me and introduced himself. I apologised for the mix up and he smiled, and said.

"These things happen, forget it."

When we got to his car he said he had to stop at his home for a minute before we went to his office. When we arrived at his house he ushered me into the kitchen.

"Take a seat I'll just be a minute." He said.

As he disappeared into the front part of the house, I sat down and noticed a large Cock a too Parrot in a cage which was on the Kitchen Counter. It was staring at me intensely, and I thought. That's all right fella I know how you must feel.

It was obvious the Bird Cage had not been moved for some time and not cleaned for even a longer time. The floor of the cage was covered in a thick coat of bird droppings which had over flowed on to the Kitchen counter. Amazingly the bird appeared perfectly healthy with a thick coat of feathers and a sharp eye. I felt the cage was far too small for a bird of that size, and I thought I hoped they don't do any food preparation on that counter. Just as I was thinking of trying to make friends with the bird Gaw came back and we continued into town to an office on Cook Street, where he opened the brown envelope which contained my parole papers. It was a document outlining the rules to be followed while I was on parole some of them are as follows.

While on parole, I was not to possess any fire Arms, or Explosives. I was not to associate or fraternize with any known felons. I must engage in finding employment, and when such employment was found I was not to quit without permission, and I was not allowed to get fired. I was not to leave Vancouver Island without permission. In short I was still in prison but without bars. Gaw told me to read the papers and when I was finished he ask me if I had any questions. I said I didn't and handed the papers back. He pushed them over to me and said.

"You keep them, and follow the instructions carefully, and you won't have any trouble from me."

I sat there looking at him for a minute, and I said.

"I'm guessing that you know this is not my first parole?"

And he said

"Yes I know that. What happened on your first parole?"

I thought he knows the administrations version, but he doesn't know mine, and it's good he's asking me. I told him about the other parole Officer and what I thought of him, and why, and I didn't want to have anything to do with him at all. I also told him I didn't want my family to have anything to do with my so called rehabilitation, because I didn't trust any of them.

Kazoonie

I was surprised when he said he agreed with me, and didn't go into a rage about me telling him what I wanted, which I knew the other Parole Officer would have done. I decided to go a little further and so I said.

"Look, I'll tell you everything I'm doing or have done, if you tell me everything that you're doing so I don't have any surprises, okay?"

He looked at me and thought it over for a minute, and said.

"All right that sounds all right to me. Well it's getting late, and this short notice they've given me has left me a little unprepared for your accommodation for the night. Come on."

We drove down town, towards the inner harbor. We didn't talk too much I just gazed out the Car Window, and was surprised at the changes the town had made in six years. Finally we were coming up behind the Empress Hotel, Victoria's best and most famous luxury hotel at the time. Gaw said.

"We'll go into the drive in section of the Empress, and get you a room for the night."

I was completely taken aback by this, nobody but nobody I knew had ever stayed at the Empress, not even the drive in section.

"You're kidding?" I said completely surprised that the government would be footing the bill or even thinking of it. I laughed and said.

"Can you afford it?"

"Well the first night, yes the second night no." He chuckled.

"I'll pick you up at ten tomorrow."

The Motel Room was small, but it was furnished a little more high-end than other motel's I had been in. The linen was crisp and clean and the bed had a thick down filled cover on it, and I had the best night I had had in a long time.

The next day, Gaw arrived and picked me up, and we drove over to his office where he went over the conditions of parole again. I ask him about my money which my Mother had given me, and he explained that he would be hanging on to it for now, and I was not to worry about it until I was more established in the community. He told me I was going to stay in a boarding House on Fernwood Road and he would be paying the rent until I got a job. I didn't bother thanking him because I knew he was just doing his job. I was still reserving judgement about what was going on because it was too early to do otherwise. My first thoughts were about the previous officer and his open distrust of me and the other cons under his charge, and I kept trying to figure him out, and all I could get was a lot of unwarranted distrust on my part. I would just have to wait and see.

"Come on we'll go over to the Boarding House on Fernwood Road, and get you settled," he said.

When we arrived, I discovered it was a large older house run by an elderly woman who explained the rules, and showed me my room. The room was equipped with a double bed and a dresser with a mirror. There was a window facing the back yard. Gaw obviously had dealt with this woman before, and while I was looking the room over he engaged her in conversation which I couldn't hear. I assumed it was about me, and I left it at that.

While Gaw waited out in the car, she laid down the law about the rules of the house. I was to be at breakfast, dinner and supper at a set-time, and live in guests were not allowed in the kitchen or her living quarters during off hours without her permission without exception. The telephone was not to be used without permission, and distance calls were not allowed. I thanked her for renting me the room, and she just nodded her head without commenting.

I went out to the car and Gaw asked me if I was satisfied with the arrangement. I just said, "For now." I noticed we were in my old neighbourhood right across the street from the Victoria High School, and on a bus route which went right by the house. The location was just a few blocks from the house where I had spent all my younger years.

On the way back to town I realized I was wearing the only clothes I had and I needed to do some shopping. The money that was put in my account, and saved for six years would have to be spent on this to start. When we arrived back at his office, he told me the rest of the day was mine, and asked me what I was going to do. I told him about my lack of clothes and that I was going shopping. He ask me about money, and I told him about an income tax return I got back shortly after I had started doing my time, and the few bucks I had left over from my prison canteen fund, and how I thought if I was careful I could probably last for a couple of weeks. He laughed and said.

"Okay, be at my office tomorrow, and we'll start trying to find you a job."

I left, and proceeded down town to Eatons Department store on Douglas Street, and bought a couple of work shirts and some casual pants, and the usual toilet articles, soap etc. along with a heavy jacket. This took most of the afternoon, so I found the Fernwood Bus Stop and headed to my new home.

In the morning I woke up and washed in the bathroom down the hall from my room. I went down stairs to the kitchen, and found the Kitchen table laden with plenty of everything required for a very hearty breakfast. There were three other guests at the table. Two of them looked like young high school students, and the other was a young man probably in his twenties. I was to find out later that the youngest was a ward of the court and was only a twelve year old black female. Everything about her suggested she was much older, and wiser. The young boy was another ward of the court who by coincidence was the son of a man I had known for most of my younger years a surprising coincidence. It left me wondering what sort of bad luck he had had with his marriage etc. The young man had a strong European accent, and was employed as a painter, and was the friendliest of the group. I decided from the very start that it wasn't in my best interest to cultivate any friendships here, and proceeded to do just that.

The next day, I walked over to Gaw's Office to find out what my next move was to be, and he told me to go down to the Unemployment Office, and to get interviewed for any available jobs. When I arrived at the office, I remembered what my brother Alan used to say. (I'm going to the slave market today to see about a job.") I had been there on several occasions in the past, and had never been hired for anything. I really thought that this attempt would be a waste of time to.

When I arrived I approached the front desk, and was issued a slip with a number on it and told to wait to be called. When my turn came up I was greeted by a very friendly clerk. Who made me feel at ease, he ask me what sort of employment I was looking for, and I told him anything I could get, and that I was not trained for anything specific. I deliberately did not tell him about the jobs I was trained to do in the Pen. Because I knew I would be ask about where I was trained etc. and one lie leads to another and another lie until it comes out and the distrust sets in with your employer, and the circle keeps going around and never ends from one job to another. The clerk informed me that there wasn't anything available at that time but my name would be put on the list for anything in the future. I wasn't a bit surprised.

The next day I was back at the Parole Office to tell Gaw what had transpired at the Employment Office. He told me not to worry, and that he had a job waiting for me. He said he would pick me up in the morning and show me where it was. I ask him what I would be doing and he told me it was lathing an apartment building just off Hillside, and Cook. I told him that I didn't know anything about lathing and he said.

"That's okay, they'll teach you."

When we arrived I was introduced to a young guy who was the Foreman of the Subcontracting business. He had two other men working there along with himself. He ask me if I had ever done this type of work, and when I said no, he told me not to worry, and handed me an apron with pockets full of nails, and a hammer. I was told to follow him up the scaffolding that surrounded the outside of the building which was about six stories high. I noticed the other guys were tacking up rolls of black roofing paper along the walls, and then nailing up rolls of wire mesh on top to hold everything in place. He proceeded to give me a crash course in lathing and left me with one of the other guys to help out. It wasn't long before I was as good as he was and I realized that none of the help was really an expert except maybe the boss himself. I had already made my first big mistake. I had not asked what the conditions of my employment were such as wages, workman's compensation etc. Later on when I began to wonder when I was going to get paid. I asked the boss and he told me the contract was based on how many rolls of paper and wire we put up and this was calculated at the end of the job, and along with how many man hours put in he would be paid a lump sum of money to be distributed amongst his employees, and like the sucker I was I just nodded and said "Okay" and walked away.

I was on the job about two weeks, and working on the second floor, when a Concrete Truck which was unloading its cargo of cement on the first floor, finished and was beginning to drive clear of the building, when something protruding from the side of the truck caught onto something attached to the scaffold. The truck pulled the scaffold right out from beneath me and I plunged into a Sand Pile which was directly below me. I hit the sand feet first and twisted to one side when I rolled over, but the height of the drop, and my weight drove my lower legs into the sand, and when I twisted I badly wrenched one of my knees, so I could barely walk never mind climbing up a scaffold. In the meantime the truck stopped, the driver got out and inspected the damage, and looked his truck over. He spoke to somebody who looked like a Job Site Foreman got into his truck and drove away. Nobody paid any attention to me at all. I was leaning against the building when my boss came around the corner and ask me why I wasn't working. I told him what had happened and he looked around at the fallen scaffold, and asked me if I was all right. I said.

"No, I wasn't and because of my leg I wouldn't be able to finish the day."

He looked disgusted, and said "Okay, I'll see you tomorrow."

I could hardly make it down town to the Fernwood Bus Stop. I immediately phoned Gaw who was sympathetic, and asked whether I needed medical care. I said a couple of days of rest, and an elastic bandage, and I should be alright. He just said, "Keep in touch," and hung up. Three days later I returned to the job site and was put back to work. The knee was still uncomfortable but I managed alright. Unfortunately the job only lasted two more days, and I was out of work. The boss told us to meet him at a local hangout restaurant down town in a couple of days when he should have the proceeds of the job for distribution. We all agreed. The day arrived and I went to get my share. I walked in and immediately saw him sitting in a booth. As I approached him I noticed his shoes sticking out and I recognized them as prison issue, after all I had made enough of them. But to this day I don't remember him while I was in there. I sat down, noticed he seemed very nervous. He started talking about my hours on the job and how much wire and paper I had put up, and then he made some excuse about being shorted by the project management. I even found myself commiserating with him about what a bad deal he got. I ask him where the other guys were, and he said.

"They came early."

"Well can I get my share know?"

A real scared look came over his face but he reached into his pocket and pulled out a Twenty dollar bill, and pushed it across the table to me. I sat there for a minute, and then realized that I had been had. The son of a Bitch never intended to pay me my so called share at all. I could feel my face getting redder as my blood began to boil. I looked up and very quietly and said.

"Is that all? I worked hard for you for a good two weeks and you slip me a lousy Twenty Bucks, and besides that I even got hurt on the job, and I got nothing for that either."

He made an attempt to get up as if to leave. I said.

"Don't you bloody well move. I'm just at the point where I'm trying to decide whether your worth killing or not."

At that point I realized he had me over a barrel I couldn't do a damn thing. I was on parole, I couldn't exact vengeance on him at all I could only walk away, and report to Gaw that I had been taken by a slimy Bastard, and hope he would do something about it. I slowly stood up being as menacing as I could. I picked up the Twenty, and said.

"You will never know how lucky you are."

I then walked out of the restaurant, and headed straight to the Parole Office to see Gaw. He was sitting in his office when I came in. On my way over I had been thinking, and consequently I was getting madder and madder.

"What's the matter with you?" he said.

"Did you check up on that Ass Hole before you sent me to work for him?"

"Oh, so that's it." He said.

"He's wearing a pair of Prison Shoes, hell I might have made them."

Gaw stared at me for a minute, trying to figure what I was talking about. Then I explained about working in the Prison shoe Shop for a couple years. I said.

"Am I right about him being an ex con?"

"Yes your right."

"What was he doing time for?"

He said, "Child molestation."

I was thunder struck I couldn't believe what I was hearing, a baby molester, the worst and vilest creature on the face of the earth, as far as I was concerned

"Why didn't you tell me?"

"Because I knew I would get the same reaction I'm getting now and that can mean possible trouble for you," he said sternly.

"What's happened to the Parole Regulation "No fraternizing with people with prison records?"

"You needed a job didn't you?"

"Some job," I said.

I told him about how he cheated me out of a fair wage, and how I was injured on the job and received no Work Man's Compensation for it. He told me to put it behind me, and come back in a couple of days to see him about further work.

When I went back to see him, he took me out to a building site where they were building rows of town Houses. I was introduced to a tall young man who was foreman of an insulating and lathing team. He asked me if I had done that type of work before, and I told him just in lathing. He said he would show me around, and get me started in the morning.

I arrived on time and started on the lathing part of the job right away. After I had finished that part, I was shown how to do the other skills of the different disciplines of his team of six men. A few days into the job, I met the partner of my boss who came over to help speed up the job, and during the time I worked with him I noticed he was a very skilled tradesman, who pushed the men very hard on the job. Never a smile or a kind word just work, and more work.

After the first day on the job I spoke to the boss about my wages, and I learned I would be paid piece meal, which means so much for each roll of wire I put up and the same for each role of backing paper applied, and the same system for the bundles of insulation, and Plaster Board. I knew then if I was to make a decent wage I would have to develop speed, and skill in my work, and as the weeks went by I did that. I was told to give the foreman a list of what I put up and they would honor it every two weeks. I was careful to keep a duplicate copy of my list, and I found I was treated fairly by my boss. I never had to deal with anyone but the young man who hired me. One incidence when my boss couldn't cover my wages after I handed in my tally sheet. He told me to go over to his partner's house in the evening, and he would pay me. I said okay, and went to his home after supper. He invited me to come in to the kitchen, and have a seat while he made me out a cheque. When he handed me the cheque I pulled out my list, and noticed a big discrepancy right away. He had only paid me for half of what I had earned. When I pointed this out to him politely, and showed him my tally sheet he got really angry and started shouting about if I didn't like it we could go outside and have it out in the yard. I looked at him, and realized he hadn't realized that I had kept a duplicate sheet and he had been caught in a poor attempt to under pay me, I just looked at him and thought not again. I felt the usual anger and frustration but because I had been through this before I wasn't surprised. I thought I'll bluff him a bit. I said.

"Why go outside?" We can start right here, and maybe I'll smash up some of this nice furniture, and break a few windows at the same time."

He looked at me in surprise, and suddenly the young lady who was sitting nearby, and who I wasn't introduced to when I came in jumped up and yelled.

"This is my house and if you do that I'll call the police."

"Well do I get paid my wages or not?" I said.

Just at that moment the young boss arrived saw what was going on, and said to his partner while looking at me.

"He's the best worker we've ever had, and he earned his money. I think you should pay him."

Grumbling to himself he picked up the tally sheet did a quick count, and wrote out my check. I realized then that this bastard had been short changing his transient workers all the time and his partner knew all about it. I don't think he was part of the scheme because he had always been fair when he was paying my wages. This one incident came about because of the change in policy of finances. It occurred to me that it was a bit of a coincidence that his partner should show up and go to bat for me at just the right time. I grabbed my cheque, and walked out the front door.

The next day I checked in at the Parole Office and told Gaw what had happened, and he said.

"Don't worry about it. I have set up a meeting for you at the Royal Jubilee Hospital Personnel Office. It's for three o'clock in the afternoon.

"Do they know about me?" I ask.

"Yes they do, but don' worry about it, just act natural."

I said, "Okay," thinking about the last time I was interviewed for a job at the Veterans Hospital, and the verbal insults I had to take from them. I decided to be ready for them this time.

I showed up at the Hospital Personnel Department on time, and was ushered into a sparse office in a brown shingled building which looked like it was one of the buildings left from the original construction. Sitting behind the desk as I walked in was an attractive personable looking woman, who introduced herself as the Personnel Officer for the hospital.

The interview was short and most of the discussion was about my past criminal record. I kept my answers to her questions as short as I could because I didn't want to upset her too much. At the end of the interview she gave me what sounded like the old dismissal. ("Don't call us we'll call you.") When I got home I gave Gaw a call and told him about it. He said he'd look into it, and let me know. A couple of days went by and I received a call from Gaw telling me to report back to the Hospital Personnel Office the next day. I didn't ask why because I thought it was just a waste of time.

CHAPTER 12

Royal Jubilee Hospital
Work in the Kitchen
And as an Orderly on the Wards

When I arrived at the office I was greeted with a very friendly smile, and told that there was an opening in the kitchen as a Wagon Man. I ask what that was, and was told I would push Food Wagons to the different kitchens on each floor for distribution to the patients, and to keep them clean as well as helping with the cleaning of the main kitchens pots and pans with the disposal of the remaining perishable foods left over from the days cooking I smiled and said.

"I think I can handle a job like that."

"Fine, now we'll go over to the kitchen and I'll introduce you to the Head Dietician."

It was a uneventful meeting, and when it was over I was told to come in in the morning for an initial orientation on the job. I realized I was hired as a Wagon Man. What I didn't realize at the time was that this was not just a job It was going to be a career that would last almost thirty years.

After about a year on the job I became tired of the monotony of the job and decided to apply for a position in House Keeping, which had become open and paid ten dollars more a month, so I filled out an application and eventually was called for an interview.

On arriving at the House Keeping Office I was greeted by the House Keeping Manager, and his assistant who proceeded to ask me a series of questions designed to find out if I was a total idiot. For example, (If you were issued with nine mops how many mops would you need to service nine wards?) Another one was (who was the Mayor of Victoria?) which to this day I haven't been able to figure out what connection that had to House Keeping at the Jubilee Hospital.

After the interview was over, I went back to my job in the kitchen, and waited for an answer. After a week the Manager from Housekeeping came to see me, and told me I had not got the job. When I ask him why not he said I was too smart, and I wouldn't stay. Then he suggested I apply for an Orderlies job. I ask him who I should see, and he suggested I go to see a Mr. Bows who was the Head Orderly, and his office was on the third floor of Center Block.

The Wagon Men had two hours free time in the afternoon before they returned to work during the supper period. So during that time I went up and found Mr. Bows in his office, and he said he had a few minutes to talk to me, and to sit down. I pulled up a chair, and told him what I was there for and I had two hours in the afternoon which I could be trained in. He asked me if I had any previous experience and I said no, but I was willing to learn with no pay expected. He said he would take the matter up with the Director of Nursing, and get back to me. I thanked him for his time, and went back to the kitchen. Several weeks went by, and to my surprise Mr. Bows showed up at the Wagon room, and told me if I was still interested to come to his office the next day and he would get me started. I thought great a step up on the job. The next day I arrived at his office. And he gave me several manuals on what is required to be a good Orderly. He said.

"When you memorize this come back, and I'll be training you on the job."

It took me a good couple of weeks to get through all the information he provided on Catheterization bathing, enemas etc. I had no idea the job was going to require a lot of hands on work with the actual patient's

Kazoonie

When I felt I was ready. I showed up, at Mr. Bows Office. He said.

"Well come on there has been a death in the Emergency Department and the body has to be prepared for the Morgue. I might as well start you off the hard way."

I nodded, and followed him down to a small room down the hall from the Emergency Department. We went in and found a body on a Hospital stretcher which was completely covered by clean sheets and a blanket. Mr. Bows yanked the covers away from the face of an elderly man, and that's when I realized I had never seen a real corpse before. The whole gesture was done without any preparation for me at all. I don't know what I was expecting at the time but the surprise of being confronted with death so abruptly gave me a faint feeling in my knees and body for an instant, and I had to quickly bring myself under control, so I didn't turn away or change my facial expression I just stared. Mr. Bows said.

"Are you all right?" I lied and said.

"O yeah I'm okay."

In a low voice, he said, "Good, let's get on with it."

Beside the stretcher was a small packet on a table. Mr. Bows said.

"This is a shroud kit, there located on all the wards including Emergency, and Medical supply." He opened it up, and showed me a folded white Plastic sheet with a bundle of ties of various lengths several cotton balls and a length of thin bandage, a plastic pan and tweezers. Bows said.

"Uncover the body, and remove any clothes."

I reached for the hospital gown he was wearing and Bow's said,

"Stop, there's some disposable gloves on the table, put them on, you will need them."

I put them on and undressed the body.

"Take the bandage, and placed a section around under the chin, and tie it at the top of the head to keep the mouth closed. Take another section and tie it tight around the penis, turn the body on its side and stuff the rectum with the cotton balls. When you have done that unwrap the sheet, and slip one edge under the body's side as far as you can, then tip up the far side and take hold of the sheet and pull it through to about half way, and at the same time wrapping it around the body from head to toe. When you are finished secure it with the various lengths of ties available.

I completed the tasks, and stood back. Bow's said.

"You did all right in that procedure but I won't be showing you again so don't forget it. We'll take the body down to the morgue know. Put a sheet over the body and cover it completely, then place a blanket on top of that. Before you go out into the hallway with the body see that all the ward doors are closed, and that there are no patients in the hallway. When you get to the elevators, and you find that there are passengers ahead of you. Don't push the body onto the elevator, wave them on and take the next empty one. It helps to avoid upsetting people who are not nursing staff."

After the little lecture, we proceeded to the floors nursing station, and told them we were leaving with the body, and then proceeded with the closing of each rooms doors

To get to the Morgue you had to cross a lane between the main hospital and the Wilson Block, which was a separate building housing the Microbiology Department with its various sciences including a T.B. Lab. the Morgue and the Autopsy Room etc. Next to this building was another building which at that time housed the Laundry, and Medical Stores as well as the Boiler House and other Maintenance and Engineering departments. After reaching the main floor, you turned to the left and proceeding down a back hallway to a small door leading to the road, you crossed the road, and proceeded to a narrow alley between the Wilson Block, and the Laundry Building. This alley was very steep, so Mr. Bows took the front of the stretcher, and I held the back so it could be navigated down the hill. On reaching the bottom it was a short walk to two large double doors at the opposite side of the building. Mr. Bow's had obtained the key to these doors from the Hospitals Main switch Board. I already knew where that was so he didn't bother to take me through that procedure. He opened the doors and we pushed the body into a room where the left wall had four large wooden refrigeration Doors. On the front of each door was a metal slot bolted to the door. During the preparation of the body there were two cards of heavy paper which had the Name, Address, Doctor, and any other pertinent information stamped on it. One of the cards was attached to the outside of the shroud. The body itself was still wearing its identification wrist band which had been issued, and placed on one of their wrists on admission to the hospital. Mr. Bow's opened one of the refrigerator doors, and looked inside. Although there were four doors each opened into a single room and behind each door was a wooden stretcher with a block of wood as a head rest, and some had leather straps to hold the bodies on, and others just had pieces of rope. This antiquated equipment was attached to the stretchers in various ways to make sure nothing fell of the stretcher during transfer. I saw at the far end of the room two other stretchers, one of which was metal including a tray which had a raised edge all around, and I guessed it wasn't as old as the others. Mr. Bow' checked behind each door and located an empty stretcher where we placed our body, and pushed the stretcher back into the cooler. I noticed that each door had an identical latch on the inside as well as the outside. I ask Mr. Bow's about it, and he said.

"From time to time you will be required to bring bodies down here by yourself, and if you accidentally shut a door behind you, you will be able to get out okay." I laughed and said.

"Has anybody ever done that?"

"No but if they did and it was at night, and there were no inside latches and there are no more deaths that night. They are going to be in bad shape the next day when someone will probably find them." He laughed, and said. "You won't get any help from your company, without those latches."

The next day, I showed up at Mr. Bow's office, and he said

"Well I wasn't sure you'd be back today."

"No problem I'm in this for the long run."

"I've got a patient on First South that needs his catheter changed."

We proceeded down to the Medical supplies Department, and Mr. Bow's asked for a Catheter Kit. Then we went to First South.

Some of the wards in the hospital were named according to what direction the wing of the building was pointing such as First South, Third West, etc. and the same went for middle blocks, Two Center Three Center, and so on.

We went to the nursing Station, and found out who the patient was, and where to find him. When we arrived, I was told to pull the curtains around the patient whenever I was treating him, and to check his wrist band, and ask his date of birth from the band to confirm it was the right patient.

Mr. Bow's placed the wrapped Catheterization kit on the bedside table and opened it being very careful not to touch anything inside. There was a paper package with rubber gloves inside, he picked them up, and carefully opened the package. Each glove's sleeve area was folded forward to allow the wearer to put on the glove without touching the outside. The catheter, and jell tube, and a Kidney Basin with a pair of Steel forceps, and a syringe with wads of small square bandages, and a small paper cup, were inside the cloth package, which I opened without touching anything inside. The Jell was squirted into the cup, and then the end of the penis was wiped with an Alcohol Swab. Before I started the cleaning process with the alcohol, I had put down the forceps so I could open the Alcohol Packet. When I laid them down I didn't notice that the tips of the Forceps had come in contact with the bed covers thus contaminating them. When I had finished the cleaning I reached for the Forceps so I could pick up the catheter and start the insertion.

"Stop,"

Mr. Bow's growled I knew right away that I had done something wrong.

"You have contaminated the forceps, and you are about to insert the catheter."

"I did," I said in surprise.

"Yes, you allowed the forceps to touch the bed clothing. You can't use them again. You'll have to go down to the Medical equipment room and get another kit. You had better hurry because you are leaving your patient half finished."

I rushed down the hall to the Medical Equipment Room, and got another kit and rushed back. Fortunately the ward was not too far away. I soon had a clean pair of forceps in my hand, and proceeded to insert the catheter up into the urethra, and push it through to the Bladder. I then inflated the bulb on the end of the catheter using the sterile water to make sure it would not fall out and hooked the free end up to a plastic bag to hold the urine. I managed to complete the procedure with Mr. Bow's expert help without any more mistakes. That evening at home I studied the procedure carefully to stamp it into my memory.

The next day I was taken down to the same ward again, First South and introduced to a young orderly who was going to give a patient an enema. At the end of the procedure Mr. Bow's took me out into the hallway and ask me what I thought of the technology that was used. I was caught off guard. I didn't want to get the orderly into trouble because what I had read in the instruction manual I had been given, and what I had observed been practiced were not the same at all. I stalled a minute before answering and realized I had to tell the truth because Bow's was watching the whole thing with me. I couldn't very well tell him that the technology was fine when I knew it wasn't even though I probably would have to work with the orderly in the future. I said lamely.

"Well, it wasn't quite the same as the manual."

Bow's shook his head and stared at me for a minute.

"Good, that technique was terrible, and I'll have a long talk with him before the days out, because he knows better."

I never did find out what happened, but the orderly left the job before I came to work as an orderly so I never had to work with him. I often wondered if I took his place.

I kept up the afternoon training including full days on my days off for about six months. Finally Mr. Bow's dropped into the kitchen one morning, and told me to come directly to the Head Nurses Office in the afternoon because an Orderly position had become available, and it was mine if I wanted it. I told him I would be there. I had no idea how hard the orderly had to work because all I had done was follow Mr. Bow's around, listened, and got to practice what I had learned when the opportunity arose. I was soon to find out that there was a great deal I had not learned or been shown.

The Head Nurse was kind. She listened to Mr. Bow's while he recommended me for the job and when he was finished she said.

"Well Me. Diener I hope you will keep up the good work and initiative you have shown in the past. Good Luck."

We left her office and went to Mr. Bow's Office.

"When do I start?"

"You'll be working in First south which is a Medical ward and you'll start Monday Morning. Here's a Time sheet, so you won't forget, and be late."

"Don't worry I'll be there on time."

"Report to me here in my office," he said.

That night I studied the time sheet, and saw that there were three shifts, Morning, Afternoon, and night. Monday rolled around, and I was taken down to the Laundry, and issued a uniform of White Pants, and White Short Sleeved Shirt. I changed, and we went over to First South, and I was introduced to the Wards Head Nurse, and then I was taken to the Ward's Treatment room, and shown the day's Work Sheet, and introduced to the orderlies as they came in. The treatment room was the center of the Orderlies Equipment, where they spent most of their time. Mr. Bow's told me to take it one step at a time, and left.

The patients on the ward were all men, and at that time the largest room contained Heart Patients and the other rooms an assortment of Cancer, Strokes, and various other Medical conditions. There were no Surgical Patients or infectious diseases.

Because of the fact there were Cancer, and Strokes, and Heart Conditions there were deaths occurring constantly with the orderlies responsibility to prepare the body and move it to the morgue left to the Orderly who could get help from the Emergency Department Orderly at night when he was on duty alone if he was available if not he had to do the job alone which at times was very heavy work.

In evening, and night shift there was only one Orderly on the ward, and when there coffee break time came, rather than leave the ward short of staff they allowed the staff to use the Ward Kitchen. Tea and Coffee etc. was left out for them for this purpose. An effort was supposed to be made to clean it up for the Kitchen Staff in the morning.

One night when I was on my break I suddenly heard the nurse on duty calling my name softly with some urgency.

"Mr. Diener. Come here please."

I immediately dropped what I was doing and went out into the hallway to find the Nurse standing with a very small man blocking her way he was obviously a patient for he was wearing a Hospital gown, and nothing else. He had a hold of her arm. I walked over and ask her.

"What's going on?"

"Will you take Mr. Smith to his bed?"

All of a sudden he starts shouting.

"Don't come any closer, your all under arrest. I have ten men here, and I'm waiting for the wagon to take you away."

I reached slowly over, and took his hand away from her arm, and led him to his bed, while the nurse rushed away to the office to phone his doctor for permission to give him a sedative to quiet him down. When we got to his bed, I ask him to go to bed in as quiet and gentle voice as I could muster, but he refused and kept insisting we were all under arrest, and his men had everything under control. A few minutes went by, and the Emergency Orderly arrived. He was a young man well over six feet tall, and at least two hundred lbs. He looked at me, and the patient, and says,

"You've got to be kidding. You can't handle this patient alone?"

He then walked over to the little guy smiled at him, and reached out with one hand and gave him a gentle push. He was standing with his back to the bed, and his legs were up against the edge. The slight push just made him sprawl onto the bed. He just lay there surprised, and too weak to get up. He said.

"My men will be here any minute now."

Then he closed his eyes, and went to sleep. The Orderly said.

"The next time, you need some help don't call me in the middle of my break."

"I didn't call I guess it was the nurse over reacting."

"O I see," he said, and laughed. "See you later," he said and left.

In a few minutes the nurse arrived, and when she saw the patient lying on the bed sleeping, a worried look came over her face she quickly checked his pulse, and said.

"He's asleep! O, well I'll give him the shot anyway it'll keep him quiet until the morning."

I gently rolled him onto his side, and she expertly administered the shot into his hip. The next morning, when I was going off shift he was up walking in the hall with a Dressing Gown on and talking rationally to another patient. When I passed him he stared at me for a moment as if he recognized me from somewhere but never spoke. I passed by, and never spoke either. The next few nights were uneventful. I learned later that he had been admitted with a severe case of pneumonia, so I assumed he had had a reaction to his medication, and along with anoxia caused by the pneumonia he had unknowingly lost his mind temporarily.

Another incident that occurred on First South was when a patient suddenly leaped out of bed when an orderly was approaching. The ward was situated on the ground floor with large windows facing out to a lawn. He hit the floor running, and leaped right through the closed glass window, and fell onto the grass, he picked himself up, and took off heading across the road for a parking lot behind the Wilson Block. In the meantime when the orderly recovered from his surprise he ran to the nearest exit and headed him off in the parking lot. The patient was exhausted by his efforts, and gave no resistance to be returned to his bed. The only injury he received when he went through the closed window was a large gash made by the glass on his chest. He also forgot about what had happened and recovered, and was released.

There was never a day went by without some small or big incident happening somewhere in the hospital. I can only relate to the ones that occurred where I was working at the time, or were told to me by those who were directly involved.

One evening when it was growing dark an employee who worked in the Laboratory was leaving a side door in the hospital heading for the parking lot when he heard a groan. He stopped looked around, and found a patient lying on the lawn. He had jumped from the fourth floor in a suicide attempt. I don't know whether he survived or not. Help was called, and he was transferred to the Hospital's Emergency Department.

Another incident which had a better ending was when an orderly was making his rounds on the ward. He entered a room and noticed a window had been left wide open he walked over to close it and found a patient hanging onto the window ledge with one hand getting set to drop three floors to an alley below. He quickly grabbed his wrist just as he let go, but he was a lightly built young man and the patient outweighed him and was not trying to help himself. So there he was, hanging on with one arm, and holding on with the other to keep from falling out the window himself, and hollering for help at the top of his lungs. Fortunately help arrived in a hurry and the patient was saved from further injury.

One day while on shift in first South, I was in the Treatment Room with one of the other Orderly's. The windows from this room faced out onto a road leading to and from the Emergency Department, and passed by a large Visitors parking lot and lawn area. An orderly from our ward was just coming to work driving down Fort Street which ran by this area in front of the hospital. A man had just brought his wife into the Emergency Department because she was acting very strange and was totally incoherent. When they arrived he placed her in a waiting area, and went to the desk to report her arrival. But when he turned his back on her she quietly got up, and walked out the exit, and proceeded to walk down the driveway and across the lawn toward Fort Street taking of her cloths as she went, by the time she got to Fort Street she was totally naked. The Orderly who was driving down Fort at the time saw her crossing the street against the traffic. He realized right away that she was probably a patient from the hospital. He pulled over to the curb, and jumped out to try and stop her. In the meantime the husband and staff noticed she was missing, ran outside, and saw the uproar on Fort Street where the Orderly was trying to cover up the woman with his light jacket. All this did was cause her to explode in a violent rage, and she was screaming, and punching, and biting him in the middle of the road. An orderly and a nurse from the Emergency Department arrived pushing a stretcher and carrying a blanket, and between the three of them they managed to strap her onto the stretcher and cover her up with the blanket as best they could. While crossing the distance back to the Emergency Department, she was screaming high pitched wails, and struggling with her arms, and legs going in all directions. It was a terrible spectacle to watch from the wards windows as they went. A while later when the orderly came back to the ward, he showed us some of his scratches and bite marks he received while trying to subdue her without injury, and there was quite a few. He told us the young nurse received a very deep bite to her chest which required Medical Treatment. He said, after that if he saw anymore naked women walking down the road on the way to work he wasn't going to stop again. We just laughed, because we all knew we would stop if required, and he was just letting off a little steam.

Time went by with incidents happening every day, and it seemed most of them occurring at night. I assumed it was because there was far fewer staff during the quiet times, and because of this you were always on the alert, and thus became more involved in everything that was happening.

One day I was asked by a Student Nurse to help her roll a patient on to his side so she could change his draw sheet, and get him settled for the night. This patient was in a single room right beside the central ward desk. The room at most times held seriously ill patients. I noticed right off that the patient's bed was cranked into a High Fowlers position so he could breathe easier, and that he was wearing a high compression Oxygen Mask which covered his nose and most of his lower face. The young nurse was bustling about making her patient more comfortable and talking to him

Kazoonie

in a friendly way although it was just a one way conversation. I noticed he wasn't moving in anyway at all so the minute she went to a corner sink to get some water to wash his face and hands. I quietly felt for a pulse, I found nothing. I then lifted the mask and could see that the man was dead. I lowered the mask back in place, and realized he had probably been dead long enough that heroic methods were a waste of time. Just then she came back with her basin of water, and wash cloth. I reached out, and said.

"Here let me have that."

She smiled gave me the basin, and started to adjust the patients pillows so he would be more comfortable, chatting all the while. I put the basin on the side table and said.

"Could I see you out in the hall for a moment?"

She paused at what she was doing. And I took her arm and gently guided her out of the room. For a minute I thought she might resist. She looked at me kind of startled by my behavior I guess. Once we were clear of the room, I said quietly,

"Your Patient's dead."

A complete look of shock came over her face.

"What!"

For a minute I thought she might collapse, but she just burst into tears. Fortunately another student nurse was coming out of the nursing station at that moment, and saw her crying.

"What's the matter?" she asked.

"Her patient died, take care of her, I'll get a nurse to carry on."

Right away she put her arm around her and led her into the Nursing Station consoling her as she went. I followed, and found an R.N. explained the situation, and an intern was called for pronunciation. I never saw the Young Student again. But the group that was on the floor at that time came up for rotation in a couple of days and left for another floor, so I don't know whether she toughed it out, and carried on after such a terrible shock. I like to think she probably did stay on because the little time I saw her working I think she would have made an excellent compassionate nurse.

Occasionally you came across some very poor nursing techniques. One of these times was when I checked the work roster, and found one of the patients was scheduled for a bath. There were two bathrooms on the ward the one closest to the patients room had a row of three toilets with their own cubicles. The bath tub was situated at the back of the last cubicle in the room. When I walked in I could hear someone talking to a patient in the last cubicle. I could make out it was an Orderly. I ran the bath, and left to get the Bath towels and clothes in the laundry room, and when I returned, I was just going to check the water temperature, I noticed there were several pieces of stool floating in the water. I was so surprised I had to look closer to make sure. Then I heard the Orderly still in the cubicle next to the tub, and I realized what was happening. This particular Orderly, had been working for approximately sixteen years without taking any time off for sickness, he always arrived on time. But the time I had worked with him I discovered his habits, and care for the patient were careless and crude and he seemed to have a slower mentality than his cohorts. I noticed that they laughed when he was the center of conversation regarding his work habits, and personal life. I knocked on the door, and ask him to come outside for a minute. When he appeared from the cubicle I noticed there were traces of stool on his hands. I said.

"What the hell are you doing?"

He shrugged and said indignantly.

"I'm helping a patient go to the bathroom, he's impacted with stool, and I'm digitally removing it for him."

"Where are your gloves?"

He laughed and said.

"I didn't have time to get any."

"Come here I want to show you something."

I took him around to the Bath tub and showed him the floating stool.

"What the hell were you doing throwing it over the Cubicle wall? God dam it now I have to clean the tub and refill it which will put me way behind in my work load. Go back in there, and clean up your mess, and put him to bed, and then tell the nurse about your patients impaction, and she will get it looked after by orders from his Doctor."

"I don't have to do that, I've been doing this for years by myself."

"Well it just came to an end because if you don't do it I will, and after I explain to the Head Nurse exactly what's going on here your duties will be coming to an end soon too."

His face became very pale, and he turned on his heel, and went back into the cubicle. He never came near me for a couple of days. When I needed assistance I got the student nurses to give me a hand. A few years later he became ill, and was forced to take some time off from work. He didn't recover.

During Coffee Breaks, and Lunch Time the men such as orderlies and cooks etc. all sat in the Cafeteria area which faced the entrance. The rumor was it was to get a better view of the female employee's coming in. One of these men had a reputation of being a bit of a ladies man, and was known to make the off comment about some of the better endowed young ladies as they arrived. One of the orderlies sitting at our table noticed a particular young lady arriving, and began to comment on the way she was dressed to take full advantage of her better attributes so to speak. Suddenly there was silence at the table. And he was the only one laughing. The man with the bit of a reputation was particularly silent. And he had stopped eating, and was growing redder and redder in complexion, as his anger grew. I gently nudged the commentator, and said.

"Cut it out your talking about his daughter."

He stopped immediately, and sat there with his mouth half open, as he spluttered, thinking fast about what to do. Then suddenly he pulled himself together, and said quietly.

"I didn't know."

Everybody started to laugh except the father. I think everybody was thinking (What goes around comes around.) I think everybody probably noticed she wasn't seen for a couple of days after that in the Cafeteria. When she did show up again her dress was much more sedate than it had been, and the father didn't join in the girl watching as enthusiastically as he had in the past.

The largest room on First South was reserved for Heart Patients and was nearly always full of patients. One day I noticed that one of the patients had been assigned an R.N. to be beside his bed in case of an Emergency. I happened to be in the room when he went into Cardiac arrest. The R.N. immediately began Pulmonary Resuscitation by exerting force to his chest in a pumping motion another R.N. inserted an airway, and told me to blow into it every four beats. I had just started when in rushed an Intern, who brushed us all aside, and started a very strenuous resuscitation procedure on the man's chest. In a few minute's the machine arrived for administrating electric shock to the heart, and he was given several jolts of electricity, but it was to no avail. I saw the man's doctor arrive in a few minutes with the man's wife for a last visit. This was my first experience with the C.A. procedure. Eventually there was a Cardiac Arrest Cart kept in a centrally located area near our ward, and when the C.A. announcement came over the intercom an orderly would rush from our floor to the scene with the cart. I performed this duty several times when I was an orderly. After about a year on First South we were transferred to Third Central with all the patients, and staff, and First South was changed to the Brain and Heart testing area, along with the Hospital Mail Room.

One evening while I was walking around checking the Patients needs in the Heart Room. I noticed a young Patient lying with his eyes closed, and one of his arms hanging over the side of the bed in what appeared to be a very uncomfortable position. I went over to have a closer look, and noticed he didn't appear to be breathing I picked up his arm, and put it in a more natural position, there was no response from the patient at all I immediately picked up his signal button, and pressed it three times in quick succession. This was the alarm for trouble which would ring in the Central Control Panel at the Wards Front Desk. I did not start the Cardiac

Arrest Procedure because Orderlies and Aids were not supposed to do this. They were not allowed to answer the phone at the Front Desk if the nurse was absent, and if they did and a Doctor was phoning in orders for a patient they were not allowed to take those orders, but were required to find a nurse to answer the phone. Failure to obey these rules could lead to dismissal regardless if it helped to even save a life. I found this out latter on when I became active in the union, and to represent employee's accused of this. Another strict rule was confidentiality. You must never discuss a Patients case outside the confines of the hospital. That could lead to immediate dismissal, even if it happened under what was believed to be completely innocent circumstances.

One of the patients in a room I was assigned to had cancer, and a collapsed lung. He had a tube running from his chest to a large glass bottle for drainage, and the bottle was sitting on a small wooden platform for stability, and held in place by sturdy wire clamps. While passing his room which was a four bed room I noticed the call light over the door was on. I walked in the room and found the patient standing by the bed holding onto the rubber tube attached to the bottle and swinging it around in a circular motion. He was yelling incoherently, and I couldn't understand what he was talking about except that he wanted to play cards, and nobody had taken up his request. I immediately dodged the bottle and platform as it came around, and grabbed it on the next pass. At the same time I gently pushed him on to the edge of his bed trying to keep the tube from being dislodged form his chest which would have caused his lung to collapse again all the time telling him we would have a game as soon as he settled down. When he heard this he sat up, and reached for a pack of cards that was sitting on his side table, and calmed right down. At this moment a young student nurse came into the room, and was standing there watching the action. Unfortunately the patient saw her to, and decided he would rather play cards with her than me. He brightened right up, and started to try and coax her into sitting down beside him. A frightened look came over her face, and she looked at me as if to say, "What do I do now?" He was a big man old enough to be her father, and he was talking to her like she was his oldest daughter or someone of that sort and I realized if we didn't satisfy him he may return to even more violence than I had previously

235

witnessed. I told her quietly it was all right and to sit down beside him and don't upset him. I told her I wasn't going anywhere, and it was going to be alright. She smiled like a real trooper, and sat down beside him on the bed he just smiled back, and started dealing the cards. In the mean time I rang the call button the required three times and an R.N. arrived I told her briefly what was happening, and she took over. She pulled up the Bed Rail on the opposite side of the bed, and speaking quietly she told the Patient it was time for his afternoon nap. Surprisingly he just looked at her smiled vacantly put down his cards, and rolled into bed to an inaudible sigh of relief by everyone in the room. When I came to work the next day I noticed his bed was empty, and I inquired what had happened to him. I learned that the young Orderly who relieved me for the evening shift ran into some trouble with him and received a punch in the face. The Head Nurse phoned his Doctor, and complained about his bouts of violence. When the Doctor found out about this he had him transferred to the Bay Center for Psychiatric Patients and I learned latter he had died from his illness.

Third Center Orderlies were used occasionally in the Psychiatric center, which at that time faced the entrance to Bay Street, thus the name Bay Center. Usually we were called in the evening or at night when they were short of Orderlies, and required help with unruly Patients, or to help with the Electric Shock Treatments. One evening I was called to go over to the center and when I arrived I was told that a patient had gone into a bathroom, and wouldn't come out. The bathroom was a long narrow room with a toilet at the far end. It was so narrow that two people could not walk side by side to the toilet this made it impossible for one orderly to remove her without injury to either one. The plan was to get her out of the Bathroom across the hall to an empty room onto a bed, and to give her a sedative. Then take her back down the hall to the Isolation Ward, and a secure room. Myself, and the other Orderly decided that he would go first into the Bathroom and grab her around the waist making sure to pin her arms, and I would follow immediately behind him and grab her legs pinning them so she couldn't kick me. Everything went well until my partner grabbed her around the chest he missed pinning her arms, and when I grabbed her legs she began throwing punches at me right and left.

Neither of us could let her go, so I ducked my head down and stretched her out so most of her punches just bounced of the top of my head. We picked her up easily, she wasn't a fat women, and hustled her across the hall. As planned the nurse was there with her sedative at ready. We threw her on to the bed, and pinned her down but when we managed to get her skirt up so the nurse could administer the shot into her hip, we found she was wearing a thick elastic pair of panties which the fine needle wouldn't penetrate without breaking so there we were struggling with this poor women while she was screaming at the top of her lungs finally we managed to hold her, and get enough of the elastic down off of her hip so the nurse could make the shot. MY partner was yelling, "Don't let her go yet." I assured him I wouldn't. We had to hold her until the shot took effect. In a few minutes she stopped screaming, and lay quietly so we let her go and got up and stepped back. She suddenly jumped of the bed and grabbed a folding chair by the bed and swung it at my partner. But fortunately the shot had taken effect enough that he easily stopped it and it dropped to the floor. We both took hold of an arm a piece, and skidded; her down the hallway on the waxed floor, because she refused to cooperate, and walk.

As the years went by a couple of other incidents come to mind of occurrences in the Psychiatric ward. I was called over with another Orderly from the Emergency Department to assist the Orderly on duty in case we were needed. When we arrived we were told that a male patient in isolation was refusing a shot to calm him down, and we were instructed to stay out of sight by the side of the open door. The Nurse went in to the room with the Orderly on duty, and asked the patient to cooperate. The Orderly positioned himself at the top of the mattress which was all the furniture there was in the room, so that when the patient got up to approach the Nurse he would be behind him. The Patient got up, and immediately made an aggressive lunge at the Nurse. The Orderly was on him from behind, immediately grabbing him by the shoulders and knocking his feet out from under him. As soon as he dropped to the floor we rushed in and subdued him. He was completely taken by surprise, and immediately gave up, and submitted to his shot like a lamb. Compared to the lady in the bathroom it was very efficient, and controlled. Another case where three Orderlies were called over to the Bay and along with the two orderlies on duty the five of us were going to give a patient a bath. At the time I thought what on earth do we need five men to give a bath for? When I saw the Patient I realized it was entirely necessary, because he was over two hundred lbs. and very muscular and stood at least six foot four. He was flushed, and wild eyed, and kept asking questions about what was happening, he didn't seem to be intimidated by the five men surrounding him at all. I found out later that when he was admitted to hospital he had given the two Police Officers a very hard time when he assaulted them. One of the wards Orderlies explained what was going on, and he accompanied us quietly to the bathroom. When we got there he was told to undress, but he said no and just stood defiantly. I thought here we go, and got set for a areal battle. But he just stood there laughing at us. One of the Ward Orderlies began undoing his shirt buttons, and he let them strip of his cloths without resisting at all. He kept right on talking absolute nonsense, and stepped into the bath tub without any resistance. But he wouldn't lie down in the water so the tub was drained, and the shower spray was used. Slowly three of the Orderlies left the room thinking I guess that because of the Patients passive behavior they weren't going to be needed. When the Orderly who was doing the washing was finished, and was reaching for a towel I turned, and took a couple of steps toward the door. The Orderly immediately panicked, and shouted.

"Don't leave me, don't leave me."

I turned to see what was happening, and found a very frightened man standing with a pleading look on his face staring at me. I quickly said.

"It's all right I'm not going anywhere."

He was obviously terrified of being alone with the Patient, and I don't blame him at all. The Patient laughed, and said to me.

"I like you. You have all the right answers."

I just nodded my head, and said as confidently as I could.

"Yeah I do."

Between the two of us we got him cleaned up, and dressed in Hospital Pyjamas, and back to his room without incident. On the way back to third

Center I felt a great feeling of relief that everything went well without a hitch, and the tension of being on guard every minute of our encounter with the Patient flooded away. I thought to myself I wouldn't want that job for all the money in the world.

A couple of weeks later while I was up in the Cafeteria taking a coffee break I found myself sitting across from one of the psychiatric Orderlies who I had worked with in the past. I noticed when he lifted his cup of coffee up to take a drink he had to use both hands because of an intense tremor he had. I asked him.

"What are you doing over here?"

"I'm not working at the Bay center anymore I'm working up in the "O.R I needed a change it was really getting to me. Ten years of the Bay is enough for anybody."

"Yea, I can see that you can hardly hold your Coffee Cup?"

"That isn't the half of it he mumbled."

I changed the subject because he was getting more agitated as the conversation continued. I thought he was on the brink of a nervous breakdown, and knowing something about the job he had left it would better if I didn't bring any old memories back to him. A few years went by, and he was forced to retire because of the onslaught of Alzheimer's disease, and I never saw him again.

I was involved in a couple of incidence involving Patients in the Memorial Pavilion. On the way home from work one evening I noticed an elderly man dressed in pyjamas and kimono walking erratically down Bay Street. The first thing I thought of was a possible escape from the Psychiatric Ward. I pulled ahead of him, and waited till he came level with the car. I got out, and asked him where he was going, and if he wanted a lift. He spoke very quietly looking kind of dazed, and said.

"I'm going home."

He then turned, and started walking down the side walk. I took him gently by the arm, and said.

"Come on you look a little tired. I'll drive you the rest of the way."

By this time I realized by his actions he wasn't a patient from the Bay, but one from the Memorial Pavilion, which had a ward for Dementia Patients. So I just drove around the block, and directly to the Pavilion Entrance. I said.

"Here we are back home."

I helped him out, and sat him on a visitors bench, and walked a couple of feet to the reception desk, keeping him in sight all the while I was doing it. I explained what was going on to the receptionist, and she called on the intercom for assistance. The Patient never spoke, just sat there quietly. In a few minutes a Nurse appeared, checked his wrist band for identification, and led him away. I continued on home.

One evening I was crossing the road between the Wilson Block, and the South Wing, when I heard someone calling out that he couldn't get the door open. At first I couldn't make out where it was coming from because there was nobody else in sight and it was beginning to get dark. As I started to continue on my way, I heard it again, this time I realized it was coming from above me. I looked up and saw a Patient standing on the fifth Floor Fire Escape Platform. I knew it was a Patient because of his attire, and the fact he was standing there with a silly grin on his face, yelling he couldn't get the door open. I immediately yelled back, not to move, and I would go inside, and open the door. I looked around, and I saw there was nobody else in sight, so I ran through the South Wing Door's and down to the security Office which was halfway through the hospital. Fortunately there were two security personnel there, and when I explained what was going on. They quickly responded, and the three of us ran down to the South Wing main entrance, where we split up with one officer taking the stairs to the fifth floor while we went outside to talk to the Patient. The second officer climbed the fire escape while I talked to the Patient. All this took only about ten minutes and we had him down, and safe. We found that someone had pinned a note to the back of his Kimono, stating his name, and what ward he was on in the Memorial Pavilion, and would the finder please return him. I never did find out how he managed to get as far as he did without being spotted on the Hospital Grounds.

One day while we were all attending what was called "Report" which is where the outgoing shift reports to the incoming shift, all important occurrences which happened on their shift so a steady flow of information can be transported to the incoming shift to keep the quality nursing moving at all times. This occurred with everybody gathered around the wards Reception Area while the Head Nurses and Student Instructors read off the list of important occurrences. Suddenly one of the older Nurses collapsed, and began to have convulsions. It happened so fast there was a slight pause before one of the Registered Nurses grabbed an airway from a nearby drawer, and inserted it. My- self and the other Orderlies picked her up and took her to a single room which was empty and right next to the Reception area at the time. I was rather surprised to find out later that this was not an isolated incident, and she was diagnosed as an Epileptic. How she managed to keep this secret, and perform her duties without incident for so long was surprising. She retired a short time later.

I spent about three years as an Orderly, and during that time there were countless incidents happening. Never a dull moment!

CHAPTER 13

Unionization of the Hospital

Morgue Attendant

1St Autopsy

Checking for Possible Infection

One day while perusing the list of openings for the staff on a bulletin board outside the Cafeteria, I came across one which struck my interest. It was a job in the Hospitals Laboratory as a Morgue attendant. The job had a two year wage increment, which led to your top wage instead of three years like everyone else in the hospital. It also was about Fifty Dollars a month more than I was presently making, and had no shift work, just eight to five, five days a week. At the time I thought these conditions were great. But I didn't have any idea what a Morgue Attendant did or what was required for this job anyway. I decided I would apply for the position mainly because of the wages, and straight day shift with weekends off. I filled out an application form, and dropped it off at the personnel office on the way home. The next day, I found that nearly all the Orderlies who worked in the hospital were talking about the new position, and that most of them had applied for it. There were quite a large group of Orderlies in the hospital who had graduated from the Veterans Hospital, and the other large hospital in Victoria St. Josephs, who both had training schools for Orderlies. The Jubilee relied on the military and these two hospitals for most of their recruits, and did not run a school for Orderlies. A few managed to get hired under unusual circumstances because of a shortage of people with the necessary training like myself. In the three years as an Orderly I only met one other person who was hired under these conditions and even he was eventually fired for making too many mistakes on the job.

Eventually the Chief Orderly fell ill, and died, and was never replaced, and then the Government started a School for licensed Practical Nurses to help with the shortage of Registered Nurses. At this time the Hospital Employees Union was in the process of signing up the Jubilee Hospital which only had an association representing the employee's. The Jubilee was the last big hospital in the province to join the union. When the time came to negotiate for a new contract with the hospital the employee's used the Medical Lecture Room, with the hospitals permission of course. The membership would get up and give the executive ideas for presentation to the Hospital Board of Director's. All this would take a few hours, and then we would all go home, and wait for an answer. In the time of my association with the Hospital Association representing the Employee's we never gained a better wage contract then what the Union gained for the Hospitals they represented. The joke which always came up when it was over was that our committee always went to management, and pointed at what the Union got , and demanded the same, and invariable the hospital agreed, and it was over no fuss no bother. What was overlooked was the size of the union who had the money from thousands of union members to pay for the infrastructure of their organization, compared to that, we didn't stand a chance to advance our ideals or goals to keep up with the rate of inflation. As far as the nurses organization was concerned at that time any kind of labour action was unheard of, and the expression "What about the Poor Patient, always came up at their negotiations, and they would immediately settle for whatever they could get.

The Hospital Employees Union eventually was successful in signing up the Jubilee Hospital, and after a while they were successful in bringing the Licensed Practical Nurses wages to almost the same rate as a first year Registered Nurse. This caused a bigger shortage of nurses, and a new generation of nurses began to appear. The doing away of the starched and pleated White Uniform's soon appeared, and the nurses with

Bachelor and Master's Degrees began to appear everywhere. The Nursing School's attached to the bigger hospitals were closed, and the Colleges and Universities picked up the slack. Rules regarding marriage while in training and the live in restrictions in some hospitals were gone. Licensed practical nurses were given the right to apply for training, and graduation after only two years to become an R.N. compared to three years with no Licensed Practical Nurse training. Suddenly without the live in nursing schools the wards were in need of more Licensed Practical Nurses and to help this situation a lot of orderlies were fired or quit, or transferred to other jobs with in most instants a lower pay rate. In the meantime the nurses association grew more powerful, and commanded a louder say in the negotiations at the contract table, and today are a voice to be reckoned with. What with the increase in technology in hospitals today. I think what goes around comes around.

A couple of weeks went by, and I was told to attend an interview in regards to the Morgue attendant's job. It was to be held in the annex. A separate Brown Shingled Building used for Interns quarters, and various other offices such as Pay office etc. This interview was to be held on one of my scheduled days off so I got dressed up in my Sunday go to meeting clothes, and showed up on time. When I arrived I was ushered into a small room, and introduced to the Head of the Histology Department, which is the department in charge of the study of tissue, and another gentleman who was the Head of the Laboratory.

The Head of Histology was a technologist who learned his trade on the job, and rose up through the ranks from Morgue Attendant to head of his own department with several employees under his command. He was an Englishman. The Head of the Laboratory was also an Englishman, who controlled the whole Laboratory, and all of its different science departments as well as hiring, and firing staff etc. I was to learn he was a fair but very complicated man indeed.

The head of the laboratory was sitting behind a desk, and the Histology supervisor sitting to one side of him. He said.

"Have you ever had any experience working as a Morgue Attendant?"

I said, "No, the only experience I have had which is remotely associated with the position, is I'm currently employed here as an Orderly, and this job puts me in the position of taking care of the dead before delivering to the Morgue.

"I see, well I have your Hospital employment record here and it states that you have been a hard working employee with a good record of punctuality on the job."

"Thank you, I'm pleased to hear that my efforts are appreciated." He smiled, and changed the subject. He flipped over the pages of my record, and asked the usual questions. Then he said.

"Have you got any Hobbies?"

"I like to go fishing. I have a small Aluminium Outboard Motor Boat, and a trailer, and I go out whenever I can."

"That's great I like to go fishing to, I have a small boat like yours, and I like to go out once in a while to see if I can catch something. I haven't been too successful though, but it sure relaxes you."

I nodded in agreement. Then he got serious, and said.

"Well Mr. Diener that'll be all, we'll let you know in due time when we've made our decision, we have quite a few other applications to go through."

We all stood up, shook hands, and I thanked them for their consideration, and left.

Three months went by without any word so during this time I had given up on the success of my application even the other applicants had stopped asking me if I knew anything, and then one evening when I was just getting ready for the change of shift report, a R.N. called me to the reception desk, and told me I had a phone call. I picked up the phone, and it was the Personnel Officer. When she told me I was the successful applicant tor the job. I said.

"Well, I had forgotten about it. I just told myself I was not a very convincing candidate at my interview."

She laughed, and said.

"They thought you were the best that applied for the position, and there were quite a few applicants. Congratulations. The Lab. will be getting in touch with you tomorrow for an orientation, and to tell you when you'll start."

I thanked her and hung up. I sat there kind of stunned by this change coming up realizing it was probably going to be the last position I was going to hold in the hospital, and I didn't have any idea what I was getting into. Sitting here writing this I realize if my situation had been any different I don't believe I would have taken the job.

The next day I received a call from the Head of Histology telling me to come to his office in the Lab. on Monday Morning around nine. I checked my work schedule, and found that this was a day off for me so I told him I would be there on time. He said.

"Fine there's a couple of autopsies scheduled, and I want to see how you react under fire so to speak, and he laughed at his little joke. Of course I didn't have any idea what he was talking about because I had never been to an autopsy before.

Monday rolled around, and got into my white's and reported to the Lab. I didn't have any idea what was going to happen, so I thought I had better wear the hospital issue clothing rather than my own in case I might be required to perform some work.

When I arrived I was shown around the Histology Department, and introduced to the staff as well as a quick explanation at what was being done and why. The Laboratory was situated on the fifth Floor which was the top floor of the south Wing. Access was obtained by stairs or two Elevators, to the reception area.

After my quick tour of Histology, we went down the elevators to the Main floor, and crossed the street, and entered the Wilson Block, which was a two story building. The first Floor contained the Micro Biology department and the Basement the Autopsy Room, and Morgue, and T.B.

Lab. as well as washrooms. As the years went by some of these departments were changed of course.

There were large renovations in the entire Laboratory system as science and technology improved in the years I worked there. We walked through the Biology Department, down a flight of stairs, and I found we were in front of the Morgue to my left, and the Autopsy Room, which was straight ahead. To the right was another corridor which went down to the washrooms, and the T.B. Lab. The T.B. Lab. was just an empty room at this time.

I was ushered into the autopsy Room, and found myself staring at a Stainless Steel Table, equipped with a sink and Garbage disposable unit at one end. The top of the table had several Stainless Steel Trays, which were perforated for drainage with space beneath each tray for the run off to enter a large drain hole in the center of the table which sat on a center pillar eliminating the need for four legs, and the various pieces of plumbing were hidden inside. In the middle of the room was a square concrete pillar for roof support. I then noticed that the ceiling was very low, and I discovered later on that if I reached up I could easily touch the ceiling. So I estimate the ceiling was less than eight feet high. There were two large sinks one on each side of the room. They were unusual, because they were made out of porcelain, and because of their condition, were out of date, with multiple small cracks, and were both discoloured from white to the more creamy color of old age. The small cracks did not go through but made it almost impossible to keep them completely clean. At one end of the room was a green chalk board with a list of the various Body Organs and height and weight etc. embossed on one side. There were multiple bits, and pieces of cupboards, and shelves around the walls, and one table with a Tape Recorder. At the far end alongside the table and close to the floor was a large vent with a dusty screen. Scattered around the room were plastic buckets with organs being saved for some reason or another. They were labelled with names and numbers. The shelves contained along with varied odds and ends smaller pots which I assumed were the same.

When we first walked in the room, I noticed a small man dressed in a gown with an apron over the top of that. He was wearing ordinary Tan Colored Leather Work Boots. On his hands he was wearing a pair of rubber Maid Kitchen gloves used by cleaners. He was leaning on the table smoking a cigarette. The cigarette had a long ash hanging on the end ready to fall any minute onto the Autopsy Table. On the Autopsy Table beside him was a body with the chest, and abdominal cavity wide open showing some of the organs that were visible in the body, I was introduced to him, but I didn't bother to shake his hand, and he didn't take off his blood covered gloves. I just stood there looking, and feeling very uncomfortable. While my boss, and him were talking I noticed another stretcher off to one side with another naked body, and I assumed it was going to be autopsied too. My boss explained to me that Mr. Jones was the Morgue Attendant over at the Veteran's Hospital, and had been hired to cover the Autopsy Duties while the job was vacant. When I realized he was working at both hospitals I realized that he had more than he could do with just Autopsies besides all the backup duties that went with the running of the Jubilee Morgue, cleaning etc. I spoke briefly to him about the job, and found out he was going to teach me for five days the fundamentals of Autopsies, and then I was on my own. The boss said.

"That's it for now. You will report to work on Monday, and get started."

When we stepped out of the building I felt the cool air on my face, and breathed in the fresh air. I realized the smell of the Autopsy Room was going to take some getting used to.

"Well! What did you think of that? The boss asked, do you still want the job?"

"Yes I'll give it a whirl, and see how it goes." I said.

"When you don't have any Autopsies to do you have permission to sit in the back, and read as long as the reading material is about the job. And you are required to learn all you can about being a Prosector." Prosector? I asked.

"Yes one who dissects the Human Body," he said. I'll see you next Monday when your formal training will begin,"

And he walked away towards the Main Building.

The next few days were spent working at my usual duties up stairs on the ward, and listening to the comments, and crude jokes about my new job. I received a nice goodbye from the Head Nurse, and some of the senior Student Nurses thanked me for the help I had given to them on the job, and I was out of the Orderly Business.

On Monday I arrived wearing my Orderly Whites, but I had bought a cheap pair of Leather Oxfords with thick rubber soles, because I had noticed the attendants Boots had a lot of blood stains on them, so I carried the new shoes to work in case I needed a change. I went upstairs to the Laboratory, and the boss greeted me with a smile, and we went down stairs. We found a body on the table waiting for me. The boss said.

"Well I'll leave you to it," and left.

At the end of the table where the sink was, I noticed there was a Stainless Steel Stand with a three quarter inch piece of plywood with a black water proof coating on the exposed surface, and the top was covered with cork, like a kitchen cutting board. This was lying in the top of the Stainless Steel Stand with a rim to keep it from being dislodged, but allowing it to be separated for cleaning purposes. On the top of this board was a Scalpel fitted with a large disposable cutting blade, a long stainless steel one piece slicing knife a pair of forceps, and a pair of tweezers. At the head end of the table was a shorter one piece Autopsy Knife, and a Stryker Saw hanging on a portable stand. The Saw had a Stainless Steel Blade with the curved edge traveling only half of the blade while the other toothed surface was at the back of the blade with a much smaller cutting edge. The Saw was a Reciprocating Saw, it didn't travel in a full circle when in use only back and forth on the blades cutting surfaces, which ever surface was in use at a very high speed. This was used for cutting Bone. There was a larger round blade with teeth on full surface for cutting large bones, which was only used occasionally. In a few minutes the Chief Pathologist arrived, and the autopsy began. The morgue attendant made an incision, from the far shoulder to the Xiphoid Process at the bottom of the Sternum, and up the other side of the Chest to the other shoulder. Then he lifted the skin away from the internal organs as he made another incision straight down through the abdominal muscles to the Symphysis Pubis, just over the bladder, keeping the skin and muscles of the abdomen up so as not to cut any of the internal organs. The incisions he made looked like the letter Y when he was finished. Then he trimmed the skin, and muscle back from the rib cage, and upwards to expose the sternum. When this was done, he used the Stryker Saw too cut the Rib Bones and Cartilage so he could lift out the sternum exposing the Heart and Lungs. There was a roll of heavy string hanging from the ceiling on a make shift wire frame. He pulled a length down, and cut it off. Then he reached into the upper Chest Cavity, and put his hand around the Esophagus, and Trachea along with various blood vessels coming up from the heart, and slipped the string under the bundle and tied them off. He then reached down just above the Diaphragm, and cut through the Aorta and Esophagus and the Inferior Vena Cava. Then with the help of his short Autopsy Knife he took hold of the section at the top and gently pulled the Heart and Lungs out cutting any adhesions as he went. He then placed this block of organs into a large pan, and proceeded to remove the Bowel. When that was done the Liver and Stomach and the Pancreas was next, and then both Kidneys with Adrenals, Ureters, and Bladder with the Prostate. Of course the Bowel was tied off with string wherever a cut was made to avoid spilling Fecal Matter over everything. In short this system was called the Three Block System

In the meantime the Pathologist had finished reading the Patient's Chart, and had dictated any pertinent information into the machine on the table at the front of the room. He then came over to the Autopsy Table, and took the first block of organs out of the pan and placed them on the cutting board, and began to carefully examine and weigh each organ as he examined the system. After he had dissected each organ he would take small sections and place them in a small plastic container which was numbered, and labelled with the Patients Name, and the Pathologists Name, and filled with formalin for fixation, and preservation, and would be sent to the Histology Department where the tissue would be trimmed to fit into cassettes for the making of Microscopic slides for further examination. The attendant asked the Pathologist if he wanted the Brain for examination. I was to find out later that not all cases had their Brains removed for study purposes, because if it was not pertinent to the Patients illness it was not needed. This rule was only for Hospital Patients, Coroners Cases,

Police Cases, and Private Autopsies the Brain was always done because of the lack of Medical records, and other obvious reasons like Murders, Suicides etc.

The morgue attendant asked me to lift the Head up, and when I did he placed a heavy Rubber covered block under the back of the Neck. He then took a Scalpel, and made an incision across the top of the Head. Starting from behind one Ear, and ending behind the other Ear. He then lifted the Scalpel by gripping the edge of the incisions, and pulling with a steady pressure so as not to tear the Scalp, and with the help of the Scalpel he gradually pulled both sides of the incision clear of the skull. Then he took the Striker Saw, and made a horizontal incision. One in each Temporal Area, and he joined each side by cutting completely around the Skull. These cuts were very shallow just enough to allow the Skull to be broken loose by a gentle prying with a sharp steel wedge type tool made for this task. This was all done to avoid damaging the surface of the Brain. Once the Skull Cap was removed, any Dura that had missed being cut was cut loose, then the frontal part of the Brain was pulled gently forward, and a pair of curved Autopsy Scissors was inserted into the Spinal Canal below the Medulla Oblongata, and the spinal Cord cut. I was to learn later the use of certain tools for different areas was just a matter of that person's preference. The years went by and I learned more, I followed that rule with much better results in most instances. When he had severed the Cord he gently cradled the Brain in one hand and scooped it loose to be placed on the board for dissection.

While all this was going on, the Pathologist was weighing different organs like the Liver and Brain, and was calling out the weights so they could be placed on the Chalk Board, so the attendant was stopping every once in a while with what he was trying to show me, and I was finding out he was a man of very few words, and I was a man with a lot of questions. It became very apparent that I had a great deal to learn, and a very short time to do it.

When the Brain was removed, the attendant took me over to the body on the stretcher, and said.

"Okay you start this one."

At first I thought he was kidding, so I laughed, he just handed me the Autopsy Knife, and said.

"Measure him."

And I got the Tape and did that. Then he said.

"We've only got one table, so we'll have to do the Autopsy on the stretcher."

I unwrapped him, and put a Green Plastic Bed Pad under his head, and wrote his Autopsy Number, and name on the Chalk Board, I looked around for the Specimen Pot, and realized it hadn't been done yet so I made one, and put a proper label on it, and some formalin in it.

In the meantime the attendant had gone over to the Pathologist at the table, and I heard the Pathologist asked him how I was doing, and to my surprise he told him I was going to be just fine. That gave me a little more confidence, so I picked up the Autopsy Knife, and made my first incisions and removed the Sternum, tied of the top vessels like I had been shown. Of course I was much slower and tentative than he was. He had done it all very quickly even while trying to describe to me what was going on.

I managed to get the Heart, and Lungs free without any difficulty, except being very slow. By the time I had done this the Pathologist was back from his dictation of the first case, and was waiting for me with an exasperated look on his face. In the meantime, Rip had cleared away the Cutting Board debris, and quickly moved the first block over for him to get started. Then he came back, and quickly removed the Bowel and I had time to wrestle with the second block. With the morgue attendant helping me, I managed to keep ahead of the Pathologist, and he left without a word. Because the Veterans Hospital Attendant was just on call at the Jubilee Hospital, he wasn't getting paid overtime, and we were running late so he went, and phoned up Histology, and explained the situation to my boss. When he got off the phone, he had a big smile on his face, and said chuckling.

"He's coming down to show you how to wash up the place. That's another rule that must not be broken, you must clean the place up before going home, and you must finish your Autopsies. You now, sewing and washing that sort of thing. If you just leave it you'll have disease around here in no time, and that's a real bad situation."

Each body's removed organs were placed in Large Green Bags which were tied shut. The Bodies Cavities were suctioned, and the Bag placed in the cavities. The Sternum was replaced, and the Skin was then sewn tightly back into place, with a simple over and under stitch. The Brain Cavity was filled with an absorbent material to catch the remaining Spinal fluid, and keep leaking to a minimum. The Skull Cap was then placed back on the Head using the ledges created by the first two horizontal cuts, and then the scalp was pulled together and sewn tightly. The outside of the Body was then washed, and the shroud under the body on the stretcher was replaced. Both Bodies were then returned to the Morgue. The Admitting department was then phoned, and told we were finished so they could release them to the appropriate Funeral Home. The Funeral Homes then removed everything we had done so they could embalm the Body.

In a few minutes the boss came down, and he gave me a quick course on how to wash an Autopsy Table, and Floor, and clean the instruments. Bleach was the main antiseptic mixed with water. Bleach and water along with Clorox Dutch Cleanser which was sprinkled on the table to help remove some of the more difficult Blood Stains. This solution cleaned, and sterilized the table thoroughly. The different Stainless Steel Containers were placed in the large sinks and left to soak in the bleach and water, while the table was being done. I was told to put all the instruments except the saw of course into a tray, and cover them with the bleach solution, and leave them over night. This was the only thing which was wrong with the procedure. I found in the morning that the Bleach literally turned all of the metal surfaces black from its corrosive action if left over night. So I inquired with the Medical Supply Department, and they recommended a substitute which performed very well by cleaning the blades of the instruments without the corrosive results even when left over night. Everything else that was dirty was washed, and rinsed with a hose. The floor was equipped with two drains for washing down the floor. I found a large squeegee, and a Mop and Bucket. My Boss showed me how he wanted the table done but he said.

"Use some common sense for the instruments, and the floor, and don't leave anything dirty overnight." And then he left.

Over the years I developed a thorough cleaning procedure which was a quick, and efficient. To find out how it was working, I went to the Biology Department, and ask the Technologist who was also an R.N. who was in charge of infection control in the hospital, to come down periodically, and check for contamination. She showed a little reluctance to do this because it had never been done before. But when I explained to her that there was no way I could tell if the place was really clean if I didn't have some tests done, besides I had to go up to the wards throughout the day. She argued that the Patients records were available when they died, and if they died from a contagious disease, they would be isolated, and warnings posted. I told her she was forgetting about the D.O.A.'s I received from the Coroner, and the various Police Departments that didn't have Medical Records or an apparent cause of death. She looked at me for a minute, and said.

"Yes your right I over looked that I'll take care of it for you."

"I'll let you know when I don't have any cases scheduled." I said.

In a couple of days I got in touch with her, and she came down with several Petri Dishes and placed them in places where the possibility of infection might arise. After a period of time she picked them up and took them away to the Biology Department, and after another short wait of a few days she reported that the growth in the dishes was negative, and I was not to worry about it. This pleased me very much. It showed I was working in a fairly clean environment.

An example of the unknown dangers of Coroners, and Police cases, was when an elderly Chinese Gentleman was sent in by the Coroners Department for Autopsy. He was found lying on his apartment floor with a peculiar Burn to the top of his head which had no explanation. On Autopsy it was discovered that his lungs were riddled with a bad case of Tuberculosis, and during the dissection process by me, and the Pathologist no protection was done until the disease was discovered. I'm sure the infection was in the air while we were working with no face masks on or suitable air conditioning available. Just one air vent for removing foul air but no vent bringing in fresh air. Everything in the room must have been in contact with the disease one way or the other. The Saw had been used, and small invisible particles would have been in the air. A condition of employment was I was subject to an X-ray once a year for several years before they decided not to continue the practice anymore. The mysterious burn was not diagnosed at the time of Autopsy. Later on I mentioned the case to a representative of a Funeral Home. He explained it was the custom to burn the top of the Head with a Hot Iron to seal in the soul, and to give the people some sweets, and some change at the Funeral so they could have a good taste in their mouths and some money in their pocket when they left. I don't know if this is true or not, but I could not detect any sign of humor coming from the story teller, so I assume it is. In any case I don't think it was a bad idea at all. I relayed the explanation to the Pathologist, and I don't know whether he reported it or not. I do remember that the Admitting Department kept getting phone calls from anonymous people, and the Police Department changing the Patients name. I think this was a clumsy attempt to stop the Autopsy so I just used the name on the tags that came with the Body. No more was heard about it.

CHAPTER 14

Viewing of Bodies by Relatives

Signing over the Disposal of Newborn Infants to the Hospital

A Few Situations Regarding Bonuses

The Difficulties of Picking up and Transporting the Bodies to the Morgue

From time to time, I received phone calls from the Admitting Department asking me to bring relatives over from their offices to view their relatives for the last time or from people sent by the police to make identification. In the latter case I do not remember any Police escorting these visitors to this unpleasant Job even from as far away as Port Alberni over a hundred miles away.

In one of these cases an elderly gentleman arrived, and explained he had been sent by the R.C.M.P. to make a formal identification of his next door neighbour from the town of Sidney which was located approximately twenty miles away. After it was over and I was showing him the way back to the Main Entrance of the Hospital. I offered my condolences for the loss of his friend. He suddenly stopped, and turned, and said.

"Oh, that's not him."

I looked at him, and saw that he was perfectly serious, and it took me by surprise. I stammered, and said.

"But you just identified him."

"I know, but that's not him, he's gone," he insisted.

I could see that was the last word he was going to say so I didn't ask him any more questions. It was the way he explained it. Too me it seemed it was something he believed that the man's soul was gone and so it wasn't the man he once knew just his remains and he didn't know them at all. He said.

"Thanks for your help, I can find my way back know, have a good day." And smiling he strode away. I often wonder about what he meant and whether I was right. I guess I'll never know.

One of the saddest duties I had to perform was assisting at the Autopsies of young Babies who suddenly die for no obvious reason, and the Coroner orders an Autopsy. Some of these Babies parents were of very low income, and couldn't afford the expense of a funeral, and so they sign the documents authorizing the hospital to dispose of the infant for them. After the Autopsy was finished the infant was placed in a vat of formalin for preservation and kept for a while until two or three were collected. The Babies little bead chain identification band was left on so the body could be identified. A local Funeral Home who volunteered their services was then contacted, and they would make a little box to hold their remains which were wrapped in plastic and placed in the box. The Funeral Home then billed the hospital ten dollars to cover the cost of plywood for the box and gas for the car to transport the case to a local graveyard for burial. There were only two cases which problems occurred. One was a case where some digging was taking place on a neglected edge of the graveyard, and they unearthed a wooden box containing three infants who were buried in an unmarked section of the graveyard. Of course the startled and shocked shovel operator called the R.C.M.P. and after some investigation, they soon traced the bodies back to the hospital. Every case that has an Autopsy performed on it is recorded in a ledger with all the pertinent information recorded. I was on my vacation at the time and my relief, said each infant had its name band in place, and so proper identification was easy to establish and that's the last we heard of it. Another case came up later on when we received an infant who had been signed over to the hospital, and before I ask the

Funeral Home to come, and pick it up a young man and woman arrived at the morgue with a beautifully built Wooden Cedar Coffin, the exact size of the infant, and lined with a velvet cloth, and painted with an ornate design. They ask me if their son had gone yet, and when I realized what had happened, I knew there may be an incident brewing here. I had not been informed of their arrival by Admitting or anything, and they wanted to see their son when their son was not in any condition for viewing at all. I ask them to take a seat on a leather sofa outside the Autopsy room, and then I sat down and explained that the hospital was not a Funeral Home, and there were no conditions for viewing bodies. Then I ask them to leave the casket with me, and I would place the infant in for at least a better showing. I suggested that they go up to the Hospital Cafeteria for a coffee or something, and to come back in a half hour and I would be ready. They stared at me for a minute, but agreed. I thought I detected some suspicion about my actions but I wasn't sure. When they were gone, I immediately retrieved the infant from the vat, and dried it off, and wrapped it in a sheet to make sure no sutures were showing. I got some green plastic Bed Pads, and carefully wrapped his little head so the sutures didn't show there either. I placed him in the coffin, and covered him with a white Knit Blanket. Fortunately I had a collection of sheets, and blankets in the washroom off the Autopsy Room. I draped a sheet over a stretcher, and put the Coffin there. I had just finished when the parents came back. I ushered them into the Morgue, and told them not to touch the baby because of the Autopsy. I ask them if they understood, and they said they did. I lifted the top of the Casket, and stepped back. They stood there smiling, and talked about how good he looked in the box, and looked very pleased, which was a big load of my mind. In a few minutes they left arm in arm. I think that my efforts brought some closure that they had done the right thing. I really hope so.

In a few years the Pediatric Center was closed, and transferred to another of the cities large hospitals, and I did not have to assist at any more infant Autopsies which was a great relief.

One of the duties I had to perform was to go up to the wards and pick up the deceased, and bring them down to the Morgue. At that time, I was not equipped with a proper stretcher equipped for this job. It was a high priced piece of equipment, and the budget for the Autopsy Room, and the Morgue came out of the Histology allotment, so of course I seldom received any new high priced pieces of equipment. It was at least ten years before I finally received any thing that wasn't essential for the running of the Morgue. As far as equipment was concerned, instrument's such as knives, scalpels, and scissors etc. of course were essential.

Building Maintenance was a separate item, which I didn't have anything to say about. There was no heat in the Morgue at all. There were times in the Morgue during the winter where I didn't remove my winter jacket at all, only when I was assisting at an Autopsy. Air Conditioning was pathetic. There was an exhaust fan on the roof which had to pull the fumes up two stories through a screen, and vent before being released into the outside air. This vent was situated too far away from the Autopsy Table to be of any use at all. There were dozens of buckets, and pots full of formalin on shelves in the Autopsy Room, and they contributed to the smell of Dead Cadavers in all sorts of Autopsy conditions, and even when we were not performing Autopsies, you could cut the air with a knife because of the smell of Formalin permeated the room at all times.

The ceiling of the two rooms in the Autopsy area had what looked like four inch hot water pipes covered with a protective sleeve this sleeve had been broken in several areas due to various small renovations, and painting that had gone on over the years, and one day they came down, and told me I would have to close the Autopsy Area, because they were coming to close off the area so they could remove the Asbestos Pipe Covering on the exposed pipes. I had been working under these dangerous conditions for several years without even a mention from the administration of the hospital, and I believe it was only because of a large renovation going on in the main area of the hospital that they did anything at all. I was told I would have to go over to the old Veterans Hospital for a couple of days, and open the old Autopsy Room there. I thought.

"Oh, well what's new?"

One day I received a call from the Intensive Care Ward, requesting a pickup so I went into the wash up area and picked up a Sheet and a Blanket. I then proceeded across the hall to the Morgue for a stretcher.

When I arrived at the ward I found all the curtains pulled around the beds in the room which was full of patients, and there wasn't much room to maneuver the Stretcher. The room was built for about four patients, but due to overcrowding they had put another bed over against the wall on the far end of the room. Because this room was full of critically ill patients, there was more than the usual amount of nurses bustling about doing various treatments. I was quickly told where the deceased was, and I went to work quickly putting the stretcher alongside the bed. I reached over, and pulled the Cadaver onto the Stretcher, and tied it down with the ropes attached to the Stretcher for that purpose. I covered the body, which was wrapped in a Plastic Shroud, and properly tagged then I covered the body with a Sheet, and Blanket. When I grabbed the head end of the Stretcher I had forgotten that most of the Stretchers had fixed wheels at that end preventing the Stretcher from turning at that end. This allowed the Stretcher to be manoeuvred in a straight line, and when being turned by a single person. Without this arrangement the Stretcher would constantly drift to one side. When I pulled the Stretcher sideways, I fully expected it to come out sideways from the wall but because I had it against the wall the two fixed wheels didn't turn and over the Stretcher went with the body strapped on the top. An audible gasp was heard from the Nurses. A second went by when nobody moved. Then I quickly grabbed the Stretcher, and gave a heave, and lifted it up, Body, Sheet, and all into the right position. Grabbing the proper end, I was gone out the door before any one fully realized what had happened. I was rather surprised when I didn't get called up stairs for an explanation. I guess the Nurses were just too busy to complain. Needless to say from then on I made sure about the wheels on all the stretchers before I ventured onto the wards again. The body must have weighed around a hundred lbs. and the stretcher another thirty or so. To this day, I don't know how I managed to get it back up off the floor so fast. The shock of the situation must have taken over I guess.

Before I got the job as Morgue Attendant, It was up to the ward to take any deceased patients to the Morgue. Of course the job of taking them down at night was still their responsibility. But the wards were constantly complaining about my not responding to their requests at five or less minutes to the quitting hour. They never complained to me about anything that wasn't to their liking. They would phone up the Head of Histology, and complain to him, and he would relay it to me. I would then explain that I was trying to finish up a busy day in the Autopsy Room, and I couldn't possibly do their bidding without increasing the amount of over time I would have to work. It was a very rare week when I got home from work on time I was usually at least an hour late. The hospital paid time and a half, but all this did was raise the amount of taxes I had pay each year, and at times my pay check was usually lower than it would have been if I hadn't worked any over time at all. After standing at the Autopsy Table, and cleaning up all day with no Coffee Break, and fifteen minutes for lunch I was exhausted by the time I got home. The Union Contract stated that I didn't have to do unnecessary overtime, but I never invoked that clause in my discussions with my boss.

One day in the middle of the afternoon on a particularly busy day, my boss arrived at the door waving a letter around, he said.

"You are in trouble."

"Wadaya mean I'm in trouble? I haven't done anything wrong."

"I've got a letter here from Mr. Brown," he said,

Then he handed it to me. Mr. Brown was the Hospital Trouble Shooter. The letter stated that he had received a complaint from the Head of the Emergency Department about a Funeral Hurst being parked in front of the Emergency Entrance, and this was not acceptable at all, and that I was responsible for this, if I couldn't do my job more efficiently I should be replaced.

I handed the letter back, I could feel the blood had rushed to my face, and I felt very angry. I said.

"A few days before this incident referred to in the letter happened. The hospital changed the rules regarding the releasing of Cadavers to Funeral Homes, and I was not to release any D.O.A. Bodies that arrived in the Emergency Department before being transferred to the Morgue without a Pink Authorization Form signed by the Emergency Department, and I had received an Interdepartmental Letter stating that all the Funeral

Kazoonie

Homes in Victoria had been notified to this effect. I was busy with three Autopsies the day this incident happened, and when a Hurst arrived at the Morgue to pick up the case in question the driver didn't have the required papers. I told him about the change in procedure, and he would have to go back to the Emergency Department, and bring me a copy. He said he knew nothing of the changes. So I suggested I could help him with loading the body in to the Hurst because he was by himself, and he wouldn't have to bother me twice because he would just drop of the form, and leave. He readily agreed to that, and after loading the body I hurried back to the Autopsy Room where the Pathologist was doing my job and his own as well. In the meantime the Agent from the Funeral Home gets into his Hurst, and drives over to the Emergency Department, without telling me he was going to drive his Hurst over. I just assumed he would walk."

My boss just smiled and said.

"O, well just forget it there wasn't anything you could do. I'll explain it to Brown. There's nothing to worry about."

The thing that annoyed me about all this, was the fact nobody in the Emergency Department bothered to tell me what had happened, and nobody had consulted me about whether there little plan about changing the method of releasing the bodies was going to run into difficulties at the start. I think the Emergency Department didn't want to be involved with the Admitting, and releasing of bodies to the Morgue. They obtained a small victory when I came on the scene by transferring the job of picking up bodies during the day, and transferring them to the Morgue, and going down to the Morgue with the Funeral Rep's to get the back of the identification tags signed by the Funeral Home Agents, and bring them back to admitting, and sign the papers as a witness to the transaction, and make sure they got the right body. This was all transferred to me. I also think the Admitting Department got some of the responsibility and paper work for D.O.A.s to the Emergency Department which they didn't like at all, and I believe the Emergency Department was annoyed after all the negotiating that they still would have some involvement. The bottom line was they were hoping my arrival would unload the whole thing on me, and give him more time to do the Emergency paper work for the living, and the

Admitting Department had the same ideas. In all the years I was there doing the job, I did not have any trouble or complaints with the Admitting Department. I was never talked to by the Head Nurse in the Emergency Department, and whenever I saw her on the job she smiled like nothing had ever happened. I made a point of having nothing to do with her as long as she was in charge. When she did retire the next Head Nurse would consult me if she wanted my cooperation, and I made an effort to respond as best I could.

One day I was called to the Chief Pathologists Office. When I arrived he asked me to sit down, which I did tentatively. He said,

"John, I've decided to give you three Hundred Dollars every three months, because you are working so hard by doing a lot of extra work for me and the other Doctors. I would advise that you do not tell any of the other staff of this arrangement. Every three months, Jan. my secretary will call you up when it's ready."

He shook my hand, and I thanked him profusely, and I left hardly believing my good luck.

Eventually they decided to hire someone to help me. I was the senior employee, and my wages were a little higher than his. I was told to train him on the job. He had no previous experience as a Pathology Attendant so for the first month I had to do the job as usual, and train him at the same time. I didn't mind this because I knew as he became better on the job, I wouldn't have to work so much overtime, and things would be done quicker, and easier, as time went by, and I didn't have to train him anymore. I decided I would share my Bonus with him, so I told him about it, and of course he was delighted. The mistake I made was I didn't tell him about why I was getting the bonus. I just split it down the middle. Over the course of a few years I gave away several hundred dollars to him. Because I didn't tell him the reasons why he was getting this money he assumed it was coming to him directly from the pathologists and I was just the delivery boy. The fact that it was coming out of my pocket to him because of the help he was giving me on the job never occurred to him.

One day while I was on my annual vacation, and he was running the Morgue, I dropped over to the hospital to pick up my Pay Check. I decided to go over to see how he was doing on the job. When I arrived I found the Autopsy Room in the usual state of array after an Autopsy. He looked very pale, and stiff. I said.

"Hi, how are you doing?"

"I hurt my back undressing a body, I can hardly move."

I looked at him more carefully, and realized he was in deep trouble. I said.

"Yeah, I can see that, I said sarcastically. I'll get you a Wheel Chair, and take you to emergency."

"I can walk over their okay." He insisted. Just help me get my Boots off, and get my shoes on."

I thought Jesus he's being stupidly stubborn, but I helped him anyway.

"Phone up the boss and tell him I have to go to Emergency." He said.

He got up carefully, and walked out the door very slowly with a great deal of pain showing on his face. I phoned up the head of Histology, and told him what had happened, and went home.

The next day he phones me, and asks me to cut my holidays short because my partner had been admitted to hospital. I said I would. Three or four days later, when I could grab a few minutes I went over to see him, and found him lying on his back, his face was flushed, and he looked very uncomfortable.

"How are you doing?"

"Not very good, I'm booked for surgery to-morrow morning. My Doctor came to see me on Emergency. He examined me, and said I had just pulled some muscles in my back, and told me to go home, and get some rest, and I would be all right. I told him it felt like it was more than that because of the amount of pain I was in. He finally agreed to have me admitted for ten days so I could get some physiotherapy treatments. They would come in every day for the last few days, and jerk my legs up and down. It got so I couldn't stand it any longer, so I refused the treatments.

The Physiotherapist reported it to my Doctor, and he came in to see what was going on. When I told him I couldn't stand it any longer, he got a Neurologist to look at me. He just lifted my legs up and I screamed in pain, and he said."

"I'm scheduling you for surgery tomorrow morning."

After his surgery, I went over to see him in a rehabilitation area to see how he was doing. I found him looking a little dishevelled, and lying on his bed.

"Well how are things going?" I ask.

"Not so good a few days after my surgery I noticed my ankle and foot were numb, and I lost some of my balance. I told the surgeon about it, and he said it was nothing, and I was lucky to be walking at all. It seems I ruptured a lower disc in my back, and it hemorrhaged and the bleeding and swelling hasn't subsided yet."

I realized then that his problems were just starting so I didn't comment on it at all. I just said.

"Don't worry it's early yet, it'll get better when there's a little more healing.

As the years went by those words were proofed to be as wrong as I could get. I knew he was going to be off work for a long time with Physiology Therapy so I went to the head of histology and told him I wanted some help until Jim recovered, and was able to return to work. It wasn't long before they hired an Irishman who said he used to drive Limousines for a Funeral Home in Belfast, and worked in the Ambulance Business in Ontario before coming to Victoria.

When it came time for Jan to give me the bonus, my partner was still not able to work, but he was walking around with the help of a Cane, so I ask him to come over to pick up his share. I had decided to give him One Hundred Dollars, because he hadn't been at work for the full three months, and the remaining Fifty Dollars to my new partner, who didn't know anything about the arrangement.

When Jim arrived he assumed that he was entitled to his entire share. I believe he still thought I was still just the messenger boy. I explained why he was short was because he hadn't been there doing the work, it didn't seem to take effect he didn't say anything he just told my new partner in a roundabout way that he was the one giving him the money. I then realized what I had done, by not telling him it was coming directly from my pocket, and I was doing them a favour by giving them anything at all. To late the idea it was coming from upstairs was cemented in their minds. He was even going on about what a big favour he was doing him.

During the next year, I decided I needed some extra cash for some renovations I was doing around my house so I thought I'll tell my new partner he'll have to forgo his money for a while because I was short of cash. When I told him he got real mad, and said I was a Chintzy Bastard. I couldn't believe my ears. I tried to explain what was happening but he was in no mood to listen, as far as he was concerned I was keeping his share of the money that came from upstairs, and I had no right to do that. It was the Head Pathologists week to do Autopsies and we had one scheduled for the middle of the morning. So I told him we'll talk to the Chief Pathologist and he agreed to that, but I could see he thought he was going to get his share. When he came down I brought up the subject right away. I told him what had happened and he told him that the money was given to me a long way before he was hired, and it was for service beyond my regular duties done for the Doctors. The look of shock that came over his face was pathetic. He said nothing, and went back to work. He tried to bring it up later on in the afternoon, but I wasn't having any of it. I think he finally got the message, because during Lunch Time his wife arrived, and I saw him, and her having a serious conversation in the parking lot at the back of the Wilson Block. When lunch was over he came into the office, and apologized for his actions, and it was never discussed again. I was going to carry on with sharing the money when I was able to get my renovation bills paid, but after that I decided to hell with both of them and never shared again.

One day the Chief Pathologist called me to his office, and told me he was working as a Professor at the University in his spare time, and he wanted to run a class for the Biology Department Students in Neurology, and part of the course was the Anatomy of the Human Brain, and he wanted me to collect all the Brains from Autopsies that weren't needed for examination at the time. This would mean a lot of work for me. I would have to remove the Brain and fix it in Formalin. Fortunately I had saved all my used Cutting Boards, Knives, Scalpels, and Forceps, so I had enough to go around for approximately six to seven students who would come every Wednesday evening to dissect and study brains under the doctor If more than that showed up they would have to double up.

After the class was over they were to put the brains back into numbered buckets, until the following week. Every Wednesday after quitting time, I would empty the buckets into a vat of Formalin, then I would rinse the brains off by running cold water into the buckets until the fumes subsided. I would then lay out the instruments on the Cutting Boards on the Autopsy Tables, and the Stainless Steel Shelves situated beside the new Steel Sinks. The Autopsy Students would arrive after I had gone home so I would not lock the doors to the Autopsy Room. When I arrived back to work the next morning I always came a little earlier so I could start the regular work without getting too far behind. I would empty any water still in the buckets, and replace the Formalin from the Vat. Then clean and put the Cutting Boards and Instruments away until the next week. This went on for about three months, and I was given a Hundred Dollars for that. I felt that the money was not nearly enough for all the work I had to do, but the fact that my services was helping in a small way towards their education gave me some satisfaction even when one Wednesday night after a very busy day I had to put the students into the back Autopsy Area because setting up for them had put me away behind in my regular duties. I was cleaning the front Autopsy Area when they began to arrive so I had to stop now and then to usher them away from where I was working so they wouldn't have to walk through the wet bloody floor or touch anything in the area. One of the Young Female Students was late, and I just caught her in time before she walked in to the dirty area. I was dressed in a Plastic Apron, and a Green Operating Room Gown, and a pair of Yellow Rubber Boots, and I was wearing Rubber gloves. When I got her around to her area I heard her say in a loud voice.

"Who's that weird guy out the front?"

She didn't make any attempt to lower her voice, so I had the impression she wanted me to hear her derogatory outburst, because I was no more than a few feet away from where they were working. I didn't respond, I just put it down to being very rude, and the fact she didn't know that she was there partly because of my efforts on her behalf.

Another incident that happened because of a very inconsiderate University student was when he was hired as Summer Relief in the Morgue and Autopsy Room. He didn't tell the management that he could only be available for one week out of three, because he was going away on another job he had obtained on a Cable Ship. On the last weekend of his first weeks work there was a rash of deaths, and the Morgue coolers were full. Two of the deaths were D.O.A. and arrived on Friday. Both of these deaths were drug over doses. The rule of the Morgue was. Because of overcrowding, Bodies in the Cooler should be taken out, and the warm ones put in to cool down. This rotation will help prevent Autolysis occurring over a long weekend. When the Relief Attendant didn.t observe this rule which was written on a large notice board and attached to the wall of the Morgue for everyone to see, and as this was the second time he had relieved me in the summer, he knew about it. Late Monday Morning I received a call from Histology asking me to come back to work because the relief didn't show up, and nobody could do anything about it when it was learned by a few phone calls what had happened. I of course went in to bail them out. The first thing I did was check the bodies outside the cooler. The Morgue was full all available Morgue stretchers were full, including several from the Emergency Department. I found the two D.O.A. Cadavers were in advanced stages of Autolysis, so I got them inside as quick as I could if for no reason than to cut back on the smell. Why the Hospital Staff who delivered some of the bodies from the floors did nothing about that I'll never know. Then I phoned admitting, and told them what was going on, and ask them to get the Funeral Homes moving on picking up any cases that were going to them. The next step was to phone up Histology, and find out what Pathologist was doing Autopsies that week, and to phone him, and let him know I was at work, and explain why I was so late in calling.

He told me the R.C.M.P. wanted to be present for the two D.O.A. cases but couldn.t come until the afternoon. I said fine I'll be ready then.

When the R.C.M.P. arrived I had both bodies in the Autopsy room waiting for them. I ask the Constable if he recognized the cases as the ones he had sent in for Autopsy. I pulled back the sheets covering them, and a shocked look came over his face. He said.

"That's them, but they weren't in that condition when we sent them."

I I explained that overdoses of drugs usually caused a faster Autolysis rate on the body. I don't know why, but previous case's had shown this phenomenon to me before. The R.C.M.P. did not complain, and we heard no complaints from anybody who might be concerned. I felt that the relief person, and the Hospital Personnel who could have done something about the constant overloading of the Morgue could have made an effort to get the bodies that were left out of the Cooler moved as quickly as possible into the Refrigeration System. It was the usual problem that nobody wanted to address the problems in the Morgue or allocate any funds unless it was absolutely necessary. The Morgue came last. I managed to get a new surface put on the Autopsy Room Floor which improved cleanliness, and I had the back room turned into a makeshift office with shelves for linen etc. and a counter for paper work. When the amount of Autopsies being done doubled, I rummaged around in the used equipment storage area of the hospital, and got some Stainless Steel Counters, and Sinks left over from the O.R. installed along with two new Autopsy Tables which were equipped with built in suction and Air Ventilation, and Garburators. Eventually a homemade Fume Hood was attached to the existing single Ventilation Shaft which helped a great deal when filling Specimen Bottles with Formalin. That job, was given to me about halfway through my time spent working in the Lab. Any job in the Lab. that nobody else wanted to do always seemed to wind up with me. We wound up supplying Doctor's Offices, and the University, and any other facility which was sending specimens to the Histology Department. I'm sure during this time it must off amounted to thousands of plastic containers which we filled, and labeled, and placed in boxes we obtained from the Hospital Supply Warehouse, next to the Wilson Block. I made arrangements with the workers in the

Warehouse to save us any suitable boxes that they had emptied during their working day. They always seemed to come up with something. It certainly saved the hospital a lot of money for containers.

The Histology department ran a lottery at the end of each year, and each contestant had to guess how many specimens went through the department for the year. The last year I was there the amount was well over Thirty Thousand Specimens. I don't believe of course that they all came in the containers we filled, but I'm sure a good percentage did.

Another job I was given was to take X-rays of Breast Biopsies. Somebody decided that after a Breast Biopsy in the O.R. the tissue would be sent for an X-ray so that the Pathologist would be sure to find the area of suspicion in the tissue so he could take a piece to be put on a glass slide for microscopic examination, and confirmation whether it was cancer or not.

I was told to go to Medical Imagine for a crash course on how to use a Portable X-ray Machine. I spent a couple of days with a Veteran Technician taking pictures of various articles, and determining depths etc. I was given a couple of charts on this subject, and a Lead Apron to wear, and an X-ray Machine. The pictures were not taken on the large X-ray plates, but on the straight film which was easier to store and handle. This went on for a couple of months until they set up an X-ray system in the O.R.

There were times when we would receive gunshot victims from the Police or the Coroners and the Pathologist would decide he wanted an X-ray done to locate a Bullet. Or the person had multiple fractures, and the Pathologist would decide he wanted to make sure he had located all the breaks, so I would have to phone the Medical Imaging Department, and tell them I was coming over with a body. This was done so they could reserve a room for me. This was at times a difficult procedure because I had to push a Stretcher up a very steep grade, and halfway across the hospital to get to the department, and then the positioning of the body on the table was usually left up to me. When the procedure was completed the body was left on the table until the Radiologist read the X-ray and when he agrees the pictures were clear. "When this was done I would pick up the films and take them back with the body to the Morgue where the Pathologist would examine them for the information he needed, and I would get on with the initial dissection. Eventually a portable X-ray Machine was stored in a corner, and an X-ray Technician summoned to do the picture taking in the Autopsy Room, this was a great time saver and a lot easier on me.

Behind the Morgue Coolers was a basement which was full of various discarded pieces of equipment from the Lab. One section of this was used for storing the Glass Slides from the Histology Department. There was a lot of stuff stored there by one of the Pathologist who had worked in the Lab. for years, and when he decided to go to the Veterans Hospital to work full time, he wanted to take some of his possessions from the basement. Just when this was about to happen, I received instructions from my boss in Histology to make room in the basement to store slides. At the same time I was instructed to dispose of all specimens stored in the Autopsy Room that were more than a year old. So I went to work cleaning out a section of anything that wasn't Lab. equipment.

One of the things I found was a beautifully built Model Airplane, which was equipped with a motor. After I examined it, I decided it was too valuable to just throw away so I phoned my boss, and when I told him about it, he said he would be right down. When he saw the plane he said.

"I'll take that."

And he went back up stairs. It wasn't long before I had cleared out a suitable area for storing the slides, and so I went back into the Autopsy Room and proceeded to throw out the old specimens, taking up space. One of these specimens was up on a top shelf. I checked the date on it, and found it was over a year old, so I disposed of it.

The very next day the Pathologist who owned both the specimen and the Airplane, shows up at the Autopsy Room looking for his specimen. When I told him what had happened he was very annoyed. A short time after he had left I received a phone call from him asking about his Model Airplane. This really put me in a spot, so I told him I would go and look for it, and call him back. Instead I called up the Histology Boss, and told him what had happened. He said.

"I can't give it back to him all I wanted was the motor. I threw the rest away."

"That's not my problem I haven't told him that you took it. I said I'd look for it, and call him back."

"Okay, forget it I'll explain to him what happened," and he hung up.

The next day the Pathologist arrived, and asked me to give him a hand with some of his belongings in the basement. I went with him around to the back, and he pointed out a Skeleton which was hanging on a hook attached to a metal stand.

"That's what I came for."

I unhooked it, and followed him out to his car, which was a light blue convertible. I went around to the trunk expecting him to follow me but he didn't he got behind the wheel instead, and told me to sit the Skeleton down on the seat beside him. The Skeleton was being used as an instrument for teaching but at some time in the past, it had been used as an instrument of fun at some hospital social gathering. It had Cotton Batting glued over its Eye Sockets as Eye Lashes, and a cigarette dangling from its mouth. Just as he was about to drive away, the Technologist who was in charge of teaching the Student Lab. Technologists came around the corner of the building. She was shocked to see the Skeleton sitting there, and she said.

"You are not going out of the Hospital Grounds with that sitting beside you?"

He looked at her with a look of "Mind your own business," and said.

"Got more sense than some people I know."

And drove away out on to a very busy street without looking back, words cannot describe how ridiculous the Skeleton, and the Dr. looked. It was hilarious.

CHAPTER 15

Problems with the Pathologists

Nursing School

Fainting at Autopsies

A few years had gone by, and during that time I had very little problems with the Pathologists. One problem was occasionally the Pathologist on duty wouldn't finish the cases which came up during his time in the Autopsy Room and on his last scheduled case for the day he would leave it, and tell me he would do it first thing in the morning before the other Pathologist came on duty. This would always put me behind and the new Pathologist would never wait to find out what was going on he would just be angry, and want to know what the hell I was doing to be so late.

One day after a very difficult week the above mentioned problem occurred, and when the doctor walked in he never ask why I was late he just laid into me in a particular nasty way. This knocked me back on my heels and I decided I had had enough and I said quietly.

"I don't deserve this I'm going to have my coffee Break."

I glanced up at the clock on the wall to make sure it was near the time of scheduled Coffee Break. I saw it was, and I said to my partner.

"I'm going to Coffee now take over, and when I get back you go."

He was so surprised when I said that, he just nodded, because when the Doctor walked in we never went for scheduled breaks, we always stayed, and worked until he was gone. I just took of my Boots and Aprons and went to Coffee leaving the Doctor speechless. When I came back exactly fifteen minutes later, making sure not to exceed my time in the Hospital Dining Room, The Doctor wanted to have a talk with me. I could see he was subdued and didn't want to make me any madder, but I wasn't having any of it, I just ignored him, and told my partner to take his break, and I would take over. He declined, and I didn't insist. I put my gear on, and went to work. After the Doctor had gone, and the cleanup completed, he told me that he had told the doctor that I did a lot of extra work around the Autopsy Room when he was asked what was going on, and that I was trying to distribute the load more fairly. At any rate I did not hear about the incident again.

A couple of years after that I was assisting at a Forensic Autopsy where a person had been stabbed multiple times. This case had attracted several Police Officers to attend, both Municipal Cops and R.C.M.P. Before the initial steps were started the Cops, and the Pathologist who happened to be a female, and the Forensic Pathologist for the Victoria area were all standing around talking shop, and exchanging information. The body was on the table, and I was waiting for the work to start, when a sergeant came over, started looking the stab wounds over. I recognized her from other cases, so I struck up a conversation about the shape of the wounds, and I pointed out that the shape had a sharp edge and a dull edge which pointed out the knife was a single edge weapon.

While we were talking the Pathologist came over, and immediately started reprimanding me for discussing the case, and warning me about the oath of confidentiality we were all under. I was completely taken aback by the anger she displayed, and the total nonsense of it all. There was absolutely no breaking of any confidentiality. We were there to gather information about the cause of death for the Police Officers, and if I couldn't point out some piece of evidence to a Police Officer who after all is a ranking Officer. I wasn't concerned about the fact that I might be reprimanded for talking about a case which was not part of my duties. I was really annoyed about the way she did it in front of all these Detectives. It was a belittlement, something which embarrassed me. I got very angry, and blurted

Kazoonie

"Jesus" under my breath, and walked away. I glanced up at the clock on the wall, and saw it was Twelve Noon. I went into the washroom, and began taking my work gear off. She saw me, and said.

"What are you doing?"

"I'm going to lunch."

"You can't do that I want to start the case now. I need you here."

I could see panic on her face as she spoke, but I just kept taking of my gear. The Police were watching what was happening with surprised looks on their faces.

"I need your help, don't leave now," she repeated.

The tone in her voice had changed she was asking me politely, and not angrily. So I nodded, and put my gear back on, and said, sarcastically.

"Are you ready now?"

"Yes I'm ready," she said.

After my part of the dissection was over, and I had a few minutes I stepped into the office to get some towels. The Sergeant followed me back and said quietly.

"You know she was annoyed because the tall R.C.M.P. Blood splatter Specialist didn't pay any attention to her when she tried to be nice to him."

I was completely surprised by this observation. I laughed, and said.

"Your kidding, I didn't notice anything."

Oh, yes she played up to him quite a bit, and he just ignored her."

I just shook my head in disbelief, and got on with the job.

The next day she came down to the Morgue, and gave me Two Hundred Dollars in a envelope. She also gave my partner Two Hundred Dollars, even though he wasn't on the job the day before because his hours had been reduced to part time. When she handed me my envelope she said.

"This is a little something for all the help you have given me in the last few years."

I just took the money, and said nothing my partner was of course surprised and pleased. I put this gift as a throwback to the money that I was already getting every three months. I didn't think it was for anything she thought I was doing special at all, and I still don't. I think she had time to think over what had happened. And realized she was wrong, and it was a peace offering. She couldn't very well have given it to me and not my partner for fear of creating more animosity.

Over the years there were a few incidents that occurred, and I'll talk about a few of them now. A young man was brought in for autopsy because there wasn't an obvious cause of death or any Medical History. Everything was routine until it came time to examine the brain. When I placed his head on a rubber support I noticed a small black dot in the middle of his forehead. I had noticed it before, but I hadn't thought it was a trauma, but on closer examination I determined it was a bullet hole caused by a small caliber weapon. The strange thing was there was no blood on his clothing or face. Just to make sure I pushed a probe into the mark to see if it was a hole. I noticed the black staining of the tissue was the usual burn mark caused by being shot at close range. I said.

"Doctor I think this man has been shot, he's got a bullet hole in his head."

The Pathologist looked at me in surprise, and came over to see what I was talking about. As soon as he saw the mark on the forehead, he did what I had already done he probed it to make sure it was a hole. When he had done that he said.

"Open up the skull but don't take the brain out until I've had a look."

Then he hurried over to the phone, and phoned the Coroner's Office. He was obviously excited and annoyed at the same time. The phone was a Speaker Phone, and because his gloves were bloody, he didn't want to pick up the receiver so all he had to do was press a button on the phone, and dial the number using a pencil's rubber end. When the party he was phoning answered he just spoke into a built in receiver without contaminating the phone. The conversation went something like this.

"Hello this is Dr. Smith, about that case you sent in. I found a Bullet Hole in his head."

"O, yes I forgot to tell you, they found a Rifle on the floor beside the body." "What caliber was it?"

"It was a 22."

"Thank you." and he hung up.

On his way back to the table I could see he was furious. He was muttering to himself.

"He forgot to tell me."

He glanced at me, and said.

"Get me a Basin, I'll take the Brain out, and I want you to put it in the cooler until I'm able to examine it."

I watched him take it out, and I could see that the impact had shattered part of the base of the skull, and the Bullet had shattered causing extensive damage to the internal Brain tissue, this would make it extremely hard to find the remains of the Bullet without firming up the tissue. 22 Caliber Bullet's do not usually pass through the skull, they shatter into many small pieces or one badly compressed piece. To find all the small pieces it is better to have the Brain X-rayed because the lead shows up very clear, making it easy to locate.

Another case I was involved in was when a badly decomposed body was brought in. The tissue on the head was almost all gone but there was a hole showing that the Cadaver had been shot in the head. The Pathologist on duty was not a Forensic Pathologist, and all he was interested in was sending the Skull to the Chemistry Department to have the bits of remaining tissue removed chemically. I had some experience in this, and when I mentioned it to him he insisted that the technologist's in Chemistry were more knowledgeable about this, and he wanted them to do it. When I pointed out there was no exit wound in the skull, he ignored me, all he was concerned about was the fact all the evidence pointed to the fact that the Cadaver had been shot, and that was the cause of death period. He told me he wanted the skull cleaned up, and in one piece so he could give it to his son for Medical school. It was not my place to argue with him so I did as I was told. When I arrived in the Chemistry Department, and delivered it to the Technologist, and told him what the Pathologist wanted he said he didn't know anything about it. I told him I was just doing what I was told and left the Skull with a very mad Technologist.

A few days later I received a call from Chemistry to come, and pick up the Skull, and it was in a Tissue Corrosive Solution, and he didn't have room in his Fume Hood to store it, so I picked it up, and took it back down stairs.

After a couple of more weeks went by I rinsed it off and found the tissue was softened but far from cleaned off the bone. As I was working on getting the remaining scraps loose I heard something rattling around in the skull, and with a little shaking I managed to get the remains of a Bullet to fall out through the Eye Socket.

I immediately went to the phone, and called him up about the found Bullet. It was a larger Bullet than a 22 but it was obviously a hand gun slug, by its shape. I wasn't surprised too much about my find because there was no exit wound, and the Brain had completely autolyzed, and disappeared. He wasn't concerned about my find at all he was only interested in the preservation of the skull which I dried out, and he picked it up in a few days.

I wasn't involved in any Coroners hearing or legal activities concerning the case. I don't know whether one was even held. I just did as I was told, and forgot about it. There were a few of these cases done by Non Forensic Pathologist's while I was on duty, and they were a little slip shod at best. There were two Pathologists that were highly trained in this field, and the difference was like night, and day in their work compared to the others.

A few times in Murder cases and no experts were available at the hospital. An expert would come from Vancouver, and do the job. He always brought his own equipment, and did the case from start to finish all I had to do was clean up afterwards. Towards the end of my job at the hospital they began to ship most of the big time murders to Vancouver for Autopsy. I never heard of any repercussions happening about any of the few cases handled by Pathologists who weren't Forensic Pathologists. One or two were murders but they always got convictions. I don't believe anything that happened in the Autopsy Room would have made a difference along that line.

After I had worked in the Autopsy Room about a year, the Chief Pathologist decided I needed further Anatomy and Physiology training, so he told me to go to the Nursing School and take these subjects. So I went over to the Nursing Residence, and met the Instructor, and she gave me a schedule of the classes which were held in a classroom built behind the residence. I had to purchase a text book on the subject's and I obtained another book from one of the students who I had worked with when I was an Orderly.

The day of class I found I was in a class of about thirty young girls, and there were no other men there taking the course which surprised me. The instructor was a tall older Nurse who over the next six months I found to be a very pleasant and knowledgeable teacher.

The course was to be taught using the systems method. Each system of the body would be taught one at a time, and after completion of each one, an exam would be given using the multiple choice answer method.

One of the systems that was being taught was the reproductive system, and for some reason I'm not sure why the instructor decided to organize the pupils in groups of five with the idea in mind of having the students collaborate in answering the questions, instead of the usual individual method. One of the questions on the sheet was "How many Sperm does the Male produce in the reproductive process. There were five possible answers to pick from. All ask for an approximation. When we had all come up with an answer the four female students had picked identical answers, and mine was completely different. After a short discussion on the subject I stuck to my answer and the girls refused to change theirs. So we just agreed to disagree and left it at that.

After a short wait of a few days the instructor decided to change the routine of marking the papers from marking them herself and grading them and then handing them back, to handing out the papers, and then reading the answers to the class as a whole so the students could mark their own papers.

When the reproduction questions came up I found that I was right, and the other four girls were wrong. There was a strange silence for a few seconds as everybody turned to look at me because I was sitting in the back of the class. Then out of the quiet came a clear voice.

"One for Mr. Diener."

I did well in most of my final exam, but the last part was a disaster it was mostly about Fluid, and Electrolyte Balance. I crammed for my final exam, and didn't give myself enough time for the last system. I thought what I was doing in the Autopsy Room had nothing to do with fluid and electrolyte Balance. The Doctors could worry about that, so I never studied it at all. I passed with just over a seventy percent mark. The instructor told me I would have done a lot better if I I had spent some time on that last system. I thought "Hell I would if I didn't have a full day's work to perform as well as having to go to school nearly every day as well as going home to a wife and three kids. As far as I was concerned I felt like enough was enough, besides there was nothing in my job description about going to school.

A few months later I was called up by the Anatomy, and Physiology Instructor, and asked if I could obtain a Kidney for them to show to the class. I said I would try. The next Autopsy that was performed I told the Pathologist about the request, and he said it was all right. He had taken his required sections and there was plenty left for a demonstration.

When I arrived at the school with the specimen, I found the class in session. I handed the instructor the specimen, and she addressed the class, and said.

"Mr. Diener from the Laboratory has brought over a Kidney for demonstration to the class. I was standing there wondering what she meant by her statement "Mr. Diener has brought over a Kidney for demonstration," when she called the class up to the front of the room at the rate of ten at a time to see the Kidney, and I was going to explain what they were seeing. I was trapped, so I drew on what I had learned when I was a student, and winged it.

When I got back to the Laboratory I told the Chief Pathologist what had happened and he just laughed, and told me not to worry about it.

No Autopsies except Police and Coroners cases are performed without an Autopsy Permit. The permit is written to include teaching purposes to allow for the occasional incidents like this. The Autopsy also has to be requested by the doctor in charge of the patient with the families signed consent on the permit. All this paper work was done by the Hospital admitting Department. The Hospital did not do Autopsies without the request of the doctor. The only exception to that rule was if the family wanted the Autopsy, and the Doctor didn't. Then the family would have to pay the Pathologist his fee for services before he would agree. This was accomplished by the Admitting Department phoning me, and I would ask the Pathologist if he agreed, and how much he wanted for the job. When the Autopsy Permit was signed along with the Cheque and delivered a time would be set and the job carried out. This did not happen very often, but when it did the Pathologist eventually gave me about Fifty Dollars for my efforts. There was never any agreement between me and the doctor on my being paid. They just paid when they got around to it, and I wasn't going to say "no."

One of the teaching services carried out at the hospital was the attending of Nursing Personal which was mainly Nursing students, and Biology Students from the University. These groups were accompanied by the instructors.

The head of the Laboratory was usually the Pathologist who handled the arrangements for the University Students which consisted of my keeping them out of the Autopsy Room until he arrived to give them a little speech about fainting, and feeling nauseated. If this happened they were to leave, and sit on the leather bench outside until they settled down. Nobody in attendance would comment on this because it does happen occasionally, and to faint could result in further injury because of the Hard Terrazzo floor. The other exception to the rule was, I was to drape the body with sheets, and leave an area clear for dissection. I'm not sure this made much difference.

During one of these Medical and teaching Autopsies I was told that an Intern who was doing part of his internship in the Lab. would be the teacher. Unfortunately he didn't set the time for this to be the first case of the morning. I had just managed to get the first case off the table, and covered, and set aside and the teaching case on the table when the students arrived. The Intern was late so I stopped them in the hallway outside, and I gave them the speech about nausea, and fainting. I told the Nursing Instructor to keep her charges outside until I called them in she agreed. I went back into the Autopsy Room and started to clean up the place as best I could before draping the body. A few minutes went by when suddenly the Autopsy Doors swung open, and in walks the Instructor and the students. The Students were all first year Students still taking their Anatomy and Physiology, most of them couldn't be much more than eighteen or nineteen right out of High school, and had never seen a dead body before. Because of the first Autopsy, and virtually no Air Conditioning you could have cut the air with a knife, it smelled of drying blood and fecal matter, all the smells of death. To top it off I had not had time to cover the case, which was an elderly male. As soon as the class saw the naked body on the table they just froze. At that moment the Intern came through the office door, and said.

"Open him up John."

I picked up my Autopsy Knife, and walked over to the table, and started to make my first incision. I must have been a sight to be-hold wearing my green Blood soaked Gown over my Plastic apron, and Blood Spattered Rubber Boot's. I hadn't had time to change them, between Autopsies.

I heard a thud, and gasps from the Students, and looked up to see what was happening just in time to see at least six or seven of the girls fainting and collapsing onto a very hard floor. I noticed a lot who were still standing were trying to help them up. Some were standing but were on very unstable legs.

I looked over at the Intern who had a very disgusted look on his face. The Student Instructor was rushing about trying to calm the ones still standing. Finally the disaster was over. Very few of the students came back to finish the session. A week later I was told there would be no more teaching lessons to Students with less than three years training.

I believe that when the Intern came down to do the Autopsy he found the class waiting in the hall way, and sent them in not knowing I wasn't ready yet. A little more preparation might have made a difference as far as the shock effect was concerned. There were a few more incidents over the years. An occasional fainting but I think the one described was the worst.

I had one incident where two young R.C.M.P. constables were brought to the Morgue for a case by a tough Sergeant one of the Constables was a female. They looked fine as the procedure went on, but about half way through the Young girl turned a little green, and said.

"I think I'm going,"

I looked up quickly because that usually meant they were going to faint. I told the Male Constable to escort her outside to the bench, and she could come back later if she was up to it. He just smiled put his arm around her, and started toward the door. All of a sudden they both stopped, and he turned and said.

"I don't think I'm going to make it either."

I dropped my Knife, whipped my gloves of, and rushed over to help. I got there just in time to offer support. They staggered out to the bench, and sat down before they fell down.

When I got back to the table the sergeant said nothing, it was like he couldn't have cared at all. They both came back in about twenty minutes, and even though they both looked green around the gills they stayed to the end.

CHAPTER 16

Wage Dispute

Blood in my Urine

A Kidney Stone

A Suspicious Autopsy

Rude Relatives and a Few Difficult Times

Final Closure

I had been doing the job for just about three years when the association had one of their bargaining sessions with the Hospital Management, and came to an agreement after a couple of weeks. In those days, Management and the leaders of out Association left the disclosure of the various wage increases to the supervisor of the various departments in the hospital. When I had some time I went up to the Histology Department to see my immediate supervisor. When I discussed it with him and he talked about increment basis and quoted a calculation for three years. It was not anywhere near my top wage in three years. I said.

"Wait a minute I have a three year increment basis not a four year one. I'm the only one in the hospital that's got that."

"I'm sorry your Association must have overlooked that, this is the only information I've got."

And he showed me a list with my name on it along with my new wage rate, and the fact that I would reach my top wage in another year. At this point, I was very angry, and frustrated. I said nothing to my boss, because he had no authority in these matters. I went back to the Morgue, and calmed down enough to plan a course of action to see if I could get it corrected.

I decided to go to the President of the Association. When he heard my story he was apologizing all over the place about what had happened. He explained that his bargaining committee just assumed that everyone in the Hospital Association was on a four year increment basis, and because of that my situation just slipped by them all together. He said he would arrange a meeting with the Personnel Manager, and get it straightened out immediately.

In a couple of weeks I got a phone call to show up at the Personnel Office. When I arrived the Association President was there. He told the personnel manager what the problem was, and she just smiled, and said.

"No, there is nothing I can do about it, we all bargained in good faith and an agreement was reached. I'm sorry that Mr. Diener was over looked, but the hospital is not responsible for that. The Association is." I said.

"Well if that's the case I think it's the first time in history, that a person or association or anything else actually bargained an innocent persons wages away, and at the time the rest of the party's involved received a wage increase. I'm going backwards here if this keeps up I'll be working for nothing.

The Personnel Manager was the one who hired me, and she knew of my past history, and reputation, she was watching me intently, and could see I was very annoyed. She was showing signs of nervousness, so I decided to cool it. The President of the Association got up and thanked her, and then we left. I said

"Well that was a waste of time. What do we do know. You guys got me into this mess, and I want you to go to the head of the hospital if necessary to get it straightened out."

He looked at me with embarrassment written all over his face, and said.

"Don't worry it's not over yet. I'll get an appointment with Mr. Butcher, and we'll discuss it with him."

The next day I went up to see the Chief Pathologist the head of the Laboratory, and explained the situation to him. He listened to what I had to say, and when I finished he said.

"Let me know how you make out, and if it's not satisfactory, I'll see what I can do. I arranged the three year increment with management, and I expect them to honour it."

I thanked him and left. Three weeks later I received a call from the Association President telling me that the hospital had agreed to honour the original employment conditions.

One evening after a hard day's work my back began to give me a lot of trouble. It got so I could hardly finish my work. I went into the bathroom next to the Autopsy Room, and noticed my urine was black so I immediately collected some in a specimen bottle, and phoned up the Lab. and ask for Urology. A technologist answered the phone, and I ask her if she would mind testing some of my urine for blood. She said.

"Sure, bring it up, and I'll phone you when I'm finished."

I dropped the specimen off, and it wasn't long before she phoned me back to confirm my suspicions.

The next day I made an appointment to see my Doctor. He sent me to see a Urologist, he had me admitted to the hospital for a battery of tests to try to determine what was causing the bleeding.

For the next ten years I was subjected to several cystoscopy examinations including a water cystoscopy, where the Bladder is distended with water. They checked my Ureters, and took ultrasounds, and X-rays of my Kidneys. A Pathologist took an interest in my case, and dropped by my bed to tell me they found something in my right lower ureter, but they don't know what it is. He said.

"I think it could be T.B. because of the job you do."

I thought thanks Dr. that's all I need.

Finally the bleeding stopped after about a week, and the Urine cleared up. The Urologist called me into his office, and sent me into his bathroom to collect a specimen. When he looked at it visually he determined I was cured, and said.

"Well I have a story for you. During the war I was training as a pilot, and on one of my solo flights, I crashed the plane on landing. I wasn't hurt, and when I climbed out, my instructor gave me a lecture, and told me, don't do that again, and that advice is the same for you." I left his office not knowing what was wrong.

About one year later the same thing happened again, and I went through the whole procedure again. It was like clockwork approximately every year for the next ten years the bleeding then the tests I even had a Cat. Scan and they couldn't find anything. After about five years of this pain and bleeding, and poking, and prodding, I threw up my hands, and said to myself enough. So when the bleeding would start I decided to just wait seven days, and if it didn't stop I would go to the doctor, but it always stopped. Finally one evening during one of my bleeding sessions, I went out to the corner super Market, and while there I began to experience excruciating pain, along with the urge to void. So I rushed home thinking this is different than my past experience I immediately went into the Bathroom, and attempted to void. Out popped a large blood stained object, and I experienced immediate relief. I thought what the hell was that? So I got a large wooden Spoon much to my Wife's disgust, and fished the object out of the toilet. I found I had passed a Kidney Stone about the size of a large Thumb Nail, it was flat, and one side was studded with numerous bumps. From that day on the bleeding stopped along with my constant back ache. I had been to a Physiotherapist on several occasions. I had taken four months off from work with back pain so bad I could hardly get out of my car when I arrived at home in the evening. When I determined that the stone was behind the whole thing. I couldn't believe that all the experts couldn't find one large Kidney Stone passing very slowly through my Ureter for years with all the tests that I had endured. As far as I'm concerned the only explanation is one word "Incompetence." I was even sent to a Doctor in our city's Rehabilitation Hospital to examine me because of my Back Pain. He showed me some of the X-rays taken in the past, and pointed out that there was nothing wrong with the disks in my back. Even I could see that they were all normal. Finally he told me it was probably my Facet Joints in my Spine, and told me to wear a back brace, and I could go back to work. Of course that was no help at all.

One afternoon I received a call from a Pathologist who told me he had received a call from the Coroner who had requested an Autopsy on a car crash victim, and he wanted to do the case late in the afternoon. I knew this meant overtime but I couldn't say anything. This kind of request was why I was getting the bonus. He told me when he would be down, and he even arrived a bit early. Because of that I had not undressed the body yet. But I could see by the outward condition of the body's clothes, and his face that it looked like a typical car accident victim. I ask the Doctor if I could undress him, but he wanted to take some notes first. When he was finished I began to take his blood soaked clothes off. As soon as I started to move the body about a very strong smell of Alcohol filled the room. I estimated at the time that I had never smelled anything stronger than this before, and I pointed it out to the doctor. He just nodded, and said nothing.

While removing the clothes I noticed he had a lot of fractures of various parts of the body. Some of them were compound, and had caused some blood to leak onto his clothes. It was obvious that he had a flayed chest. The ribs were broken, and the heart was ruptured, and the plural cavities were full of blood, along with this and the obvious fractured skull, his death must have been instant. As soon as I had opened the chest the smell of alcohol increased two fold. It was more than obvious that he had been drinking heavily before he died. I collected the usual Forensic Specimens for shipping to Vancouver, and set them aside to take upstairs before I went home. The girls in the front office would place them in a fridge kept there for such a purpose, and a courier company would be summoned to take them away in the morning.

When the Pathologist was finished with his examination, and was heading out the door. He said,

"It's late I'll take the specimens upstairs for you so you can go directly home when you're finished."

This caught me completely by surprise because in the years I had been working there, no Pathologist had ever volunteered to take specimens upstairs for me. At the time I thought well isn't that nice of him, and said.

"Oh it's all right I'll only take a minute on my way out."

He smiled, and insisted it was no trouble at all, and picked them up and walked out the door. I felt pretty good about it because I was going to get home a bit earlier than I thought.

Two or three weeks went by, and I was having a heavy day in the Autopsy Room. It was late in the evening, and I had to sew up and wash the cases, and clean the Autopsy Room before I went home, when the phone rang. It was the Pathologist who had helped out with the forensic specimens. He asked.

"John, can you come up to my office for a minute?"

I thought not again. I was annoyed because he was causing me to work longer hours again, I thought this better be good.

"I have to change, so I'll be a minute or two."

"That's all right I'll be here,"

When I arrived at his office, I was tired, and annoyed, and not in any mood to be kept over for nothing. The Pathologist was sitting behind his desk, and a man wearing an overcoat was sitting in front of him. It was a small office so I had to sit very close to him. He was introduced as a lawyer, who wanted to ask me a few questions about the car accident victim that we had autopsied. I was so tired it took me a second to remember who he was talking about. I said,

"What would you like to know?"

I was trying to be polite, and even remember the case. Right away he's looking at me intensely, and firing questions at me so fast I couldn't think about the first question before he was asking me another one. The first few questions were about the routine of what we did with the Forensic Specimens when we were finished with the Autopsy. So I managed to answer. I managed to answer those questions all right. I noticed he had this large sheet with what I presumed were questions written on it because when I managed to get a word in edge wise he'd write down something on it and then go on berating me. Finally the questions started to get to actually accusing me of losing the specimens, and trying to get me to say things which were a lot of nonsense to me. He seemed to be angry with me because it was all my fault the specimen had went missing.

I was still under the Parole Regulations when all this was going on, and if I had of been put under suspicion who knows what could have happened to me. I don't know why the Pathologist did take the specimens away but I'm sure it wasn't as a favour to me. I never heard anything more about it just another mystery of the conveniently missing specimens.

There were times when I had to show bodies to grieving relatives as well as the identification sessions which I have mentioned earlier in the book. The view area was just as crude as everything else around the Morgue. When I first arrived and had to show bodies to relatives. I was literally ashamed of the conditions I had to work with. One of these cases was when a young man went down to Willows Beach at night and killed himself. In the morning I was out in the hallway in front of the Autopsy Room. When I glanced out one of the windows lining the outside wall, I noticed two of the technologists standing in the parking lot. One of them seemed to be comforting the other one. I wondered for a second what it was all about, but went about my business for the day. I found out later on that one of the Technologists was the sister of the young man who committed suicide. She worked in the Biology Department directly above me on the first floor. Somebody must have alerted the department about what had happened, and sent one of the girls to intercept her before she came to work, not knowing that her brother's body was just down stairs.

Later on during the afternoon, I received a call from the First Memorial Funeral Home from one of their agents who used to work in the hospital as an orderly. He said he wanted to bring in the boy's Mother so she could see her Son. I said I would make an exception to the unwritten rule that a viewing of this type of case needed the Coroners permission, and he must explain to the Mother that the hospital was not equipped for the viewing of bodies. As he had worked in the hospital he knew about the conditions of the Morgue, but he agreed, and said he would be coming over directly. At this time there were no facilities for proper viewing just a cold bare room. I took the body out of the cooler, and put it on a stretcher. Fortunately there were no other bodies being stored outside the cooler. I draped the body with a sheet, and blanket, and waited.

When they arrived I was introduced, and the agent said he would wait outside. I escorted the obviously grief stricken Mother into the Morgue. When I moved her up to the stretcher she suddenly sprawled herself on top of the body, and began crying hysterically. It was one of the old stretchers, very unstable. Fortunately I was standing next to her, and had time to grab the stretcher to keep it from tipping over, it wobbled quite a bit. When everything quieted down I tried to help her back off of her son, but when I started to try, and help her down from the stretcher she became really angry, and pushed me away, telling me not to touch her. That's when I became annoyed and decided she had finished her viewing. I left her lying on top of her son, and went out and got the Funeral Agent, and told him his client was hysterical and that she had attacked me and I wanted her out of there now. He hurried in, and went up to her and as soon as she saw him she calmed right down and let him help her, she looked a little embarrassed but didn't even look at me or make any attempt to apologise. Later on I made a point of telling the agent that that was the last time I would give any more viewings of this type. After the Autopsy was done, and the daughter was back to work, the coroner delayed releasing the body. I bumped into her one day, and she asked what the delay was, and I told her I didn't know but there was nothing unusual about it. Then I told her I didn't have any control about what the Coroner was doing, but I would tell the Pathologist about her concerns. I didn't mention her Mothers hysteria or her outrageous behavior. I followed through on my promise, and it wasn't long before the case was released.

Another incident occurred when a very large group of family members arrived with the Coroner for a viewing without giving me any notice at all. The body was of a young woman who had been murdered, and was badly mutilated. Because of the poor viewing area, and the condition of the corpse, I told the Coroner she would have to wait until I could make the case a little more presentable. I made them all wait outside in the hallway while I rushed around trying to clean up the bleeding so no blood was visible, and putting proper covering in place etc.

I had finally got the Maintenance Department to install some sliding curtains so I could hide the view of the Coolers, and any other bodies stored outside. Finally I was ready, and the family began filing in. I was careful to station myself at the head end of the stretcher so that nobody could touch her head because of the extent of her wound, and the Autopsy, and I didn't want anybody getting blood on themselves, that would be a catastrophe to say the least.

Because of the large amount of viewers, and the curtain arrangement cutting of most of the available space it was crowded around the body. The Mother was grieving heavily, and she wanted to be at the head end of the table so I had to tell her not to touch the body. She was being shepherded around by one of her daughters, and when she came up to see her daughter, I noticed she was very unsteady on her feet so I reached out to steady her. The young daughter suddenly started to scold me that she was looking after her mother, and she was perfectly able to handle the situation. I could see she was angry, and didn't want any help so I didn't say anything to her I just walked away, and told the Coroner that I had other things to do, and as far as I was concerned the viewing was over. She was taken a back a bit, but she didn't say anything she just hustled them all out, thanked me and left. The Coroners service never asked for a viewing without calling me first again.

A few years went by, and suddenly the Hospital Chaplin began to appear at the occasional viewing or to give people belated last rights, and finally they built a viewing area with a waiting area equipped with a sink and comfortable sofa. There was a window in the wall so viewing could be accomplished without going into the viewing area. A door led into the room so visitors could go and stand by the stretcher if desired. The lights in the ceiling were recessed, and could be dimmed if necessary. A new policy was established that the Hospital Chaplin must be called when a viewing is requested. So I was spared most of the escorting, and involvement with Hysterical Relatives. The Housekeeping was light, mostly a little dusting and floor mopping. The difference was like night and day. I suspect the Chaplin had something to do with this change because whenever I brought the subject up it fell on deaf ears.

One particularly cold winter we had a very heavy snow fall, and I was called up to one of the wards to transfer a body to the Morgue. When I reached the steep alley way between the two buildings across the back road, and started down I found the path was very slippery, and I was being dragged sliding down the hill way to fast, and when I reached the bottom, I had to make a very sharp turn. The Stretcher I was using over ran the sidewalk hit a snow bank sideways, and the rope came loose on one side of the stretcher, and the body just slipped off into the snow. Rigor Mortis hadn't set in yet, and the body was very heavy making it far too unwieldy for a man to lift. I had to leave it there, and go for some help. Fortunately some of the Maintenance Men, and Ground's Keepers were out shovelling snow, and one of them was just around the corner, and he didn't mind giving me a lift. When I thanked him he said.

"All in a day's work," And walked away laughing.

One evening I received a call from the Head Pathologist asking me to come in to the Wilson Block, and get the key to let him in because he was bringing in a body. I didn't ask him what it was all about I just told him how long it would probably take for me to get there. He said that's all right he hadn't finished at the scene yet.

When I arrived at the hospital I had to get security to let me in to the Wilson Block. I didn't have any trouble because everybody knew who I was.

When Dr. Thornton arrived in his Volkwagen Camper I was waiting for him at the back door. He was accompanied by a Detective. I was just standing there waiting for a company that the Coroner and the Police department usually used to pick up bodies for them at the scene of crimes. I said.

"Where's the Body?"

The Pathologist said.

"It's in my Van. I'll give you a hand."

I was mildly surprised at this, but then again the Pathologist was not a man to worry about things like that, so I just shrugged, and walked over to the Van. As he slid open the door, I didn't see a body just several large green Garbage Bags.

"Here it is," he said.

I picked up one, and found it heavy, and I noticed there was one inside the other for strength. Altogether there was about four or five bags. We took them inside, and put them on to the Autopsy table. The doctor said.

"We're not going to do an Autopsy tonight John. I just want to examine the contents of the bags, and I'll do a more extensive examination in the morning."

I started emptying the bags, and found a young woman's head in one, and various other parts of her body in the others. Whoever had dissected her had a fairly good idea how to do it because it was done neatly.

I had not ask any questions up to then but when the doctor had finished he volunteered that the young girl went missing, and when the Police went over to her husband's house they found the bags scattered around the house under the kitchen sink, and other not very good hiding places. It seems she married him so she could get into Canada from India, and when she got settled she left him. That was obviously a fatal mistake. I followed the case in the newspapers, and was astonished at the light sentence he received for literally slaughtering the girl.

Another case I was involved in was when a young teenage girl attacked her mother in a rage with a knife and stabbed her several times, and left her head hanging on with just a few strips of connective tissue. She was given a sentence far too lenient for the savagery of the crime

Over the year I had to develop a very thick hide to tolerate the stupid and senseless jokes that came my way because of the job I did. It got to the point that my youngest son even thought it was funny. One day when my wife came over to the hospital to pick me up she brought along my youngest son. I hadn't quite finished my clean up, and I was taking my dirty garbage over to the Incinerator. I was still wearing my Blood Spattered Gown and Rubber Glove's. As I walked out the back door my Wife was just driving up. My son was about ten year's old at the time, and was sitting in the back seat, when he saw me he lowered the window, and yelled at the top of his voice.

"Hey "D" what you got there the Head and the guts?"

I couldn't believe my ears or my eyes. He thought it was very funny, and was laughing at his own poor joke. I glanced at my Wife, and I could see by the look on her face that she didn't think it was funny either, needless to say I had a talk with him about his poor taste of humor he never ever tried it again.

I had been on the job long enough to know full well the stupidity of some people's humor, and I tolerated it as best I could, but I was not going to hear it from my own children, and up to know none of them have tested me. I went to a Tea for a long time employee who was retiring, and her Husband was there. He was a retired Naval Commander, and an official at the B.C Government Parliament Buildings. I had worked with his Wife who was a secretary in the Admitting Department, and I thought was a very nice lady, but when she introduced her husband to me. He smirked, and said sarcastically.

"Oh, yes the Body Man."

I looked at him, and thought this guy doesn't know me, and I don't know him. What kind of a crack was that, and left his wife's Tea. I'm mentioning this because of the stupidity some people showed about the work that goes on behind the scenes that nobody wants to know about, and is just as important as every other Hospital Service. During the peak of my time in the Autopsy Room, we were doing on average Four Hundred Autopsy's a year and that was done in about Two Hundred and Fifty days with all the National Holidays included. Towards the end of my job at the Hospital the amount of Autopsy's being done had dropped off to about Two Hundred and Fifty.

I had no idea at the time what was going on, until one day when one of the Pathologists was talking on the phone, and the Physician mentioned that he had received instructions to cut back on the amount of Autopsy's he was requesting, and so had all the other Doctors who had privileges at the hospital. She got very annoyed when she found this out, and hadn't received any such request. I don't know whether that was the only reason she was annoyed because there were some Pathologists who didn't care whether they ever saw another Autopsy again. One of the reasons I guess was the fact that a Autopsy was the longest test in the Lab. and took a lot of money, and staff to complete. The Histology staff had to prepare several slides for each case I know because I broke down each sample the doctor took from each case he did and some of them took a lot of specimens.

The bottom line is if you don't do an Autopsy when someone dies. How can you determine the exact cause of death for sure? A lot of experts can argue that last statement by saying he had Cancer or he died of a Heart Attack etc. but the law says when a death certificate is signed it has to have a correct cause of death on it not just natural causes. I find it strange that one year we are doing four Hundred Autopsy's and two years or three years later were doing two Hundred. We sure got a lot of smarter Doctors all of a sudden. I think it all boils down to dollars and cents, and costs had to be cut somewhere, and what better place than the Morgue? I was sixty years old, and struggling to do a job which a much younger man should have been doing, and I realized it was time to retire and let my Younger Female Assistant take over. I made an appointment to go over to the Personnel Department to find out what my Severance Pay would be and also a seminar which the Provincial government was holding at the Victoria General Hospital to explain the Retirement Pensions that the Government made available, such as the Provincial Superannuation Pension, and Federal Old Age Pension. Of course there were some decreases in two of my pensions because I had decided to retire at Sixty years of age instead of the compulsory age of Sixty five. After careful consideration of the sort of financial situation I would be left in if I retired five years earlier. My Wife and I decided to go ahead and do it.

MY retirement party was held in a local restaurant and I was given a resounding send off by a large percentage of the staff in the Royal Jubilee Hospital Laboratory. Dr. Thornton made a speech in which he mentioned how much I didn't like Lawyers. I don't know where he got that idea from so I assumed that was related to the missing Autopsy Specimens. I never said anything to him about it, but he was entirely wrong. I have no dislikes about Lawyers at all, and of course he left everyone in the dark because of that. Fortunately nobody ask me what he was talking about.

A pathologist had to attend a funeral of one of his compatriots on the mainland but he took the time and went out of his way to drop by the reception to make a kind and humorous speech about how he was always careful when he was down in the Morgue because I was standing behind him with a big knife. He also made a comment of the fact that he had officiated at his compatriots Autopsy, and that he had been thanked by the man's relatives for the good condition he had been returned to them. He said he wanted the people at the reception to know. I know he meant well but I cannot help feeling that I know I tried to return every case and in some instances in better shape than when they came in after an Autopsy. I feel the whole effort was all in the interests of possible improvement of Medical Science, and I didn't care what anybody thought about it all. When I think about this I must say.

"Thank you, Doctor for your kind support."

Me and my Wife were picked up in a Stretch Limousine and taken to the Restaurant, and when it was over we were taken home the same way, compliments of one of the private companies employed to transfer cases to and from Hospitals and local Funeral Homes. To this day I am greatly appreciative of the wonderful send-off I received from the Laboratory Staff, and all the great cooperative assistance I received when I was there for over twenty years.

A few weeks of retirement went by, and I received a phone call from the Histology Supervisor asking me if I could come in for a few days and help out in the Morgue and Autopsy Room because my replacement had taken sick. I said I would but just until she came back or until they could get a suitable replacement. I was signed on as a casual employee and to my surprise this on call work lasted for nearly four years. Even after they hired an assistant to the regular full time attendant who I was told was taking leave because of stress on a regular basis. Finally I had enough of explaining I was only helping out, besides my wife was beginning to question me about what I was doing. Asking me if I was retired or not. Finally the next time they called from the hospital I said "No."

During this narration I have deliberately left out the development of my personal life in regards to my family, and my part in my life regarding my Wife and my two Stepsons and my son. My wife, a strong personable woman built a home for me and her children with unflagging strength and determination and met all the worries and difficulties that came her way without flinching. I don't believe I could have survived without her. I look back over the last few years and say my life started out bad, but I managed to build a small place for myself, and if I can do it anybody can.

CPSIA information can be obtained
at www.ICGtesting.com
Printed in the USA
LVOW08s1607010317
525651LV00003B/12/P